THE LITERACY COACHING CHALLENGE

SOLVING PROBLEMS IN THE TEACHING OF LITERACY

Cathy Collins Block, Series Editor

Recent Volumes

Reading the Web: Strategies for Internet Inquiry
Maya B. Eagleton and Elizabeth Dobler

Designing Professional Development in Literacy: A Framework for Effective Instruction
Catherine A. Rosemary, Kathleen A. Roskos, and Leslie K. Landreth

Best Practices in Writing Instruction
Edited by Steve Graham, Charles A. MacArthur, and Jill Fitzgerald

Classroom Literacy Assessment: Making Sense of What Students Know and Do
Edited by Jeanne R. Paratore and Rachel L. McCormack

Fluency in the Classroom
Edited by Melanie R. Kuhn and Paula J. Schwanenflugel

Reading Assessment, Second Edition: A Primer for Teachers and Coaches
JoAnne Schudt Caldwell

Literacy Instruction for English Language Learners Pre-K–2
Diane M. Barone and Shelley Hong Xu

Tools for Matching Readers to Texts: Research-Based Practices
Heidi Anne E. Mesmer

Achieving Excellence in Preschool Literacy Instruction
Edited by Laura M. Justice and Carol Vukelich

Reading Success for Struggling Adolescent Learners
Edited by Susan Lenski and Jill Lewis

Best Practices in Adolescent Literacy Instruction
Edited by Kathleen A. Hinchman and Heather K. Sheridan-Thomas

Comprehension Assessment: A Classroom Guide
JoAnne Schudt Caldwell

Comprehension Instruction, Second Edition: Research-Based Best Practices
Edited by Cathy Collins Block and Sheri R. Parris

The Literacy Coaching Challenge: Models and Methods for Grades K–8
Michael C. McKenna and Sharon Walpole

Creating Robust Vocabulary: Frequently Asked Questions and Extended Examples
Isabel L. Beck, Margaret G. McKeown, and Linda Kucan

Mindful of Words: Spelling and Vocabulary Explorations 4–8
Kathy Ganske

The
Literacy
Coaching
Challenge

**Models
and Methods
for Grades
K–8**

**Michael C. McKenna
Sharon Walpole**

THE GUILFORD PRESS
New York   London

© 2008 The Guilford Press
A Division of Guilford Publications, Inc.
72 Spring Street, New York, NY 10012
www.guilford.com

Printed in the United States of America

This book is printed on acid-free paper.

Last digit is print number: 9 8 7 6 5 4 3 2 1

Library of Congress Cataloging-in-Publication Data

McKenna, Michael C.
   The literacy coaching challenge : models and methods for grades K–8 /
Michael C. McKenna, Sharon Walpole.
     p. cm. — (Solving Problems in the Teaching of Literacy)
   Includes bibliographical references and index.
   ISBN: 978-1-59385-711-0 (pbk. : alk. paper)
   ISBN: 978-1-59385-712-7 (hardcover : alk. paper)
   1. Reading (Elementary)—United States. 2. Literacy—United
States. 3. Reading teachers—In-service training—United
States. I. Walpole, Sharon. II. Title.
  LB1573.M392 2008
  372.41—dc22
                                   2008006577

For Chris Jennison,
insightful friend and able editor

About the Authors

Michael C. McKenna, PhD, is Thomas G. Jewell Professor of Reading at the University of Virginia. He is the author, coauthor, or editor of 15 books and more than 100 articles, chapters, and technical reports on a range of literacy topics. His books include two that were coauthored with Sharon Walpole: *The Literacy Coach's Handbook: A Guide to Research-Based Practice* and *Differentiated Reading Instruction: Strategies for the Primary Grades*. His other books include *Assessment for Reading Instruction* (with Steven Stahl), *Help for Struggling Readers*, *Teaching through Text*, and *Issues and Trends in Literacy Education*, among others. Dr. McKenna's research has been sponsored by the National Reading Research Center and the Center for the Improvement of Early Reading Achievement. He is the cowinner of the National Research Conference's Edward Fry Book Award and the American Library Association's Award for Outstanding Academic Books. He has served on the editorial board of *Reading Research Quarterly*, and his articles have appeared in that journal as well as in the *Journal of Educational Psychology*, *Educational Researcher*, *The Reading Teacher*, and others. Dr. McKenna now works extensively with literacy coaches in Georgia and Virginia.

Sharon Walpole, PhD, is Associate Professor in the School of Education at the University of Delaware. She teaches undergraduate courses on language and literacy development in kindergarten and first grade, master's courses on content-area reading instruction and on organization and supervision of the reading program, and doctoral seminars on literacy and educational policy. Dr. Walpole has extensive school-based experience, including both high school teaching and elementary school administration. She has also been involved in federally funded and homegrown schoolwide reform projects and has been studying the design and effects of schoolwide reforms, particularly those involving literacy coaches. She works closely with the Reading First initiatives in Delaware, Virginia, and Georgia, and is coauthor (with Michael C. McKenna) of *The Literacy Coach's Handbook* and *Differentiated Reading Instruction*. She has written articles in *Reading Research Quarterly*; *Journal of Educational Psychology*; *Reading and Writing Quarterly*; *Journal of Speech, Language, and Hearing Services in the Schools*; *Early Education and Development*; and *The Reading Teacher*. In 2007, Dr. Walpole received the Early Career Award from the National Reading Conference for Significant Contributions to Literacy Research and Education.

Preface

What a difference a few years can make! Since its inception in the 1990s, literacy coaching has evolved into a complex and sometimes confusing maze of possibilities. The questions we hear from practitioners are all about traversing this maze: What are the main models of coaching? Which are research based? Which offers the best fit for our school? Once we decide, how do we get started? And once we begin, how do we maintain our momentum?

As we planned this book, it was evident that many school leaders had outgrown the need for an introductory treatment of coaching. They were prepared for an in-depth discussion that would help them answer the questions we have just raised. Our work in schools and university settings convinced us that although definitive answers to all of the questions are not yet possible, enough progress has been made to offer real guidance through the maze of choices. This has been our principal goal. Our work in federally funded elementary school reform efforts has connected us with hundreds of talented coaches. It has also connected us with school and district administrators, policymakers, and other researchers who are interested in coaching to improve teaching and learning. We are convinced that we need to generate and implement many specific coaching initiatives. One size will never fit all when the goal is supporting excellent teaching. In this book, we invite you to consider the many choices that you might make in the design and implementation of a coherent coaching program.

We begin by exploring six major models of coaching, which are not necessarily limited to the area of literacy. Our discussion is intended to provide an objective survey of coaching innovations, how and why they developed, and the contexts where they are most appropriate. It will be evident to any reader that our conception of coaching is always about professional development, and our thinking is grounded in the belief that through enhancing teacher expertise, coaches can improve instruction and thereby help bring about greater student achievement. Accordingly, all of these models place professional learning at the forefront.

Because teacher learning differs from student learning, we think it essential for coaches to understand the distinction so that they can plan and provide experiences in which teachers will actively engage. We detail key principles of adult learning and the qualities that distinguish adults from children as learners. These differences are especially important in school settings because the preparation of coaches has typically focused on how children learn. With this idea in mind, we found the Standards of the National Staff Development Council useful for organizing our discussion.

We then move to the discussion of providing the leadership needed for professional learning to occur. Such learning must be situated in real-life school contexts, and school leaders must relate general content to the specific applications necessary for achievement growth. Toward this end, we examine the concept of distributed leadership and the importance of developing productive links between coaches and administrators. Because school contexts are also defined by curricula, materials, and assessments, it is important to consider these dimensions of the school setting in detail. The issue of reading assessments receives special attention in this book, for we believe that coaches must understand the major types and appropriate uses of available assessments if they are to interpret them properly and use them to guide their coaching efforts.

On this foundation, we devote the remainder of the book to important questions concerning the coach's role in professional growth. We begin with coaching cycles, in which teachers consider new ideas (theory), observe them demonstrated, practice their application, and receive feedback on the effectiveness of their implementation. These cycles offer coaches a framework that contains many choices, and as coaches become familiar with the choices, they can be adaptive to specific needs and contexts. We turn next to classroom-level coaching and present case studies to focus on three grade levels (first, fourth, and seventh) with substantially differing demands. We next take a step back to explore grade-level coaching, this time using three different levels (kindergarten, third, and sixth) to illustrate key ideas and issues. After examining sixth- and seventh-grade contexts in some detail, we turn to coaching in the middle grades. Although most of the coaching principles already introduced apply to middle school settings, the features that distinguish these from the elementary contexts—scheduling, teaming, subject specialization, and adolescent development—call for a separate discussion. We close this book with a careful look at what our experience suggests is a central issue for literacy coaches: contending with reluctant teachers. Though there can be no definitive solution to this problem, we offer many suggestions from research and from the field.

We sincerely hope that this volume meets the needs of coaches who confront the array of issues challenging ongoing professional growth. We have endeavored to balance theory and research with practical, real-world application. We believe that it is only through this balance that coaches can be instrumental in effecting positive change.

Contents

CHAPTER 1

Models of Coaching

There is no doubt that coaching is a hot topic in professional development (Cassidy & Cassidy, 2007). In fact, though, *coaching* may be so ubiquitous a term these days that members of the literacy community may not understand one another as they use it. *Coaching* is a strategy for implementing a professional support system for teachers, a system that includes research or theory, demonstration, practice, and feedback (Joyce & Showers, 2002). Such a thing is easier said than done. As we have worked with coaches and with coaching, we have come to realize that we must propose and define multiple models for coaching, and we must support schools in choosing a coaching model even before we assist them in using one. In this first chapter, we compare and contrast several models of coaching. Our goal is to get you thinking about models that currently exist and to provide a strategy for understanding and incorporating new models into your thinking. We are certain of this: There is no one right coaching model for all settings, *and* there are models that would be poor choices. Time spent considering which coaching model to use in a specific setting is time well spent; given the fact that *coaching* is an emerging and evolving term, you may also be well advised to create a coaching model specific to the circumstances of the setting in which it will be implemented.

COACHING STANDARDS

We are surely not the only ones considering flexible definitions of *coaching*. One way to evaluate coaching models is to test them against coaching standards. Standards reflecting the positions of professional organizations are important because they can guide university program development and in-service support for educators. We have been impressed with the evolution of position statements and standards for coaching endorsed by the International Reading Association (IRA);

a brief overview follows. You may also want to download and study the standards for yourself. They are all available online (see Figure 1.1).

As we read the coaching standards, we note how they constitute a snapshot of the evolution of coaching over time. We make this claim by working backward from the two most recent sets of standards: the standards for reading coaches (IRA, 2004) and the standards for middle and high school coaches (IRA, 2006). Both of those documents represent a gradual scale-up from competence in the intact, diverse classroom, to specialized knowledge of the needs of struggling students, to an understanding of the needs of other classroom reading teachers, to an understanding of the needs of content area teachers. For many literacy coaches, this progression actually matches their own professional history; many coaches began their career in the classroom, earned Master's degrees as reading specialists, served struggling readers, and then began to work in leadership roles and in site-based professional development for teachers.

Here is our view of this evolution (see also Walpole & McKenna, 2008): The standards themselves are actually additive. Literacy coaches must begin with the characteristics of excellent classroom reading teachers (IRA, 2000a). They must have taught in a classroom informed by deep knowledge of literacy development, assessment, instruction, and materials. That classroom-based excellence is not enough, though. Literacy coaches must have additional understanding of the needs of struggling students—the more focused skills of reading specialists (IRA, 2000b). These reading specialists must be able to apply this knowledge to support classroom teachers and to assume instructional leadership roles. Finally,

Title	Date	Web address
Excellent reading teachers	2000	*www.reading.org/resources/issues/ positions_excellent.html*
Teaching all children to read: The roles of the reading specialist	2000	*www.reading.org/resources/issues/ positions_excellent.html*
National Staff Development Council's *Standards for Staff Development*	2001	*www.nsdc.org/standards/index.cfm*
The role and qualifications of the reading coach in the United States	2004	*www.reading.org/resources/issues/ positions_coach.html*
Standards for Middle and High School Literacy Coaches	2006	*www.reading.org/resources/issues/reports/ coaching.html*

FIGURE 1.1. Standards important to coaching.

reading coaches (IRA, 2004) add an additional area of specialization to those encompassed by reading specialists: they understand how to work with adults, enacting the National Staff Development Council (NSDC, 2001) *Standards for Staff Development*. And those reading coaches who work in middle school and high school settings (IRA, 2006) add to this list a deep understanding of the structure of knowledge in the content areas of English language arts, mathematics, science, and social studies, as well as scaled-up notions of how to evaluate teaching and learning within and across classrooms and disciplines. As we initially considered these standards, we wondered whether they only described individuals with superhuman knowledge and skills (Walpole & McKenna, 2008); as we have worked with excellent coaches, though, we have met individuals who do answer this comprehensive call with wisdom and grace.

To start our own work on understanding multiple coaching models, we had to define what would constitute a coaching model in the first place. Neufeld and Roper (2003) propose two general types of coaches: *change coaches* and *content coaches*. *Change coaches* work mainly with administrators. They help administrators reorganize resources and build leadership and understanding related to site-based goals; in essence, change coaches set the stage for coaches of teachers. *Content coaches* work once resources are generally well allocated. While they interact with administrators, their focus is more squarely on the teachers. They help teachers to learn new ideas and to implement them during instruction. Then, content coaches provide formative feedback. These broad categories of work with administrators or teachers are important, but they are insufficiently nuanced for us to really describe the choices that individual districts, schools, and coaches make as they define their own models.

We assume that coaches can and should work with both administrators and teachers; influenced by Neufeld and Roper's work, we wanted to get more specific. We listed broad characteristics that would be present in various specific models, but that would constitute real choices. We constructed the criteria listed in Figure 1.2 to reflect our thinking: A *coaching model* is a set of guidelines for professional developers who provide ongoing formative support for teachers; those professional developers are called *coaches*, and their specific roles in schools vary. A coaching model includes a logistical plan for collaboration with teachers and specific strategies for designing, understanding, and reflecting on teacher instruction. It provides for knowledge building, instructional planning, and observation of teaching. It is informed by strategies for assessing student achievement.

All of these features sound very positive in the abstract, but coaching itself assumes an uncomfortable truth—many problems in student achievement are likely related to poor instruction. Increasing the quality of instruction means addressing these problems. Coaches are in schools to do just that, but they do it with specific teachers at different rates and in very different ways.

- Establishing a role for the coach
- Building knowledge for teachers
- Choosing instructional strategies
- Making instructional plans
- Reflecting on instructional quality
- Assessing student learning

FIGURE 1.2. Characteristics of a coaching model.

SELECTED MODELS OF COACHING

Different models might emphasize some specific criteria over others, but all take the stance that improving student achievement is important and is accomplished by improving instruction. We describe models that stand out for us in the literature, and we also include our own take on the strengths and weaknesses of each model. We have organized the models in an order that corresponds to their relative intrusiveness, a topic to which we return at the close of this chapter.

Mentoring New Teachers

One of the most long-standing (and perhaps ill-defined) forms of coaching is the *mentoring of new teachers*. Given that teachers develop expertise over time, perhaps in stages ranging from the novice who consciously implements rules for teaching and learning, to the expert who can automatically and fluidly adapt to new situations (see Block, Oakar, & Hurt, 2002, for a description), it makes sense for districts and schools to establish mentoring or induction programs to link novices and experts in coaching relationships. The realities of such relationships focus attention on the nuts and bolts of teaching in a very situated way—*mentors* simply help novice teachers to keep their heads above water and to integrate themselves within the context in which they are working (see Figure 1.3). This fact may evidence a general failure of mentoring programs for new teachers—they may tend to simply reproduce the status quo in a school rather than serve as guides into the profession of teaching or agents of instructional improvement and change (Achinstein & Athanases, 2006).

These criticisms of new-teacher mentoring aside, mentoring is a form of coaching that can stimulate thinking about coaching. Mentoring is a one-on-one relationship, planned to link an experienced teacher with a beginner. It is always nonevaluative. Mentoring relationships entail honest, safe opportunities to share confusions and frustrations. They are likely to evolve into coplanning sessions, with the mentor and novice sitting side-by-side, organizing for instruction. In the best mentoring situations, mentors respond to the needs of their partners in flexible ways; they might interpret achievement data, form instructional groups, observe and provide feedback, model instructional strategies, or create materials for instruction. Overlaying all other mentoring activities, mentors listen. They provide a safe space for novice teachers to share their fears.

Given the fact that induction into teaching is difficult, mentors are well positioned to be received by new teachers. The strength of mentoring (its flexibility and responsiveness) is also its weakness. Mentoring, done well, is very expensive. Mentors are usually classroom teachers who take on additional responsibilities to support their novice partners. They must have release time to provide assistance during the instructional day, and they must have additional time after school to work with their partners. Many districts respond to this expense by naming one district staff member as new teacher mentor, releasing that individual to provide mentoring full-time. That changes the coaching relationship, though, because the mentor is no longer really an expert peer. In general, mentoring establishes a relationship between two individuals, but it does not specify exactly how they will interact.

Cognitive Coaching

The "hows" of coaching are very well specified in *Cognitive Coaching* (Costa & Garmston, 1997, 2002). The "cognitive" in *cognitive coaching* signals its focus—to mediate the invisible thinking that guides a teacher's work. The goal of cognitive coaching is to facilitate the self-directed learning of teachers (see Figure 1.4).

Coaching characteristics	Model-specific choices
Establishing a role for the coach	Support and induction to work within a particular school or district
	Knowledgeable, experienced peer support
Building knowledge for teachers	Outside-the-classroom support to understand requirements, procedures, and curriculum
Choosing instructional strategies	Implement what has been chosen
	Benefit from the wisdom of practice
Making instructional plans	Coplanning
Reflecting on instructional quality	Observes and reflects on instruction
Assessing student learning	Critically evaluate student achievement

FIGURE 1.3. Mentoring new teachers.

Coaching characteristics	Model-specific choices
Establishing a role for the coach	To assist teachers to move from their current understandings to their desired understandings
Building knowledge for teachers	Consulting with teachers, based on their self-reported needs
Choosing instructional strategies	Collaboration with teachers, based on their individual goals
Making instructional plans	Collaboration with teachers, based on their individual goals
Reflecting on instructional quality	Reflecting conference, with the coach listening to and supporting self-reflection
Assessing student learning	Evidence chosen collaboratively to match the teacher's own goals

FIGURE 1.4. Cognitive coaching.

Cognitive coaches do this by learning personal interaction techniques that remind us of the strategies used by counselors. In addition, cognitive coaches engage in three other specific support services: collaboration in both planning and instruction, consulting to build knowledge and skills outside of the classroom, and evaluating to explore the quality of teaching.

At its most intense, cognitive coaching involves a coaching cycle. First, the coach meets with the teacher in a planning conference. The goal of that conference is for the coach to understand and clarify the teacher's goals, collaborate with the teacher to choose evidence that those goals are met, anticipate choices and strategies that might help the teacher to achieve his or her goals, and establish a self-assessment process for the teacher. The next stage in the coaching cycle is monitoring the event—observing teaching. The role of the coach during observation is to gather evidence chosen during planning and to document choices and strategies for the teacher. The final stage in the coaching cycle is a reflection conference, taken after the teacher has had time to reflect personally. The goal of this stage is to provide a setting for self-reflection, to share evidence collected during the lesson, and to connect new learning to future lesson planning.

To us, the strengths of cognitive coaching lie in its specific strategies for building relationships with teachers and for engaging in reflective conversation about teaching. In fact, we think that all coaches would be wise to read Costa and Garmston's work. Another strength of cognitive coaching is that it is flexible with regard to instructional focus. A cognitive coaching cycle could be used to support virtually any teaching goal.

We can also upend those strengths and call them weaknesses. Cognitive coaching encourages relationship building with teachers and reflection on teaching, but it does not specify anything about what or how to teach. It may be inappropriate to implement cognitive coaching when teachers are selecting goals for instruction that are inconsistent with current research; a series of many coaching cycles could move an individual teacher toward setting research-based goals, but that would be a very costly model to adopt for a school.

Peer Coaching

Joyce and Showers (1996) developed this well-articulated coaching model, which has evolved over time; *peer coaching* was designed and redesigned to build a bridge between formal professional development and classroom implementation. The model assumes that an instructional leader (e.g., a principal) has a concern about achievement and identifies an expert outside of the school to select and present a broad-based instructional strategy targeted to address the concern. It then engages the entire school staff to implement the strategy and model it for one another. Like cognitive coaching, peer coaching is also flexible in general about what instructional strategies are targeted, but the model includes choice of a specific schoolwide focus (see Figure 1.5).

The quality that makes peer coaching unique is the coaching itself. After the instructional strategy has been demonstrated in traditional outside-the-classroom professional development, teachers act as coaches for one another. Here's how it works: The principal ensures that teaching colleagues form groups of two or more. These collaborative coaching teams meet to discuss instructional goals and to develop specific lesson plans. Then, they observe one another as they implement these lesson plans. In fact, Joyce and Showers assert that the "coach" is the teacher teaching the lesson; the observer is being coached by observing, and no feedback is

Coaching characteristics	Model-specific choices
Establishing a role for the coach	Peers coach one another
	Demonstrate instructional strategies
Building knowledge for teachers	Outside-the-classroom sessions with an external facilitator
	Observation of teaching
Choosing instructional strategies	Collaborative up-front effort of the principal and external facilitator
	Schoolwide focus
Making instructional plans	Collaboration within each coaching team
Reflecting on instructional quality	Personal reflection, in private
Assessing student learning	Not specified

FIGURE 1.5. Peer coaching.

provided from the observer (Joyce & Showers, 1996). This is an interesting change in perspective from other coaching models.

Peer coaching has much to recommend it. It is relatively inexpensive to implement. It is unlikely to be perceived by teachers as threatening. It is likely to build cohesive relationships within the instructional team. Peer coaching is especially appropriate if one very specific instructional strategy (e.g., guided oral reading, reciprocal teaching, concept mapping) has been identified as appropriate for schoolwide attention. Surely a principal-initiated peer coaching model ensures more consistent implementation than a traditional one-shot inservice presentation; however, the downside of peer coaching is that it assumes one concept or strategy implemented across the school will increase achievement, and there are relatively few quality controls on the implementation of that strategy.

Subject-Specific Coaching

Subject-specific coaching nests all instructional decision making within a particular discipline (e.g., math, English language arts, science, social studies). In that way, subject-specific coaching honors the differences inherent in the academic disciplines and is easily linked to local, state, and national standards. That fact makes it much easier to choose a set of instructional strategies that foster academic excellence and achievement of the standards for all students. Like new-teacher mentoring, though, subject-specific coaching is a common district- or state-level strategy that is enacted in many different ways with little guidance (see Figure 1.6).

As literacy is our field, we tend to focus on that literature. Gabriel (2005) provides a model for subject-specific coaching that evolved from his work as a high school English department chair. We think, though, that this model would work

Coaching characteristics	Model-specific choices
Establishing a role for the coach	Ensure implementation of effective practices and monitor student outcomes
Building knowledge for teachers	Linked to deep understanding of curriculum and standards
Choosing instructional strategies	Nested within the discipline
	Vertically articulated
Making instructional plans	Collaborative curriculum development
	Curriculum mapping
Reflecting on instructional quality	Focused observation
Assessing student learning	Teacher-developed assessments
	State-mandated assessments

FIGURE 1.6. Subject-specific coaching.

equally well with other disciplines. He argues that teacher leaders must empower other leaders within their team, sharing the helm, but that the boat must always be aimed in the direction of expert implementation of the curriculum.

There is a strong theme about observing teachers in Gabriel's work. He encourages the subject-specific coach to observe teachers on his or her team and to help them reflect on the strengths and weaknesses of the lessons. Although he separates these observations from those of an administrator and reminds the coach not to participate in teacher evaluation or to document observations for the principal, he does suggest that a coach might see some practices that are so inconsistent with the norms of the school or discipline that the coach might have to take very specific action. He recommends that the coach try to resolve these issues personally by sharing them with the teacher and offering to help, but that if these efforts are unsuccessful, the next step would be to bring the problem to the attention of the principal. We think that this concept, however unpleasant, is important. As our coaching models become more specific and intrusive, the chance for real conflict increases. Although it does not make conflict easier to manage, it may be helpful simply to anticipate that coaches might fail to achieve their objectives with some teachers. Such is the reality of work with teachers. They are not all equally skilled or committed.

Another theme that Gabriel pursues in his description of subject-specific coaching is the need for careful, evolving curriculum mapping. He describes the map in an interesting way. A map shows various routes to a destination; it is up to the user to choose the exact route. Such curriculum maps allow teams of teachers to ensure horizontal alignment (across sections of the same course) and vertical alignment (across grade levels) so that all students have a path to the final destination. He does anticipate that the curriculum map will evolve to include differentiation within the curriculum to address achievement differences and to provide remediation for those students whose achievement is so far below grade-level expectations that differentiation alone will not provide access to the end goal.

Finally, Gabriel provides specific scenarios about how a subject-specific coach, often working in tandem with a principal, can use data. He suggests that while data analysis alone cannot determine teacher effectiveness, it can open the door to instructional change. In effect, student achievement data (both from teacher-designed tests and from standardized tests) provide a window for discussion of new goals. Data may actually be a less intrusive way for a subject-specific coach to engage teachers to really consider altering their instructional strategies.

Program-Specific Coaching

As we move toward more and more intrusive coaching, instructional strategies become more specific, and the role of the coach changes from facilitator of a teacher reaching his or her own goals to a teacher becoming masterful at a specific set of external goals. This is a controversial topic in literacy education; for instance, Hoffman and Pearson (2000) and Duffy (2004) make a very strong case that "training" teachers to follow a specific program exactly is inconsistent with the professional education of teachers. We think, though, that program-specific coaching can be part of the professional education of teachers, and concepts from program implementation are important.

In fact, *program-specific coaching* is a real coaching model, and it has been effectively applied to very different curricula (Walpole & Meyer, 2008). Program-specific coaching is targeted and outcome-oriented. It is designed to equip an individual to implement a new program with facility. Although we describe two program-specific coaching models, there are many others. In fact, almost all commercial materials available for instruction include offers of program-specific coaching opportunities, controlled by program designers, to help schools in initial implementation.

In the field of literacy, we can compare and contrast two high-profile, program-specific coaching models: Reading Recovery and Success for All (SFA). Reading Recovery is an approach to tutoring first-grade struggling readers; SFA is a comprehensive school reform for kindergarten through sixth grade. Both curricula have been recently reviewed by the What Works Clearinghouse (*http://ies.ed.gov/ncee.wwc/*) and achieved positive or potentially positive effects on overall reading achievement. The routes that they take to get there include highly program-specific coaching.

Reading Recovery has a specific 30-minute lesson frame that involves diagnostic decision making as children read progressively more difficult books, selected based on the reading strategies the teacher will encourage the child to use. Implementation of this lesson frame entails complex decision making before, during, and after the lesson. Knowledge and skills required by a Reading Recovery teacher are developed in a "train the trainer" model. That means that Reading Recovery trainers participate in extensive, specific academic work, defined by the organization and accomplished through universities. Once certified themselves, these trainers can certify teachers to become Reading Recovery teachers. Their strategies include deep understanding of the "whys" of the program, as well as extended observations with feedback—they tutor children while their trainers watch them from behind a one-way mirror (Reading Recovery Council of North America, 2004). This organized, layered coaching yields high levels of consistency in the knowledge and practices of Reading Recovery teachers (Pinnell, 1985; Pinnell, Fried, & Estice, 1990).

Success for All is a comprehensive reading program including instructional materials, grouping plans, periodic assessments, and specific requirements for 90 minutes of reading instruction in a 5-day cycle. Its designers have subjected the program to external evaluation to document its effectiveness (Borman et al.,

2005a, 2005b). The program itself is highly specified, but teachers need extensive support to implement it. SFA also employs a layered training model. Like Reading Recovery, SFA is an organized, national movement with national, regional, and site-based coaches (called *facilitators*).

SFA instruction and SFA classrooms have specific characteristics (including materials that must be displayed, instructional procedures that are used every day, and management tools), and SFA facilitators and SFA Foundation coaches use observation checklists to monitor fidelity to the program requirements. SFA coaches have ready-made tools to guide their work, and they can use a variety of strategies to support teachers who are struggling.

The role of an SFA coach is clearly specified to establish fidelity to the SFA model. Coaches do not choose curricula or strategies. Coaches have lesson plan templates specifying the type, amount, and time for instruction, and teachers are required to implement these lesson plans exactly. Coaches also receive observation templates and must conduct specific observations. They have direct support in how to monitor student achievement through specific program-embedded assessments, and also in how to use achievement data to make new grouping decisions.

Program-specific coaching models are likely to be effective in their goal—establishing fidelity to the program model. The choices they require, represented in Figure 1.7, make this fact clear. In fact, they are much more effective than simply providing teacher's editions and a few hours of training by company representatives and then having teachers make their own interpretations. Program-specific models go well beyond that, giving teachers ongoing support and opportunities for reflection and problem solving. They also provide coaches with very direct tools to monitor their work, including both student-level assessments and teacher-level

Coaching characteristics	Model-specific choices
Establishing a role for the coach	Trainer
Building knowledge for teachers	Deep understanding of how and why to implement the program
Choosing instructional strategies	External, completed by the program designers
Making instructional plans	External, included in the program
	Internal, specified for the setting
Reflecting on instructional quality	Fidelity to the program model
Assessing student learning	Program-embedded assessments
	External assessments

FIGURE 1.7. Program-specific coaching.

observation guidance. This level of direction for the coach is attractive given the debate about what coaches are doing in Reading First initiatives (Deussen, Coskie, Robinson, & Autio, 2007).

Reform-Oriented Coaching

It is to Reading First that we move in order to introduce our most intrusive model—the one that we ourselves have been developing and adapting over time. We call our own model *reform-oriented coaching* for two reasons. First, we have developed it within specific federally funded reform contexts (the Reading Excellence Act Reforms and Reading First initiatives). Both reforms targeted curriculum change in kindergarten through third grade. Both included funding for new materials, new assessments, and professional development for teachers. In the settings where we worked, districts and schools chose to use grant funds to hire site-based literacy coaches. The second reason that we call this model *reform-oriented* (and describe it as most intrusive) is that, in contrast to the program-specific coaching models described earlier, where instructional outcomes are specified in advance and both teachers and coaches know what these outcomes are and move toward them, our reform-oriented model is a moving target. The model itself must evolve and change as student achievement data dictate. In effect, it must be constantly reformed.

Our reform-oriented coaching model (see Figure 1.8) assumes several up-front decisions. First, the school community recognizes that past practices are not yielding acceptable outcomes. Second, the school has used a comprehensive, thoughtful procedure to select high-quality commercial instructional materials for grade-level instruction and for intensive intervention. Third, district and school leaders have committed to extended instructional time and schoolwide assessments. And, finally, there is time during and after the school day for the coach to provide professional development for teachers.

In our model, we are asking much of classroom teachers (Walpole & McKenna, 2007). They must be skillful classroom managers, implementing an interactive read-aloud, fast-paced grade-level instruction, and multiple differentiated small groups every day. We are also asking much of coaches (Walpole & McKenna, 2004). They must work with each of their grade-level teams to construct classroom schedules to specify how their core program will be implemented, design an assessment system to screen students for potential problems, employ flexible informal strategies to specify exactly what those problems are and how to address them, monitor progress to document the effectiveness of instruction, and understand outcome measures to chart growth over time. They must be able to interpret and represent data for individual children, classrooms, grade levels, and schools, using both cross-sectional and cohort tracking. And, finally, they must design and implement a reflexive professional support system—a system that allows all teachers to develop their knowledge of research and pedagogy through book study and to use

Common characteristics	Implementation choices
Establishing a role for the coach	Director and/or mentor
Building knowledge for teachers	Understanding of scientifically based reading research
	Implementation of whole-group instruction, differentiated small-group instruction, and intensive intervention
Choosing instructional strategies	Schools choose commercial materials for whole-group instruction
	Schools choose commercial materials for intensive intervention
	Schools choose instructional strategies for small-group, differentiated instruction
Making instructional plans	Grade-level collaboration, guided by the coach
Reflecting on instructional quality	Walkthroughs
	Observations
Assessing student learning	Valid and reliable assessment systems for screenings, progress monitoring, and outcomes
	Informal assessments to guide differentiated instruction

FIGURE 1.8. Reform-oriented coaching.

walkthroughs and observations to identify targets for professional learning. The fact that these coaches accomplish some of this work in district or regional teams, and with the support of knowledgeable state staff, mediates the difficulties in such a model only slightly.

We highlight only one aspect of this coaching model here; more specifics will be infused in other chapters. We see our reform-oriented coaches adopting one of two roles, which we have termed *director* and *mentor* (Walpole & Blamey, 2007a). They are similar to Neufeld and Roper's *change* and *content coaches*. Recall that the change coach worked primarily with the administration to reorganize the school for teaching and learning; our directors tackle that job first, establishing instructional schedules for grade-level instruction and for intensive intervention, organizing materials and assessment systems, and building knowledge about reading and the curriculum. Mentor coaches are like content coaches; they work directly with teachers, because either they or the principal has already organized the school for the difficult work of schoolwide reform.

The strength of our model is its comprehensiveness and its maintenance of choice. We see each individual school as its own project, led by a coach and principal who understand the school context. As our work with this model is ongoing and intensive, we cannot help but address all of the issues of context that arise. However, our relationships with coaches are founded on choice; we will not recommend specific commercial solutions, and we will not choose specific assessments. Rather, we provide ongoing, evolving guidelines in response to data from the field.

The strength of comprehensiveness and choice is also the major weakness of our model. It may be that this model is simply too demanding for the personnel or the institution; it may also be that teachers' resistance to the type or pace of their professional development and the requirements imposed in their classroom yield resistance too difficult to address. As we said at the start, our model is intrusive.

CHOOSING AND USING A MODEL OF COACHING

We continue to grow in our understanding of coaches and coaching; we acknowledge that thoughtful researchers and wise school and district leaders are wrestling with coaching and that they have described viable models with substantive differences. The array of choices of coaching models is larger now than it was when we began, and it is getting larger every day. To say that models abound and that they differ is not to say that all models are equal in ease of implementation or in effectiveness. In fact, there may be an important interaction—models that are easier to implement may be less effective in the long run. Geologists have long used a 1-to-10 scale to describe the hardness of minerals, with 1 being the softest (talc) and 10 the hardest (diamond). We suggest that this is a useful metaphor to describe coaching (see Figure 1.9). *Soft coaching* is invitational in nature. It engages teachers in nonthreatening, nonconfrontational ways. Teachers' professional expertise is respected and never overtly challenged. Multiple perspectives on teaching are embraced and honored equally. Problems are approached collaboratively and, while compromises are sought, teachers have the last word. *Hard coaching* is based on the assumption that instructional methods vary in their effects on student achievement and that empirical research can identify the best methods. The goal of hard coaching is to support teachers to implement more effective methods and to abandon those that

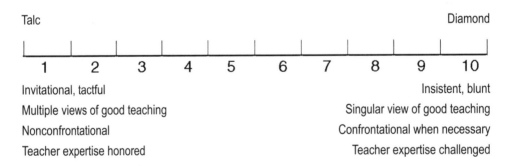

FIGURE 1.9. A hardness scale for coaching.

do not work as well. As they work to achieve this goal, coaches may encounter roadblocks and resistance. One thing is sure—the harder the model that is chosen for a given site, the more work a coach and principal must do up front to set the stage for success.

We invite you into the rest of this book with this goal: to choose or construct a model for coaching. But don't do it yet. Wait until you have thought through the ideas that we present in each chapter. At the end of your work with this book, come back to this chapter and see whether a particular model is attractive to you and appropriate for your school or whether you should construct your own. That's the stance on coaching that we take ourselves—don't be too sure too early.

CHAPTER 2

Serving Adult Learners

The term *coaching* denotes working directly with teachers to sharpen their performance. A literacy coach may have other roles, of course, such as building schedules and interpreting data, but these are really means to the same end— enhancing instruction in order to maximize achievement. The coach is therefore an adult educator, though many coaches do not see themselves as such, at least initially. When asked to give an example of an adult educator, they (and perhaps you) might suggest a college professor or a technical school instructor. These are accurate examples, to be sure, but a broader view of adult education includes all focused on-the-job learning guided by knowledgeable peers. Think, too, of the training that businesses provide for new employees. Large, successful organizations have well-developed programs for new hires and ongoing training for all members, often conducted by more experienced peers. In this case, these peers are literacy coaches. And in order for literacy coaches to be effective, it is essential that they recognize their role as adult educators and do all they can to understand adult learners so that they can better serve them. In this chapter, we discuss key principles of adult education and the characteristics of adults as learners. We also suggest ways a coach can guide teachers' learning in three contexts: the individual, the small group, and the large group. Our goal is to give you an underlying rationale for our chapter on providing professional support.

KEY PRINCIPLES OF ADULT EDUCATION

As we move to the research on adult education, we do so with a large dose of humility. We are both adult educators, but we came to these principles late in the game. In fact, we began our work coaching coaches without really grounding it in adult education theory. We planned our interactions to be coherent sage-on-the-stage shows, with relatively little understanding of the needs of our audience, their backgrounds, or their own potential to contribute important ideas. No wonder implementation was slow and/or off-base; we simply had not met the needs of our learners. We plan differently now, and we want to protect you from making some of the same mistakes that we made.

In her review of the research and theory underlying adult learning, Trotter (2006) concluded that three basic themes emerge: the influence of past experience, the importance of input and choice, and the need for reflection and inquiry. At first blush, these themes may appear too vague to give coaches the guidance they need to work with teachers. Keep them in mind, though, because they are powerful concepts once you understand them. For example, the three themes are evident in the seven principles of adult learning listed by Terehoff (2002). To be most effective, she states, adult learning requires

(a) setting up an environment for adult learning;
(b) involving adult learners in mutual planning;
(c) attending to the adult learners' needs and interests;
(d) involving adult learners in setting the program's goals and objectives;
(e) involving adult learners in designing an effective program;
(f) involving adult learners in implementing the program; and
(g) involving adult learners in the program's evaluation. (p. 70)

These principles are reflected in the *Standards for school leaders* of the Council for Chief State School Officers (1996), and they have been useful in shaping our thinking about how coaches can best assist teachers in the sometimes uncomfortable task of learning about literacy instruction. These principles inform the remainder of this chapter.

A good way to observe these principles in action over time is to view adult learning as a cycle. MacKeracher (2004) describes this cycle (see Figure 2.1), which is easy to relate to coaching. A coach guides a teacher through a planned learning experience (perhaps learning about a new instructional technique). The teacher does not accept this experience uncritically, but interprets it, assigning it value and meaning, either positive or negative. (The teacher may decide, for example, the new approach has merit.) If the teacher's response is positive, the teacher may then use the results of the learning experience to plan future actions that would have been different before the learning. (The teacher might build the technique into a specific lesson plan and then implement the technique.) The teacher then evaluates the action, based on direct observation or the responses of others. (The teacher may note that students have reacted well to the technique. If the coach observes, a postobservation conference may further reinforce the teacher's impression.) The cycle then repeats itself, building on the new learning. (The teacher may apply the instructional technique in additional lesson formats, for example.)

Knowledge of this cycle can help coaches shape learning experiences in productive ways. However, we believe that doing so requires that a coach be aware

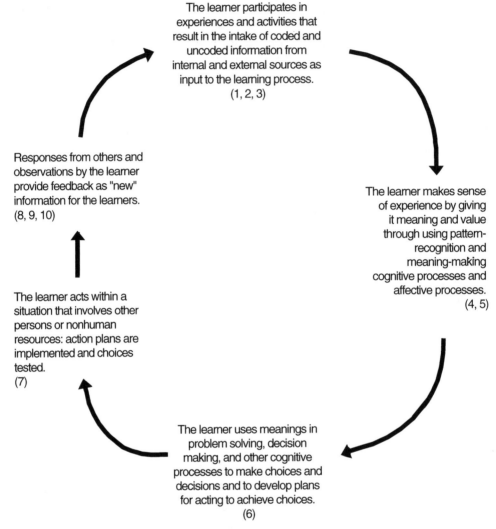

FIGURE 2.1. The basic cycle of adult learning.

From MacKeracher (2004, p. 54). Copyright 2004 by the University of Toronto Press. Reprinted by permission of the author.

of how teachers' learning differs from the learning of the children they serve. We have heard new coaches, frustrated in their roles, say, "I just want to go back to the classroom. I always felt competent there." We have also heard more experienced coaches say, "You'll see. Your teachers are just like your children. You'll learn how to teach them." There is more to this statement than meets the eye.

CHARACTERISTICS OF ADULT LEARNERS

Coaches tend to be accomplished teachers, but their experiences and preparation have focused on children. When they fulfill their role as professional developers, planning and providing for adult learning on a schoolwide basis, they are faced with "students" whose needs and characteristics differ markedly from those of children. It may be tempting to discount these differences because of the fact that teachers are more mature, more likely to be goal directed, and more capable of independent learning. The fact is, however, that teachers can provide challenges that rival those presented by children and that require every bit as much resourcefulness, differentiation, and planning. Providing professional learning for a specific group of adult learners is the job of a coach. For this reason, it is important to understand how teachers differ from children in their approach to learning.

Knowles (1989) outlines key characteristics of adult learners. His list provides a good starting point:

1. Adults need to know why they need to learn something before commencing their learning.
2. Adults have a psychological need to be treated by others as capable of self-direction.
3. Adults have accumulated experiences and these can be a rich resource for learning.
4. In children, readiness to learn is a function of biological development and academic pressure. In adults, readiness to learn is a function of the need to perform social roles.
5. Children have a (conditioned) subject-centered orientation to learning, whereas adults have a problem-centered orientation to learning.
6. For adults the more potent motivators are internal. (pp. 83–84)

These differences suggest that teaching teachers requires strategies that differ considerably from those we use with children. Children view learning as the accumulation of knowledge and skills that may be useful to them later, but adults view learning as a means of contending with the challenges of the present (Knowles, 1980). The best professional development is therefore not subject-centered, as it often is for children, but problem- or performance-centered (Terehoff, 2002). Think about our coach who said that her teachers are just like her students. We think she meant that she must provide them interesting and meaningful opportunities to work together; she must treat them as individuals, with respect; and finally, she must differentiate for them.

In adult professional learning situations, much is at stake. A particular challenge for coaches is that adults come with a wide range of experiences, knowledge, and talent. These qualities have shaped how the adults see themselves as professionals. In fact, their self-concept is central to their predisposition to learn, and their experiences have contributed to the formation of that self-concept. This is why it is important to value teachers' past experiences and to make every effort to relate new ideas to previous experiences (Terehoff, 2002). Indeed, it is difficult for many adults to separate their experiences from their total identity as human beings. When an adult educator dismisses or minimizes adult learners' professional experiences, many adult learners "feel rejected as persons" (Knowles, 1980, p. 50). For this reason, an important concept in adult education is that the personal identity of the learner is at stake. An individual's sense of identity can be profoundly changed by learning experiences (Merriam, 2001; Tennant, 2006), and teachers may be aware of this prospect. Altering their professional practice, they may reason, will alter *them*. Some welcome such a transformation; others resist. The coach's task is to help teachers perceive change not as a means of discrediting their professional expertise, but of building on it.

The first step in creating this impression is to let teachers know that they are expected to be active partners in professional development, not passive recipients. This means that affording them real choices and inviting their input is essential. Successful adult educators strive to foster a sense of self-efficacy. Indeed, a landmark review found that teacher self-efficacy is the single most frequently identified factor in successful school reforms (Berman & McLaughlin, 1980). Essentially, self-efficacy means that teachers believe their personal efforts can make a difference. It means that they feel their ideas are important and listened to during adult education experiences and that they can be effective in increasing achievement in their own classrooms. When these beliefs are in place, teachers tend to be optimistic and adaptive. In order to strengthen teachers' sense of efficacy, a coach can employ several strategies. One is to afford opportunities for teachers to teach one another, perhaps modeling a technique at a grade-level meeting or reporting on an Internet search. Teachers can help shape agendas for meetings and other professional development activities. Perhaps the most powerful way to foster self-efficacy is by signaling the progress teachers have made in terms of achievement data. In this way, teachers have direct evidence that their efforts are having a positive effect on learning.

A sure recipe for destroying self-efficacy is arrogance on the part of the coach. An advanced degree and a position that implies enhanced expertise are all the more reason for a coach to be wary about this. The coach who provides learning from the perspective of "giving teachers the word" on new techniques and applications risks rejection and failure. Because of their profession, teachers are naturally critical of those who would teach *them*. This means that the manner in which professional learning is planned and delivered will inevitably be judged by teachers. Moreover, these judgments will be shared during interactions when the coach is not present.

Schools are complex environments, and teachers have developed relationships with one another that may predispose them to be receptive or resistant. Such relationships are invisible, at first, to the newcomer who considers only the formal organization of a school. But they constitute what Simon (1947) called the "informal organization," a structure so powerful that successful change is grounded on understanding it. Getting the lay of the land as quickly as possible, by learning about individual teachers, their relationships with one another, and their histories, will better position a coach to build on or contend with the informal organization and the relationships that define it. One way to be proactive is to set up individual conferences early in the school year to explore each teacher's perspective and background in a loosely structured setting. Such one-on-one interactions can be a useful strategy for building a sense of self-efficacy; from the very start, the interactions communicate that the coach has not come with any agenda except to learn about and serve the individuals in the school.

Keep in mind that self-efficacy requires the ability to make choices. When teachers are given choices about the direction of their professional learning, they tend to opt for practical, real-world applications (Speck, 1996). For example, a coach might know that a group needs to work on improving the quality of vocabulary instruction. Real choices related to that focus include professional readings, coplanning activities, or observation of instruction through visits or video. The good professional developer also makes clear connections between new content presented today and classroom applications tomorrow. Theory can be intellectually stimulating, but it must be administered in small doses, and its medicinal value in improving instruction must be underscored. Remember that the unvoiced question in the minds of most teachers is likely to be "How is this going to help me?" As adult educators ourselves, we have learned to honor this principle by presenting new instructional strategies and then immediately providing time and activities to allow teachers to integrate them into their thinking and to make concrete plans and commitments to try them.

STANDARDS FOR PROFESSIONAL LEARNING

Unfortunately, teachers are more likely to experience professional learning uninformed by theoretical understandings of adult education and learning. Most professional learning still takes the form of isolated, stand-and-deliver presentations provided by "experts" who know little of the needs of the group. The difference between that type of professional learning and the extended service planned by a coach should be striking. However, this is not an easy realization for the coach. In our own roles to provide professional learning, we rely on standards to ground and evaluate our work.

NSDC has developed standards that reflect current understandings of adult learners and adult education. Figure 2.2 provides these standards in brief. They are categorized in three ways: context standards, process standards, and content standards. *Context standards* acknowledge that although professional learning

Context standards

- Staff development that improves the learning of all students:
- Organizes adults into learning communities whose goals are aligned with those of the school and district.
- Requires skillful school and district leaders who guide continuous instructional improvement.
- Requires resources to support adult learning and collaboration.

Process standards

- Staff development that improves the learning of all students:
- Uses disaggregated student data to determine adult learning priorities, monitor progress, and help sustain continuous improvement.
- Uses multiple sources of information to guide improvement and demonstrate its impact.
- Prepares educators to apply research to decision making.
- Uses learning strategies appropriate to the intended goal.
- Applies knowledge about human learning and change.
- Provides educators with the knowledge and skills to collaborate.

Content standards

- Staff development that improves the learning of all students:
- Prepares educators to understand and appreciate all students, create safe, orderly and supportive learning environments, and hold high expectations for their academic achievement.
- Deepens educators' content knowledge, provides them with research-based instructional strategies to assist students in meeting rigorous academic standards, and prepares them to use various types of classroom assessments appropriately.
- Provides educators with knowledge and skills to involve families and other stakeholders appropriately.

FIGURE 2.2. National Staff Development Council Standards.

From National Staff Development Council (2007) (*www.nsdc.org*). All rights reserved. Reprinted by permission. Note that online each standard is hyperlinked to additional materials and explanations.

may be independently directed, it must occur within communities of educators, continuously supported by the administration. *Process standards* require that professional learning be focused on achievement, which in turn requires careful data analysis. They indicate that decisions made in an effort to improve achievement be grounded in research and a knowledge of how individuals learn. They also stress collaboration and the necessity of matching instructional approaches with expected student outcomes. *Content standards* stress high expectations for students, awareness of student diversity, and familiarity with effective teaching strategies.

They underscore the ability to assess students in ways useful to instructional planning and the necessity of creating learning environments that are safe and conducive to growth.

NSDC takes the stance that to put these standards into practice, all stakeholders (teachers, principals, central office staff members, superintendents, and school boards) have roles. We add *coaches* to their list, and we recommend that coaches purchase the NSDC rubrics, called *innovation configurations*, to guide their thinking (NSDC, 2003). The rubrics make each of the standards quite concrete and also provide guidance for taking small steps toward improvement.

THREE CONTEXTS OF PROFESSIONAL DEVELOPMENT

Embodying these standards in coaching activities may seem a daunting task. Our suggestion is to make the task manageable by thinking about your work with teachers as taking place at three levels. These levels include working one-on-one with individuals, facilitating learning in small-group settings, and making large-group presentations. Although a coach may feel more comfortable at one of these levels than at the others, working at all three is essential to an effective coaching program. And just as a coach helps teachers set goals for their own professional development, functioning proficiently at all three levels is an appropriate goal for the professional learning of the *coach*!

Working with Individuals

The most specific and personal are activities involving a single teacher. They include observation, conferences, coplanning, coteaching, modeling, and suggestions for individual study. The power of working with individual teachers lies in the differentiation possible. A coach can focus specifically on the needs that one teacher identifies or that the coach observes. Such work is also private and may be the best way to address the difficulties of teachers who struggle; in fact, it may be the only way to support teachers who have major struggles with classroom management.

From the perspective of the coach, individual coaching might seem the safest spot for the teacher. However, teachers are often fearful about participating. Remember, teachers come to coaching situations already credentialed for their work; they may not feel comfortable discussing areas where they feel ineffective. They may be self-conscious about opening up, especially when it involves a discussion of how they might improve. They may also fear that confidences will not be honored, making it vitally important for the coach to remind them that information will never be shared (and to adhere to that principle). Another way for a coach to help teachers overcome their anxiety about one-on-one coaching is to model for them. Demonstrating a new technique reverses the typical role of coach and teacher, for it is the teacher who observes and provides feedback. For a short time, the *teacher* is the coach, and the coach is vulnerable. Such modeling is more effective with follow-up conferencing, which not only clarifies what the coach attempted to do but demonstrates how receiving feedback need not be a threatening ordeal.

Individual coaching can and should be highly specific. Observations should be narrowly focused so that the teacher need not worry about the entire gamut of teaching practices on display. Consequently, postobservation conferences can be brief and focused, starting with the positive and moving toward an agreement on what needs to be changed and a sincere offer from the coach to help support the teacher. In selecting a focus, it may be possible to find an area of compromise to empower the teacher, but a coach must nonetheless stand firm on what's important.

Coaching an individual teacher is comparable to tutoring. It is costly in terms of the time required, but it maximizes the chance of transferring new learning to classroom practice. There are more chances to listen and to provide focused responses and suggestions. Like tutoring, it can be planned on the basis of data, in this case student achievement and the coach's observations. And like tutoring, it affords a greater chance for teacher buy-in since a coach can be highly adaptive and personally responsive.

Individual coaching requires that a coach carefully plan a rationale for the work and follow a relatively slow agenda. The teacher must see the experiences as small, incremental steps—not as an overwhelming and rapid transformation. Even in the case of the neediest teacher, a coach would do well to remember that it is not necessary to change everything to change anything. This step-by-step approach will help allay fears and resistance, but it may be a good idea to begin with receptive teachers so that a coach can hone skills and allow the news to spread. ("It really wasn't so bad.") In addition, beginning one-on-one coaching with receptive, even highly skilled teachers communicates that such work is not a form of punishment. Rather, it is at the heart of the coaching program.

Working with Small Groups

A coach also works with small groups, such as teachers at a particular grade level, teachers who are new, or teachers who share a special interest. These individuals differ in their needs, of course, but they share common concerns as a group. Small groups meet to process problems, share successes, learn about new approaches, participate in book studies, and interpret data. They also allow for peer-to-peer support, a possibility hard to realize in one-on-one coaching. Small-group coaching allows a coach to build morale and shared responsibility and to afford opportunities for leaders to emerge.

To be most effective, small-group work requires an objective focus, such as curricular materials, achievement trends, or a professional book. Such a focus prevents individual teachers from feeling "naked" in front of their colleagues. They can find security in the topic and know they will not be singled out. Group interaction, particularly in the case of book studies, keeps teachers learning together rather than learning from the coach. The coach is simply providing the time and materials and participating in the learning. This is a way of communicating to teachers that they are capable of self-directed professional learning.

Small groups operate best when they meet during the regular day and have a regular schedule. Schools accomplish such meetings by having them take place during early-morning or late-afternoon contract hours, or by organizing schedules so that teacher-planning periods are congruent. When this is not possible, we know schools that hire a group of substitutes on a regular basis (e.g., every 2 weeks) to rotate through the grade levels, providing each team an hour or two of shared professional learning time. However this time is provided, it is precious. Coaches must be conscious of that and take steps to use it well.

Up-front planning of the focus of the meeting is very important. Small-group time is best used for issues that apply only to the small group. For example, in elementary school, it makes better sense for the kindergarten team to use small-group time to understand and plan for phonemic awareness instruction than for the third-grade team to do so. In middle school, it makes better sense for science and social studies teachers to study content-area learning strategies than for the English language arts teachers. Grade-level data are also well suited for small-group meetings. Coaches can share grade-level trends while providing teachers the chance to examine their own data. Alternatively, coaches can ask teachers to bring data or work samples for a particular student who is struggling in order that the group can brainstorm new approaches. Another issue well suited to small-group time is curriculum mapping or scheduling. What these issues have in common is that they are specific to the group and they are immediately useful to each member. None of them is easy work, though, and all demand careful use of meeting time.

Coaches may resist planning the logistics of small-group meetings; they may tend to see them as free-flowing problem solving. We think this ill-advised. An agenda should be copied and distributed (or e-mailed) well in advance of the meeting. Minutes should be kept by one of the participants and shared with the group. A procedure for "tabling" discussions should be adopted. In our work at such meetings, we have referred to a "parking lot," a specific physical space (a marker board or a piece of chart paper) where important ideas that cannot be addressed immediately can be "parked." This communicates respect for those ideas and also for the time and agenda established for the meeting.

While these measures seem business-like, this does not mean that the meetings need to be dull or clinical. Rather, they should be focused, practical, and targeted. The setting should be relaxed and supportive. Meetings should not end with the coach assigning teachers homework or paperwork that is not related to preparing or implementing lessons. However, the coach may leave with homework, committing to tasks that will facilitate the work of the group (e.g., finding a reference, gathering data, ordering instructional materials or books, asking about policy at the district office). At the end of a group session, a few minutes should be devoted to recapping and to next steps. Taken together, these efforts constitute attention to the specific backgrounds and needs of group members to be heard and to participate, and they produce an immediate, collaborative, problem-solving atmosphere.

Working with Large Groups

Less frequently, coaches work with larger groups, sometimes an entire school faculty. Collaboration and problem solving are more difficult when the entire school community is served at once. Presentations are more formal and topics more general, but they are important in setting the climate for constructive change and in establishing vision and consistency. They also help communicate that an initiative is truly schoolwide. Such presentations must focus on issues that pertain to all (e.g., achievement trends, school-level planning and scheduling, new curriculum or assessments). Whole-school sessions are high stakes in that they put the coach, and sometimes the entire initiative, on stage. Careful planning, consistent with adult learning and education, then, is essential.

Planning a Large-Group Presentation

If a particular topic is worthy of whole-group attention, coaches can begin to consider how to make it work for their adult learners. From the start, coaches would be well advised to consider how to maximize participation. Such participation can take the form of breaks to discuss issues in small groups, to come up with questions or concerns, or to commit to tasks or schedules to divide work.

If the goal of a session is to introduce an instructional strategy, the planning is more complex. Adults need practice opportunities, with constructive and helpful feedback *during* professional development sessions. A coach may be inclined to minimize this need, reasoning that these are adults, after all, and simply exposing them to new ideas is enough to ensure that they have mastered them. But this is not the case. Teachers require opportunities to participate in small-group activities during large-group sessions. These activities should be designed to move teachers from understanding to application. Small-group activities should afford teachers the chance to share, reflect on, and generalize their learning. Even in large-group sessions, activities could include lesson planning, role-play, or response to video.

Some coaches may be tempted to rely almost exclusively on lecture and to avoid "wasting" time on small-group activities. This, they may think, will make the best use of limited time and will not require them to yield control of a professional learning session. Research, however, suggests that this is not a productive option. In fact, a combination of content and processing is up to 10 times as effective in altering behaviors (Eitington, 1984). It is no wonder that Garmston (2005) concluded that "content is not as important as having the group process the content" (p. 53). Doyle and Strauss (1993) offer an analogy to underscore this point. Think of chewing gum, they suggest. The gum is the content and the chewing is the interaction of participants with the content. You have to achieve the right balance. You don't want to provide too many sticks of gum for teachers to chew, and you don't want them to chew a single stick so long that it loses its flavor.

Given these facts, the question is not whether to plan for processing activities but what the proper ratio between process and content should be. This, too, is a question that researchers have addressed, and again the results may be surprising. Figure 2.3, from Garmston (2005), illustrates how this ratio differs with respect to the goals of a presentation. A coach should plan differently, for example, when the goal is to build teachers' *understanding* of comprehension-strategy instruction than when the goal is to foster proficiency in a new technique for *teaching* comprehension strategies.

If the focus of the large-group session is important for all teachers and based on sound research and school-level data, literacy coaches can use an explicit teaching frame. *During* the session, they can move through the process of explicit instruction, followed by guided practice. Independent practice can come later, in individual classrooms. Guided practice amounts to opportunities provided (and carefully planned for) during the group presentation. The guidance is provided not only by the coach but from small-group members working collaboratively. Learning continues for teachers *after* professional development sessions as they apply what they have learned independently. This involves classroom implementation, of course, at times when the coach is not there to observe. However, transfer to the classroom is not automatic and may require the coach's involvement. Teachers should be encouraged to reflect on the success of a new application and to invite the coach to observe on an agreed-on day and time.

Types of presentation goals	Content ------ Process xxxx		
Awareness	---------X---------X---------X---------X--------		
Knowledge acquisition	---------X---------X---------X---------X--------		
Skills acquisition	-----------XXXX-----XXXX-----XXXX----------		
Attitude development	xxxxxxxxxxxxxx----------------------------		
Application	-----------X------------X-------------XXXXXX		

FIGURE 2.3. Content-process ratios and timing.

From Garmston (2005, p. 52). Copyright 2005 by Christopher-Gordon. Reprinted by permission.

In order to accomplish these goals for large-group presentations, coaches should consider the physical arrangements. When a coach takes time to arrange or rearrange the physical environment, this communicates to teachers that their time is valuable and will be well spent. It also communicates that the coach has carefully considered the goals and strategies that will be used to facilitate the work of the meeting. In essence, such efforts indicate that the coach respects adult learners. However, there are some issues you will need to think through.

The number of ways to set up a room may be unlimited, and the way you choose will depend in part on space and furniture. Several conventional room setups can give you an idea of the basic options. A room set in theater style, with long, straight rows of chairs, accommodates most people, but it limits interaction and there are no tabletops on which audience members can write. Unless space is extremely limited relative to the number of people, this option is not a good one. When tables are available, participants can take notes and view handouts. They can also interact with their tablemates and occasionally transition to other tables, as in jigsaw activities. Setting up a room in classroom style means arranging tables in parallel rows so that all audience members sit on one side of a table, facing the speaker. The only drawback to this setup is that interaction is still limited. Participants do have a workspace, but they can conveniently work with only the individuals immediately to their right and left. If seats are placed on both sides of the tables, then half the audience must turn to face the speaker, except during group work. One solution is to place tables at angles, so that one end of each table points in the direction of the speaker. That way, audience members do not need to move their chairs when the presenter speaks, but merely turn slightly to the right or left. If the tables are round, the same problems occur. (You may have attended a banquet featuring an after-dinner speaker and made the mistake of sitting with your back to the lectern.) Round tables can be set with chairs on one side only, if space permits, so that groups are seated in crescents and everyone can see the speaker. For smaller groups, tables can be pushed together so that all participants can see one another. This arrangement is similar to the *Harkness table*, named for philanthropist Edward Harkness. His idea was to maximize interaction and create a small learning community, while the teacher (or coach) facilitates. This goal can also be accomplished when meeting in empty classrooms, simply by arranging students' desks in a circle. There is much to consider in choosing the best room setup. The goal is to select the arrangement that permits teachers to hear your presentation comfortably and to interact easily.

No matter how much time the coach spends preparing the environment for large-group learning, anything can happen. We have encouraged coaches many times to reflect on the personal challenges they have faced during large-group sessions. Garmston's (2005) work has proved helpful for coaches who might think they are alone in facing challenges. He posits four types of learners likely to be included in the room. "Professors" want mastery and competence. They want to be able to remember the content exactly. They like facts, evidence, details, and clear organization. They will be well served by handouts. "Friends" thrive on engagement with other participants. They want to respond to content through interpersonal relations. They need emotional hooks, personal stories, and metaphors. They like opportunities to share and hands-on activities during the session. If small-group discussions are planned during the session, friends can be called on to take the lead. "Scientists" want to examine and process data. They like to hypothesize and explore explanations. They like structure, especially when it provides opportunities to inquire and reach judgments. The needs of scientists can be addressed when data are shared; they can be called on to interpret cases, or to share their own class data as an example, either for all or for a small group. Finally, "inventors" want to adapt, create, and extend ideas. They are unlikely to implement an instructional strategy in the same way as the coach models it. They want to reorganize information into new arrangements. Given their strengths, they are useful as models, or in lesson-planning discussions. They learn when they are provided opportunities to explore and generate new solutions. Garmston suggests that the effective presenter shifts focus during a presentation in order to meet the expectations of all four types of audience members. With this approach, there will be something for everyone.

Our experience tells us that few presenters are so accomplished they cannot learn from others. This judgment certainly applies to us! So, we have provided additional planning tips in Figure 2.4 that we believe will be useful. We have collected them from our own experiences (including many missteps) and from the experiences of others.

We know that coaches find making large-group presentations especially nerve-wracking. Remember the one-person band, a single performer playing a number of instruments at once? It is easy to feel overwhelmed by the need to manage every aspect of a presentation, from planning the content to adjusting the temperature. Eller (2004) argues that using a facilitator to run a teacher meeting can free the coach to focus on content and learning activities. Ideally, the facilitator is someone who is not a teacher and has no real stake in the proceedings. Eller's reasons are persuasive. In addition to helping with logistics and housekeeping, a facilitator is more interested in process than content. A facilitator can more easily put the needs of groups before his or her own needs, can listen to participants objectively, depersonalize negative events or comments, and stay calm under pressure. Of course, facilitators can be hard to find, but with some advance planning, a coach might be able to draft a parent volunteer, secretary, paraprofessional, or student teacher. It may be worth the effort. A facilitator can play one or two of the instruments strapped to that one-person band, freeing the coach to make real music.

We end this chapter with a checklist constructed around the three dimensions of the NSDC standards (see Figure 2.5). It may be helpful as a means of planning and as a focus for reflection following a session. It can also be used by a trusted colleague to organize feedback after a coach leads a learning session. If the coach

Decide on physical arrangements.

- Select (and check on) refreshments.
- Decide on and gather writing materials (markers, pads, easels).
- Back up your technology (microphone, PowerPoint, screen, lighting).
- Check out your own space (remove clutter).
- Decide how to distribute handouts.
- Package the handouts.
- Select a room arrangement that allows participants to attend to the presentation and to work with groups.

Organize your talk.

- Begin with goals. Clarify these to yourself!
- Decide on organizational structures that will help the group accomplish them, such as
  — Key questions
  — Important ideas
  — Compare–contrast
  — Problem solution
  — Combinations of these
- Decide on activities that will help teachers process the content.

Plan to get off on the right foot.

- Set up early so you can relax and greet participants.
- Send a message that you care how the session goes.
- Win them over with favors, door prizes, candy (especially after a long day).
- Consider showing a "sponge" PowerPoint as participants enter (arresting pictures, inspirational quotes).
- Put up a welcome sign.
- Greet everyone at the door if possible.
- Make sure that everyone is comfortable, and make any adjustments needed in the room (temperature, lighting, seating).
- Plan an icebreaker if this is the group's initial meeting.
- Be welcoming and thankful for the participants' time.
- Give a short and humble (funny?) introduction of yourself or a humorous story related to school.
- Share the agenda and logistics.
- Plan to engage the audience quickly in an activity.
- Make sure that directions for group activities are clearly stated and available for reference (in a handout or PowerPoint slide).

FIGURE 2.4. Tips for planning a good presentation.

- Think of a way to inspire your teachers, perhaps with a quote. (Here's our favorite, from Michael Pressley: "I cannot imagine how anything could be more demanding than teaching first grade well. It is much harder than flying a 747 or being a graduate school professor.")
- Follow your agenda notes and try to stay a step ahead mentally.
- Use PowerPoint Presenter Tools to prompt yourself to make certain points and also to remind yourself what slide is coming next. If you are not familiar with the Presenter Tools, follow a tutorial.
- Enliven your presentation with analogies, stories, student work, jokes, read-alouds, or cartoons.
- Develop strategies for tardiness, talking, negativity, and distractions.
- Plan to conclude with a recap and an invitation to continued inquiry.
- Seek a commitment.
- Welcome contact from teachers.
- Try to end on an upbeat note.
- Decide how you will form random groups. Some ways include:
  — Using playing cards or tokens and forming groups of four (kings, twos, etc.).
  — Using candy or jellybeans and grouping by kind or color.
  — Putting numbers on the handouts.
  — Organizing by birthday month (May people at this table, etc.).

FIGURE 2.4. *(cont.)*

takes the feedback and reflects on it in public at the start of the next whole-group session, he or she will surely win over some skeptics and begin to build a reflective, professional community of adult learners.

CONCLUSION

Literacy coaches are first and foremost adult educators. Their work with individuals, and with small and large groups, demands that they use an array of effective strategies that derive from adult-learning research. Fortunately, much is known about planning and facilitating activities that enhance instruction and achievement. Coaches can find guidance in standards, the experiences of others, the burgeoning literature of coaching, and research. In this chapter, we have attempted to distill the most useful lessons from these sources and offer practical suggestions for meeting the needs of teachers as students.

Context

- ☐ Did I make connections between new content and the circumstances of my school:
  - ☐ Curriculum materials?
  - ☐ Students?
  - ☐ Teachers?
  - ☐ Administration?
- ☐ Were the physical facilities appropriate?
- ☐ Did I organize my materials in advance?
- ☐ Did I begin the session on time?
- ☐ Did I remind participants of future dates and other "housekeeping" items future dates and other "housekeeping" items?

Process

- ☐ Did I monitor the understanding of the participants?
- ☐ Did I adjust my instruction when necessary?
- ☐ Did I respond to questions and comments insightfully and with tact?
- ☐ Did I provide opportunities for role-playing or other forms of guided practice?
- ☐ Did I devote an amount of time to these activities appropriate to my goals?
- ☐ Did I take the time to build rapport and establish a positive climate?
- ☐ Was my pacing appropriate?
- ☐ Did I make concrete suggestions for classroom implementation?
- ☐ Did I seek a commitment from teachers to implement the content?
- ☐ Did I elicit specific ideas for how they might do so?
- ☐ Did I ask the teachers to evaluate the session in written form?

Content

- ☐ Was the session content coherent and clearly organized?
- ☐ Did I state my goals for the session clearly?
- ☐ Did I convey the information in practical terms?
- ☐ Were my examples appropriate to clarifying new ideas?
- ☐ Did the teachers exhibit evidence of understanding?
- ☐ Did I provide adequate closure?

FIGURE 2.5. Coach's checklist for group professional development sessions.

From *The Literacy Coaching Challenge* by Michael C. McKenna and Sharon Walpole. Copyright 2008 by The Guilford Press. Permission to photocopy this figure is granted to purchasers of this book for personal use only (see copyright page for details).

CHAPTER 3

Serving Adult Learners in School Contexts

We know that if student learning is to improve, instruction must change. Learning is influenced by many factors, to be sure, but instruction is the one over which we have the most control. We also know that in order for instruction to change, teachers must embrace new approaches and apply them with diligence. In order for this to occur, teachers must become part of a community of learners in which experience is honored, choices offered, and practical application stressed. Such a community is not hierarchical. It will not work if an authority figure like a principal or coach attempts to dispense wisdom and knowledge. This does not mean that coaches and principals do not possess insights that might benefit teachers. The question is how best to facilitate teacher learning in ways that influence classroom practice. This is a question that concerns leadership. In this chapter, we explore how coaches function with other leaders, and as leaders themselves, to influence student growth.

ISSUES OF AUTHORITY

Heifetz and Linsky (2002) suggest that there are two types of solutions to educational problems: *technical* and *adaptive*. *Technical solutions* can be addressed through current levels of knowledge. They might include changing a school's schedule or reassigning teachers to grades or students to classrooms. Technical solutions can bring about clear but limited changes. Going further requires *adaptive solutions*. Adaptive solutions cannot be implemented at current levels of expertise. They require difficult new learning, they create disequilibrium, and they may lead to avoidance behaviors on the part of some. These uncomfortable changes require leadership at the building and district levels if they are to occur.

Leadership at the Building Level

Working to improve the expertise of teachers is far more than an intellectual exercise. Murphy (2004) states flatly that "there is a robust empirical link between professional development and student reading achievement" (p. 184). However, we argue that the link is not direct. This means that teacher learning affects student learning and that in order for coaches to bring about the latter, they must target the former. Since they are working in schools, coaches must also ensure that the organizational structure of the school facilitates transfer of new ideas into classroom practice.

This is not merely a matter of raising the level of knowledge. It also frequently involves altering a school's organization and culture. It may mean tactfully but relentlessly challenging beliefs that inhibit student growth, something that requires insightful leadership. An example of how the climate of a building might influence learning in subtle ways comes from a British study of secondary teachers (Hay Group Management, 2004). Teachers in 134 secondary schools were asked to rank 30 school characteristics in order of importance. It is interesting to contrast the rankings of teachers at high-achieving and low-achieving schools. The top six characteristics of each group of teachers are presented in Figure 3.1. Each group acknowledged the importance of using assessments to gauge the impact of instruction, but after that, a telling divide occurs. Teachers at low-performing schools value emotional security for both teachers and students; they noted the importance of making allowances for students because of their backgrounds. On the other hand, teachers at high-achieving schools expressed the importance of maintaining high expectations for all students and of sacrificing to realize those expectations. It is not hard to conclude that very different professional climates pervade these schools. Both are nurturing, to be sure. A coach must decide which type of climate to promote—one that nurtures through comfort and tolerance, or one that nurtures through expectation and support. The former perspective we have called *soft coaching*, the latter *hard coaching*. We argue that the discomfort teachers might experience in a climate of high expectations is the cost of promoting achievement. And in the end, fostering achievement is the best way to serve students. It is well worth the cost.

How can leaders foster both the positive climate teachers need and the expertise teachers require to enhance student learning? We begin by considering characteristics of the most effective principals. This may seem like an odd way to start since coaches have little control of the traits possessed by their principals. Or do they? We argue that many of these characteristics can be acquired as a matter of professional growth and that a coach can guide the principal toward acquiring them. Remember that in Chapter 1 we introduced the concept of change coaches (Neufeld & Roper, 2003), who work with principals. In other words, coaching may extend to administrators as well as teachers if care is taken to guide rather

Ranking	Teachers in low-performing schools	Teachers in high-performing schools
1	Measuring and monitoring targets and test results	Measuring and monitoring targets and test results
2	Warmth, humor, repartee, feet on the ground	A hunger for improvement, high hopes and expectations
3	Recognizing personal circumstances, making allowances, toleration (it's the effort that counts)	Raising capability, helping people learn, laying foundations for later success
4	Keeping up with initiatives, doing what is required, following policy	Focusing on value added, holding hope for every child, every gain a victory
5	Creating a pleasant and collegial working environment	Promoting excellence, pushing the boundaries for achievement, world class
6	Working together, learning from each other, sharing resources and ideas, investing in others	Making sacrifices to put pupils first

FIGURE 3.1. Teacher perceptions of the most important characteristics of a school. Data from Hay Group Management (2004, pp. 33, 35).

than prescribe. But coaches must first have an idea of where this guidance should lead, and this means being aware of the traits possessed by the best principals. Fortunately, research can help.

In a now-classic study that sought to identify predictors of reading achievement, Michael Kean and his colleagues (1979) looked at the correlates of fourth-grade reading achievement in Philadelphia. They knew that many factors were at work (like socioeconomic status and previous achievement), but because they had access to long-term data on children, they were able to control for many factors while examining the impact of just one. Kean et al. discovered that reading achievement was significantly related to a principal's expertise in reading, a finding that has since been supported so many times that it is axiomatic: *The more a principal knows about reading, the better the children read.*

We suspect that this is true because more knowledgeable principals make decisions that are better aligned with best practice, and they are more likely to initiate a schoolwide focus on reading improvement. Indeed, the *Standards for school leaders* (Council for Chief State School Officers, 1996) make clear that school leaders must focus on student achievement. Once this focus is established, the remaining standards can be seen as contributing to this outcome. It is easy to see that reading achievement is the most likely target.

Unfortunately, raising achievement through leadership requires far more than educating the principal. Many other traits are also important, and we rely on the leadership literature to identify them. Murphy (2004) summarizes the research that has identified these traits and organizes them into 15 categories. We have distilled the major findings in Figure 3.2. As you contrast the characteristics of more- and less-effective principals, you may wonder (as we did) whether a single individual could possess all of the strengths or all of the weaknesses that research has identified. Perhaps not. However, the chart provides an excellent tool that principals can use in examining their own habits. It can form the basis of self-reflection and goal setting that can guide principals in the direction of the ideal.

More-effective principals	Less-effective principals
Setting goals	
Has a more child-centered vision	Has a more adult-centered vision
Sets manageable, realistic goals	Favors broad goals
Sees student performance as central	Likes to see things run smoothly
Expresses goals in measurable terms	Expresses goals vaguely
Uses goals for planning	Refers rarely to goals
Asks parents and staff to help set goal	Limits goal-setting input
Communicating goals	
Periodically reviews and discusses	Infrequently discusses goals
Actively clarifies goals	Rarely clarifies goals
Has teachers who know goals	Has teachers unfamiliar with goals
Has teachers who see themselves as good instructors	Has teachers who see themselves as good managers and colleagues
Promoting quality instruction	
Insists on certain teaching strategies	Has less focus on methods
Favors interactive teaching	Content with less interaction
Assigns teachers on the basis of improving achievement	Assigns teachers bureaucratically
Supervising instruction	
Relies little on formal observations	Values formal observations
Values informal visits and meetings	Rarely makes informal visits
Often reads about instruction	Seldom reads about instruction
Often provides specific feedback	Seldom provides specific feedback
Counsels and assists poor teachers	Less likely to confront poor teachers

FIGURE 3.2. Characteristics of more- and less-effective principals.

Allocating instructional time	
Carefully sets time allocations	Less likely to set time allocations
Coordinates time allocations across teachers	Less likely to have uniform schedule
Schedules more instructional and fewer noninstructional activities	Less likely to favor instructional over noninstructional activities
Insists on time for basics	Less likely to ensure coverage of basics
Protects uninterrupted instructional blocks	Less likely to preserve instructional blocks
Coordinating the curriculum	
Highly involved in curriculum alignment	Less involved in curriculum alignment
Concerned with the continuity of curriculum from grade to grade	Tends not to focus on continuity of curriculum from grade to grade
Monitoring student progress	
Supports testing programs	Views testing as a necessary evil
Provides test results to teachers in a timely manner	Less timely in reporting results to teachers
Discusses results with groups and individual teachers	Less likely to discuss results
Encourages teachers to use test results to plan instruction	Does not emphasize the connection between testing and teaching
Setting expectations	
Holds adults accountable for student-learning outcomes	Does not hold others accountable
Requires mastery of grade-level skills for promotion to next grade	More likely to socially promote students
Being visible	
Often out of the office	Spends large amounts of time in the office
Makes an effort to move about the campus and in and out of classrooms	Less mobile
Providing incentives	
Recognizes teachers with rewards such as • distributing leadership • showing personal interest • making public acknowledgements • giving private praise	Seldom acknowledges teachers
Ensures that student rewards are frequent and that they go to a large percentage of students	Less concerned about student rewards
Focuses rewards on achievement	Less likely to reward achievement

(cont.)

FIGURE 3.2. *(cont.)*

Promoting professional development	
More likely to be directly involved in professional development activities	Often avoids professional development sessions
Follows up by ensuring that professional development methods are implemented	Unlikely to follow up professional development
Cobbles temporary coalitions of teachers to help implement new ideas	Not adept at working with teacher groups to implement
Encourages professional dialogue	Indifferent to dialogue
Helps teachers attend conferences	Resists conference attendance
Creating a safe and orderly learning environment	
Works with teachers to develop classroom management skills	Less focused on management skills
Establishes a clear and consistent disciplinary policy	Fails to set up a clear policy
Enforces discipline fairly and consistently	May be inconsistent in enforcing discipline
Involves teachers and students in setting rules	Sets rules independently
Confronts problems quickly and forcefully	Tentative and indecisive
Supports teachers with discipline problems	Unsympathetic to teachers with discipline problems
Promoting collaboration	
Encourages teamwork and collaboration	Allows teachers to function independently
Gives faculty a formal role in decision making	Excludes teachers from decision making
Informally seeks teachers' ideas and opinions	Indifferent to the ideas and opinions of teachers
Securing outside resources	
Skilled at influencing district decision making about resources	Reacts to district decisions
Actively seeks resources	Passive about finding resources
Assertively recruits the best teachers (even from other schools)	Follows standard hiring procedures
Allocates money based on goals	Makes allocations based on other factors
Linking home and school	
Communicates with parents regularly	Infrequently communicates with parents
Involves parents in school activities	More likely to ignore parent participation
Establishes programs that promote parent–teacher interaction	Fails to facilitate parent–teacher interaction
Promotes the school to community groups	Does not participate in community groups
Provides ways parents can learn about school and help their children	Does not actively reach out to parents as partners

FIGURE 3.2. *(cont.)*

Distributing Leadership

From our discussion thus far, you may have concluded that building leadership resides entirely with the principal. This is far from true. No single individual, no matter how talented, can be the sole leader of a faculty if student growth is to be optimal. "For schools to have leadership," Donaldson (2001) writes, "they need leaders–not a single leader" (p. x). Although the notion of principal-as-sole-leader was once dominant, research suggests that far more progress can be expected when leadership is shared with, or distributed among, teachers. Distributed leadership builds community and contributes to a sense of self-efficacy among teachers. As Fullan (2005) states, "The main mark of an effective principal [we might add coach] is not just his or her impact on the bottom line of student achievement, but also on *how many leaders he or she leaves behind who can go even further*" (p. 31, original emphasis). He concludes that the very best leaders "have a dual focus on performance and development of leadership in others" (p. 31).

Continuity is another advantage of distributing leadership. When leadership is vested in a single person, what becomes of a schoolwide initiative when that person leaves? In fact, Copland (2003) concludes that the single biggest threat to a reform effort is leadership turnover. By making certain that leadership is distributed, the coach and principal, working as a team, can help to ensure the sustainability of their efforts should one or the other leave.

The idea of distributing leadership may be hard for some administrators to accept. There is an old axiom among school administrators: *You can delegate authority but not responsibility*. This idea may make some principals hesitant to yield leadership power to others because they understand that, ultimately, the blame for failure falls on the principal. The alternative to distributing leadership, however, is to direct all change in a top-down, visionary manner. Imagine the pressure of being the sole source of vision and direction. And even if one could deliver, there would be little sense of professional community among those on the receiving end. In studying the characteristics of principals who fostered exceptional teacher-learning communities at the high school level, McLaughlin and Talbert (2001) discovered that none of these communities was brought about simply because the principal had a transcendent vision. Instead, these individuals worked collaboratively with teacher leaders, in effect, sharing the role of leadership. These researchers also found that the most effective principals were focused on improved learning as their overarching mission. All other decisions and actions were viewed as a means to this end. We suspect that these findings apply to elementary and middle school contexts, as well.

What, then, does distributed leadership entail? Copland (2004) identifies five themes:

> (a) a persistent, public focus on learning, (b) the use of inquiry, (c) the development of enabling structures [e.g., arranging group meeting time], (d) shared responsibility for decision making, and (e) personal participation as a learner. (p. 226)

We might add a sixth: *sharing leadership with the literacy coach*. A strong partnership between principal and coach is one of the most effective examples of distributed leadership we know of. Its importance lies in the power that resides in the principal's position. Coaches typically have little supervisory power. They can suggest, assist, and persuade, but they cannot command. A principal, on the other hand, is charged with the ability to make decisions about what teachers should do. This power has limits, of course, but it defines a position very different from that of the coach. When the principal and coach share common understandings about how teachers must change, the coach acts with the benefit of implicit "back-up" from the administration. This means that suggestions carry more weight and are less likely to be dismissed. It also means that teachers have a clear understanding that the coach works to make the principal's vision about instruction accessible and achievable by all.

Another reason that the partnering of principal and coach is vital concerns the power needed to make a reform effort truly coherent. The many dimensions of a school interact in complex ways, and an initiative can be hampered unless these dimensions operate in concert to foster change. Murphy and Datnow (2003b) suggest that the principal is responsible for "nurturing coherence" by

> (a) actively helping staff see linkages among activities and functions; (b) wiring together goals, budgets, curriculum, instruction, and staff development; (c) promoting staff stability; (d) carefully nesting the reform design into extant school systems; (e) damping down external stimuli and work demands that compete with core activities; (f) identifying and legitimizing the abandonment of requirements that run at cross purposes to reform goals; (g) linking teachers into a community of practice; (h) aligning the pursuit and use of resources with the reform blueprint; and (i) forging teacher leadership around core purposes. (p. 267)

We believe that the coach can be an able assistant in accomplishing these tasks, but the principal must assume the primary responsibility for undertaking them. The principal alone is vested with the power to make a reform initiative more coherent.

Forging a Strong Partnership with the Principal

Given the importance of a principal and coach working in tandem, how is a positive partnership to be formed? Much will depend on the experience and personalities of the two, but we believe that there are general suggestions that a coach can use to strengthen the working relationship with nearly any principal.

• *Be helpful.* Most principals will be grateful if their lives are made easier, especially during the demanding process of school reform. A coach can assist in numerous ways. One of them is to summarize achievement data and point out important trends, a subject we explore in the following chapter. Another is to help with recruiting (if requested) by examining a candidate's experience, beliefs, and orientation. It is a good idea to look for opportunities to make the principal look good. Providing PowerPoints the principal can use in meetings, talking points concerning the initiative, and progress reports to share with district leaders can do much to create a perception of worth, and even indispensability.

• *Communicate.* It is important to confer regularly with the principal. Short but frequent talks contribute to an ongoing relationship and can offer insights about the principal's philosophy, strengths, shortcomings, fears, and concerns. Such knowledge can position a coach to make decisions that protect the principal without jeopardizing the reform effort. Regular meetings are also a way to apprise the principal of successes and to prevent him or her from being caught off guard by developments that may prove embarrassing. Such meetings are also opportunities to reconfirm mutual goals and to develop a united voice.

Communication can also take the form of brief memos that describe progress in the initiative. For example, coaches who provide periodic updates on the characteristics of instruction they are targeting influence the principal's observations of instruction in subtle ways. Lists of the components of a target strategy, or lesson-planning templates that teachers have adopted for instruction are tools that can focus the principal's attention.

• *Become colearners.* Because of the connection between a principal's knowledge and student achievement, it is important to look for ways of engaging the principal in professional learning. One way is to extend an invitation to study-group meetings, with a reminder of how crucial it is to demonstrate an administrative commitment to the reform effort (Desimone, 2002). Another is to recommend materials specifically designed for school leaders. (At the elementary level, we suggest *Leadership for Literacy* by Joseph Murphy.) A tactic for leveling the playing field is to place the principal in a coaching position by requesting mentoring in leadership skills. In this way, the coach and the principal can exchange skills and enhance the expertise of each other.

• *Discuss pressure.* We believe that it is helpful for the coach and principal to discuss the pace of reform and the pressure it may place on teachers. There are definite "do's" and "don't's" to be mindful of. It is important to resist the temptation to exert high pressure to increase the pace of change. This is because teachers will probably respond with compliance, but the change is likely to be short-lived. As Goleman, Boyatzis, and McKee (2002) put it, "Essentially, the pacesetter's dilemma is this: The more pressure put on people for results, the more anxiety it provokes" (p. 73). For sustained change, leaders must strive for a middle ground between too much and too little pressure. We believe that one way to maintain this middle ground is to make reading the centerpiece not only of the formative feedback provided by a coach but of the formal evaluations conducted by the principal. We agree with Murphy (2004) that effective principals often make reading a focus of evaluations. Coaching is soon perceived as a tune-up for the "real thing," and teachers may become more receptive to a coach's suggestion. In fact, we would extend this idea to content specialists in the middle grades. If, for example, science teachers were aware that their evaluations would depend in part on observations of their use of content-area reading techniques like those described in Chapter 8, their attitudes might improve accordingly.

• *Maintain confidences.* We have stressed how crucial it is for a coach to respect the privacy of teachers by not sharing communications or observational data. This rule applies to sharing with other teachers, of course, but above all it applies to sharing information with the principal—the one individual in a position to use such information for the purpose of evaluation. However, there is also another type of confidence to maintain—between the principal and the coach. When a principal chooses to share judgments, acknowledge weakness, or confide uncertainty, the coach must not be tempted to share this knowledge. And there may well be such a temptation to share it. We have known coaches who have attempted to curry favor with teachers by sharing compromising information about their supervisor. Not only is this a shortsighted tactic, one that is likely to damage the learning climate, but the information may well get back to the principal and threaten a vital partnership. Another axiom of leadership is this: *Information yearns to be free.* If you share juicy information with just one other person, you will be surprised at how quickly your secret can be communicated widely. This a prudent point to remember at all times.

• *Be creative.* It is a good thing to inform a principal that a problem must be addressed. It is better to do so with possible solutions in mind. A coach can relieve the administrative burden on a principal and at the same time advance reading reform by thinking through problems, anticipating logistical barriers, and generating solutions that account for those barriers. For example, in *Every Child Reading*, a report of the Learning First Alliance (1998), school leaders are encouraged to establish intervention programs, but exactly how to accomplish this goal depends on the specific circumstances of a school. A coach who thinks creatively about potential plans and who approaches the principal with feasible choices is displaying good partnership skills.

Leading the Charge: First Steps toward Reading Reform

At the building level, it is important first to learn, then to plan, and finally to act. Begin by assessing the school context. No reform effort can be successful if the context of a particular school is ignored in the belief that one size will truly fit all. As Murphy and Datnow (2003a) put it, "the reform agenda must be tailored to the needs of a specific school and must be co-constructed at the site level—it must focus on what is important for that particular school community" (p. 11). This is why it is important for a coach to take stock of the context, including teachers and their backgrounds, student demographics, materials available, other initiatives in place, and the expertise and support of the administration. These characteristics define each school and make it unique. They also make it essential to adapt coaching in ways that acknowledge this uniqueness.

The planning process takes context into account and is also an opportunity for engaging teachers as leaders. Establishing a schoolwide team brings important stakeholders to the table from the outset. In a report sponsored by the Center for the Improvement of Early Reading Achievement (CIERA), Taylor and her colleagues (2004) make clear that the first step in bringing about school change is to establish a small schoolwide leadership team. The first task of team members is to become familiar with research that should inform the targeted change. This research involves not only best practices in reading but findings that concern successful school reform. Unless school leaders are cognizant of the latter, all the knowledge in the world of how best to teach reading will not lead to altered classroom instruction. This means, in essence, taking no action until that grounding is established. When it has been, the team applies findings to the achievement data for the school and produces a "detailed but simple" (p. 3) professional development plan that 75% of the teachers vote to accept. The team is then expanded to represent all dimensions of the reading program, and it meets at least monthly to sustain momentum and to ensure professional development efforts.

Leadership at the District Level

Any school reform effort occurs within a district context, and the nature of system-level support can help or hinder such a reform. One question is whether it is better for districts to take a laissez-faire stance toward building initiatives, showing a kind of benign neglect that allows school leaders to shape their own program. There is support for this stance. Ouchi (2003) found that the most successful reform efforts involved districts permitting school leaders to make important decisions regarding reform initiatives. When district leaders were too heavy-handed in mandating specific changes, the process did not work nearly as well. Of course, this idea requires that school leaders have sufficient knowledge of reading instruction, educational reform, and their own school contexts to take the initiative when it is given.

On the other hand, we feel it is important for district leaders to assume a role in the initiative, though not one that entails micromanaging the change process. One reason that district leadership should be involved is the need for a coherent literacy initiative in an era when many ideas are in play at once. School systems "do not suffer from too few innovations, but rather from too many ad hoc, unconnected, superficial innovations" (Fullan, 2005, p. 21). This crazy quilt of initiatives can threaten the success of any one of them. We have worked with one district in which so many programs were in place, it took district leaders an entire morning to summarize them for us; then, it took us several days to explain why some of the programs were working at cross purposes. This is the result of a natural tendency to seize every attractive idea and mandate it districtwide. This tendency is propelled by high-stakes testing, which "places people in a high-alert dependency mode, jumping from one solution to another in a desperate attempt to comply" (Fullan, 2005, p. 11).

Nevertheless, school districts can create an environment in which reform initiatives can flourish where they are needed most—in schools facing the challenges of poverty. Based on a study of five high-poverty districts that were experiencing unexpected success, Togneri (2003) found several common factors that appeared to be active ingredients. These districts acknowledged their poor performance and committed to a long-term effort to improve instruction. Specifically, they made decisions based on data rather than instinct. They adopted new approaches to professional development that focused especially on new teachers and that linked teacher learning across schools to curriculum standards. To facilitate these processes, the districts provided better data to schools that were truly useful in planning. The districts also redefined leadership roles. They did this by establishing groups of well-trained teachers within each school. These "cadres of instructional experts" (p. 6) were able to guide professional growth in particular school contexts, mentor new teachers, work with struggling teachers, model instructional techniques, and network with one another and with principals. In short, they performed many of the functions of literacy coaches though they were not labeled as such. Given the principal's responsibility for conducting formal evaluations, these districts made systematic observation a target of professional development for principals.

The obvious problem facing a literacy coach is how to influence district policy in these positive ways without spending too much time on district committees and initiatives. Coaches we know are inclined to stay "under the radar" of district administrators, and they try to do their jobs without attracting attention. We view this strategy as giving up without a fight. "When it comes to sustainability," Fullan writes, "each level above you helps or hinders (it is rarely neutral)" (2005, p. 65). There are certainly steps a coach might take to help ensure that district leaders are friends of the reform effort. These steps are modest in light of the power differential between a coach and the school district, but we believe they can be effective.

The first step is to become aware of district initiatives, including those that compete with the reform effort for resources and that may be based on different orientations toward instruction. Are there ways to coexist with such initiatives and minimize the damage they might do? Or, should the coach actually work with the principal to communicate why a particular initiative will not be appropriate for their teachers? It is essential to remember the chain of command. A coach would be ill-advised to approach district leaders without the knowledge and support of the principal. In fact, the coach could become the principal's liaison to the district with respect to reading reform. For example, a coach could relate a school's efforts to achieve adequate yearly progress, could summarize the reform initiative, and could extend invitations to district personnel to attend the school's professional development sessions. Even if such invitations are not accepted, it is important to keep making them as new topics and issues are explored; they serve to communicate the breadth and depth of the support that teachers are getting in the school. Fullan (2005) suggests that capacity building must occur at both the district and school levels. This means engaging district leaders in learning activities to the extent possible. When district leaders do accept, a coach should honor them when they visit and express appreciation for their support. Finally, coaches from different schools in the same district can network informally to share successes and concerns. Such interaction will make every coach better informed, and it may result in joint efforts to enhance district awareness of and support for reading reform.

Summary

Copland (2003) suggests that principals have at least three roles to play during the implementation of a reform effort. They must be "catalysts for change, protectors of vision, and leaders of inquiry" (p. 177). A coach can facilitate these roles but cannot assume them entirely, for the principal must communicate that the initiative is worthwhile and that participation is not optional. By the power inherent in their position, principals have always been "the gatekeepers of their schools' change efforts" (Murphy & Datnow, 2003b, p. 265), and their support is essential to the success of those efforts. Perhaps the most effective support, however, comes not in the form of micromanagement efforts but in the form of distributed leadership. Such strategies allow others, the coach included, to assume active roles in the change process. The same is true for school districts, which can help or hinder efforts at the school level. A coach can act in tandem with the principal to bring about more favorable conditions at the district level for the challenge of reform.

ISSUES OF CURRICULUM

Often we ask school leaders to describe their reading curriculum for us. In schools with less effective leadership, the response centers on what resources teachers teach with. In effect, curriculum and materials are the same. In schools with effective leadership, with a principal and a coach working together, we hear what teachers teach about, with the actual resources taking a secondary role. We define *curriculum* very broadly. For school leaders, the curriculum must be the overall system of goals, strategies, and resources that are garnered to support student achievement. It must be a carefully nested system, with the school functioning within the district and within the state.

Curriculum leadership entails choices, and the choices are high-cost and high-stakes. In their schoolwide improvement model, Simmons, Kuykendall, King, Cornachione, and Kame'enui (2000) suggest a series of stages, which we have listed in Figure 3.3. The choices are complex, and they are ongoing. With effective leadership, curriculum choices are made carefully, implemented fully, including time for planning and professional support, and then revisited based on their effects on student achievement. Such decisions cannot be made either by the principal or the coach alone; they must be made collaboratively by the school's leadership team or by ad hoc committees of committed teachers assembled for the purpose of curriculum review.

Classroom Materials

In schools with strong leadership, all teachers have the materials they need. Some materials, including those directly linked to the school's literacy mission, are nonnegotiable at the classroom level. They are purchased with school funds. All teachers have all of them. All teachers use all of them. They are stored in ways that are attractive and efficient. New materials replace old materials, rather than augmenting them. The physical environments of classrooms communicate much about the coherence of the curriculum and about the importance of student achievement in reading and writing. Coaches support teachers in setting up their classrooms, and principals know what must be there, and when and how it should be used.

In order to support student achievement, classrooms, including content-area classrooms, must be filled with more than commercial curriculum materials. Actual

1. Describe the context	Describe the current goals, assessments, curriculum materials, instructional strategies, and professional development opportunities. Identify weaknesses and seek alternatives.
2. Plan instructional groups, including interventions	Use data to identify children who need additional instruction. Provide resources (personnel, time, and curriculum materials) for each group.
3. Design instruction for all learners	Set goals, select materials, and organize resources to support all learners in the school.
4. Set progress-monitoring goals	Identify and schedule assessments targeted to monitor progress for all learners.
5. Evaluate and adjust	Reflect on the overall success of the curriculum, making adjustments for the next year.

FIGURE 3.3. Stages in schoolwide improvement.

books must be plentiful, organized for various purposes, accessible, and actually used in various ways during the school day. Again, as with commercial curriculum materials, money to keep classroom libraries updated must be provided by the school leadership. Web-based materials and experiences must also be provided, supported by high-quality, high-performing computers in every classroom.

Shared Resources

There are many reasons to pool resources that are only used temporarily. Shared resources reduce costs, keep classrooms from becoming overcrowded, maximize choices, and build collegiality. Book rooms can be used to house phonics-controlled and leveled readers for the early primary grades, sets of content-area trade books linked to science and social studies standards, and children's literature to read aloud. They can also house sets of texts for author or genre studies.

Effective use of shared resources can be coordinated by the coach. For example, in elementary school, teachers at a specific grade level can agree to teach specific science units at different times (as long as the knowledge is not cumulative). That way, the school can assemble very deep text resources for each unit, rather than spreading resources thinly across all classrooms. In an upper elementary school or a middle school, English teachers can agree to teach specific reading and writing genres at different times for the same reason.

District Curriculum

Effective curriculum leaders plan ahead. When new district curriculum initiatives are announced, they allocate the necessary time to plan, provide professional support, and evaluate their progress. This means, sometimes, that principals must advocate for appropriate pacing of new initiatives for their school, weighing the current demands and the capacity of the professional support system. If principals do not advocate, teachers are forced to make choices to sacrifice either the principal's building-level initiatives or the district's new initiatives. Such pressure fosters feelings of low efficacy and can damage the school's environment. The best principals work with their coaches and leadership team to gauge the capacity of the staff for change; they also foster a community in which curriculum change is constant, embedded in the workday, and expected of all. They communicate to their faculty when, why, and how new district initiatives will be incorporated into their work.

State Curriculum

The same principles apply to the state curriculum, but the pace is generally slower and the stakes higher. State curriculum initiatives are well publicized on the state website and developed by committees. Strong principals and coaches keep abreast of state-level initiatives and communicate with teachers about the processes that the state requires and the products that the state produces. Principals and coaches assure teachers that their work is consistent with the state's goals and that they are keeping up with new initiatives.

Ignoring state curriculum initiatives is a mistake; state curriculum standards and initiatives are tested in the state's assessment system. Rather than communicating a feeling that teachers must participate in the building initiatives and then be evaluated by the state, building leaders must constantly reassure teachers that the building's initiatives are consistent with the state's, that participating in ongoing curriculum reform in the building always keeps them on the cutting edge of curriculum, and that state initiatives are neither unexpected nor problematic for them.

ISSUES OF ASSESSMENT

In many schools, assessments are like the weather: Everybody talks about them, but nobody does anything about them. They are regarded as a necessary evil; high-stakes tests are given by mandate, and curriculum-based assessments are given by rote. This stance is unfortunate because the potential for using assessments to plan instruction is wasted and their assistance in monitoring a reform effort is ignored or misused. School leaders must take an active role in examining how assessments are used for these purposes. This is a process we explore in the next chapter. It is detailed work that must be driven by policy. For this reason, we conclude this chapter by examining policy questions related to a school's program of reading assessment.

Why Assess?

There are as many answers to this question as there are stakeholders with a right to know the results of assessments. They include teachers, coaches, administrators, parents, policymakers, and children. The interests of these groups vary and cannot be served by a single test. They require a broadly based program that includes measures of several kinds. We find it useful to begin with two large categories of assessments—those useful for planning instruction and those useful for charting the progress of groups. The ultimate goal of these two types of assessments is the same—student achievement. However, some tests directly influence achievement by informing immediate planning, while others affect it indirectly by informing school leaders of trends that may signal the need to reexamine what is happening in classrooms. In Chapter 4, we further delineate these two types and discuss their uses in detail.

How to Assess an Assessment

We define *assessment* as an organized method of gaining information about what children know or can do. This is a broad definition, necessarily so because of the many ways of gathering such information. The traditional notion of paper-and-pencil tests is just the beginning; to these we add observations and oral responses. The result is an array of assessment types that are complex and confusing. Sorting through them is a job for literacy leaders, for to them falls the task of ensuring that teachers get the information they need to plan instruction and that administrators get the information they need to gauge the impact of that instruction.

Characteristics of Assessments

We start by considering the characteristics of reading assessments. Figure 3.4 displays some of the more important characteristics useful in classifying assessments. To illustrate them, think of two very different ways to assess comprehension. One is the comprehension subtest of a group achievement test; the other is the retelling of a graded passage that a child has been asked to read. These assessments differ on all of the characteristics listed in Figure 3.4, yet we argue that each has the potential to provide useful information about a child's reading achievement.

Formal tests have clear-cut directions for administration and allow little or no room for teacher discretion either in how they are given or how they are scored. *Informal tests* are less structured and give the teacher wide latitude in how they are administered and scored. Often, the teacher is invited to modify the test during administration (e.g., by rephrasing a question or skipping a portion of the test). It is easy to see how our two examples are portraits in contrast. They represent the extremes on a continuum of formality. Some assessments fall somewhere in between, with a combination of formal and informal qualities.

The distinction between group- and individually administered tests is obvious, at least on the surface. Group testing is efficient but entails costs. Test formats usually require written answers because oral responses would not be feasible for a group. Moreover, the potential for students not to engage in the test and to

Formal	⇔	Informal
Group	⇔	Individual
Norm-referenced	⇔	Criterion-referenced
Timed	⇔	Untimed
Item-based	⇔	Rubric-based

FIGURE 3.4. Assessment characteristics.

mark answers with minimal thought is far higher in a group situation. For a group-achievement test, the trade-off is clear. For a passage retelling, the teacher can expect a higher level of engagement because of the one-on-one task. However, the tradeoff in this case is also clear—assessing an entire class would require considerable time.

The two major ways of judging a child's proficiency are to compare it with that of others and to compare it with an acceptable benchmark or standard. In the first case, we are interested in whether the child is performing "normally"; in the second, our interest is in whether a criterion has been achieved. In the case of the standardized test, a child's score is converted into a set of national norms (percentile ranks, grade equivalents, scale scores, etc.) for the purpose of comparing the result with that of age peers. In the case of the retelling, how well other children might have done is not the issue. The child's performance is judged against a standard of acceptability. Clearly, these are very different ways of judging performance, and the choice between them rests on the purposes of the assessment. The reason for giving the Iowa Test of Basic Skills (ITBS) is not to determine mastery of specific skills and strategies but to gauge to progress of large groups with respect to their national peers. The reason for asking a child to retell the content of a passage is to determine whether the child is able to comprehend at a particular level, information that will be useful in planning instruction.

There are two reasons for timing a test. One is for purposes of standardization. Because the ITBS is normed, it requires that time limits be observed so that testing conditions are the same for all examinees. This is important if a child's performance is to be compared with that of others. The second reason is to gauge the speed at which a child can apply skills. This is crucial in some dimensions of reading, such as speeded recall of high-frequency words. Neither of these reasons applies to our retelling example, although speeded retellings are sometimes used.

Finally, assessment performance can be judged using traditional test items, such as questions, or using more subjective approaches, such as rubrics. Our examples make the need for both types clear. Rubrics can be holistic (guiding overall judgments of the performance) or analytic (dividing the performance into important categories or dimensions). Rubrics are more subjective than test items, and they are difficult to aggregate across students. Test items are more versatile generally, but they are inappropriate for evaluating some performances, such as oral retellings, prosody, or composition.

If you return to Figure 3.4, you will see that our two examples conform to the extremes. The group-achievement test possesses all of the characteristics on the left, and retelling all of the characteristics on the right. It is important to remember, however, that many assessments have mixtures of these qualities. One example is high-stakes state-achievement tests, which are formal, timed, group measures but are also criterion-referenced. Other examples are reading assessments used by special educators to categorize learners with special needs. Like group-achievement tests, these are formal, norm-referenced measures, but they are individually administered.

Quality of Assessments

Like all tools, the usefulness of an assessment is directly related to its quality. In judging quality, we are primarily interested in two questions—whether the measure produces consistent results and whether the results address the questions we need to answer. The common terms for these concepts are *reliability* and *validity*. Measures that are reliable can be depended on to produce similar results under similar conditions. They are relatively unaffected by a scorer's subjective judgment. Measures that are valid produce results that provide an indication of the specific proficiency an examiner intends to target. Reliability is necessary for validity because without consistent results, a measure is not truly gauging the targeted proficiency. However, reliability is not enough to ensure validity. The assessment must be designed to tap the proficiency by requiring the student to apply it in situations that are similar to those the student will face during reading. To offer an extreme example, a test of addition facts (2 + 2 = __) might be highly reliable but poorly suited to reading assessment—and therefore invalid.

The reading assessments available in a school are likely to vary greatly in terms of reliability and validity. A coach should develop a sense of these qualities in order to make judgments about each assessment's utility. A hard line can be taken in appraising an assessment, insisting on high levels of reliability and abundant evidence of validity. We do not recommend this stance because of the day-to-day reality of classroom practice. Many measures, such as those that accompany commercial materials, do not offer information about these characteristics. This does not mean that they should not be used, just that their results should be interpreted with caution.

Sources of Assessments

There are at least four sources of reading assessments. These will vary by characteristics and quality.

1. *State-mandated assessments*. These are required in all public schools because of No Child Left Behind (NCLB) Act. They are group-administered, criterion-referenced measures with passing scores approved by the U.S. Department of Education.
2. *Commercial stand-alones*. These include individually administered instruments that may be norm-referenced (e.g., a special education battery) or criterion-referenced (e.g., an informal reading inventory).

3. *Curriculum-based assessments.* These are assessments built into commercial programs. They include those assessments that are integrated within core, supplemental, and intervention programs.
4. *Public domain assessments.* These are informal measures available to teachers at no cost. They target various dimensions of reading (e.g., phonemic awareness, phonics, attitudes).

We believe that all of these types play valuable roles in a comprehensive program of reading assessment. Taking an inventory of which are available is an important job for a literacy coach to undertake, and we explore this topic in detail in the next chapter.

Preparing for State-Mandated Testing

A leadership challenge facing any public school is how to respond to the pressure to perform well on state-mandated group-achievement tests. Leaders must choose between a low and a high road. The choice involves real ethical dilemmas, not just technical decisions based on the psychometrics of testing.

The low road entails extensive emphasis on test preparation. Instructional time is sacrificed to make room for test practice sessions, and the state website is scoured for released items in order to simulate test taking. Commercial test preparation programs are purchased to supplement the released items. Students are taught to be test-wise so that they can produce scores that may be higher than their true achievement might reflect. Rewards may be offered to students for putting forth effort and even for registering gains from the previous year. Contests are organized and the principal may offer rewards if targets are reached.

The high road to achievement testing is paved with the assumption that dedication to a solid reading curriculum, using research-based practice and employing differentiated instruction, will result in acceptable scores. No other preparation should be required because of the alignment between what is taught and what is tested. The pressure to perform well is translated into assessment-driven planning, more intensive classroom instruction, and better progress monitoring. Leaders accept, as an article of faith, that these actions will suffice and that testing need not be feared.

The only schools we know of that follow the high road are those where students have long done well on state tests and little pressure to improve is exerted by stakeholders beyond the school. Schools experiencing problems are far more likely to take the low road, attempting anything short of cheating to reach modest achievement goals. The impulse is understandable. It is a form of self-preservation. This quick-fix mentality is a predictable response to unrealistic demands, especially when neighboring schools have gone down the same road. We do not deny that the strategies involved may in fact yield short-term results in the form of inflated schoolwide means. But this is the illusion of success. We also know how easy it is for us, who do not face the brutal pressure to raise scores, to criticize those who detour along the low road.

What we suggest is a compromise—a middle road—along which coaching efforts can bring about instructional improvements, while measured steps are taken to optimize the testing experience without sacrificing extensive amounts of instructional time and without facilitating inappropriate test-taking strategies (such as encouraging children to answer remaining items randomly when time runs out). Our middle road is a testing policy that we believe skillful leadership can adopt in good conscience and to good effect. It entails the following components:

- Avoid costly test preparation materials that consume class time.
- Instead, encourage teachers to build in one comprehension item a week that is formatted like the state test and is based on the week's core selection. A coach can write and share these items with teachers, making their job easier. The question should be written at the inferential level—that is, the answer should be a fact that is implied but not stated in the selection. Teachers might use a transparency to discuss with the entire class how to approach the question.
- Get out the word to parents, reminding them of the importance of the test and when it is given. Suggest that they are not expected to coach their children but to get them to school well rested.
- Make certain children are well nourished on the day of the test but avoid high levels of sugar. (We know one school where children were fed pancakes and syrup on the morning of the test, a mistake school leaders will not repeat.)
- Establish clear procedures consistent with district guidelines, such as how to follow up on absences and just what teachers should permit children to do if they finish before time is called.
- Teach children positive testing strategies, such as

  —managing time during the course of a test.
  —using the process of elimination to narrow the options.
  —reading a passage prior to reading the questions, and then going back and forth between the two.

- Be aware of the oft-changing regulations concerning accommodations, and make sure that all children who qualify receive them.
- Keep up with test revisions and modifications of state policies. With the permission of the principal, e-mail state testing officials with questions you have.
- Get to know the state website and familiarize yourself with item formats.

- When test results arrive, look for patterns using the strategies we describe in Chapter 4.
- Get help in doing this if you need it. A university partnership can be useful for this purpose.
- Share results with the principal and teacher leaders after you arrive at reasonable interpretations of data.
- Use these discussions for preliminary planning.

FINAL THOUGHTS ON LEADERSHIP

The work of school leaders never ends. The goals are never accomplished, as new children and new teachers arrive each year. The demands of leadership are enormous. In a system as complex as a school, leadership cannot be vested in one individual but must be shared to be effective. While a principal is responsible for encouraging leadership in teachers, the responsibility also falls to the coach, who can do much to foster leadership skills. By sharing leadership for literacy, program ownership is shared, as well. And with such ownership comes the determination to excel in the service of children.

CHAPTER 4

The Role of Assessment in Coaching

Imagine coaching a basketball team from the locker room, without knowing the score and without seeing any of the plays. You would have little basis for advising your players, for suggesting what they should continue doing and what they need to do differently. As preposterous as this scenario may sound, something similar would happen in a school setting when reliable information about student achievement—how students are progressing and where they need to improve—is unavailable. We believe that real coaching must be focused on data if it is to benefit students. This view places us toward the "harder" end of the coaching scale we proposed in Figure 1.9. However, it is difficult to see how softer views of coaching, in which data may play only a minor role, can result in demonstrable improvements in student achievement. The purpose of this chapter is to describe the types of data likely to be most useful to a literacy coach and to suggest an action plan for gathering, organizing, and interpreting that data.

We recognize that some coaches work in settings already equipped with a well-articulated assessment system. If that is the case, the coach's role in assessment shifts from design to interpretation. In fact, it might be true that the overarching job of a coach is to support teachers to match their instruction to the needs of their children, and to pace it so that meaningful outcomes are realized; that cannot be accomplished without student-level data. It is wise, then, to check to see whether the system is conceptually sound and useful for instruction.

ASSESSING YOUR SCHOOL'S ASSESSMENT SYSTEM

It is vital to take stock of the data you have and the tools that provide that data. We begin by describing the kinds of assessments that should be in place to give teachers and administrators the information they need. Next, we outline an inventory of which assessments are available and suggest ways of viewing these critically to determine what types of information they can provide. Finally, we propose ways the assessment system might be revised so that teachers can get the information they need to help students; that same information will be necessary if coaches are to help teachers.

Step 1: Consider the Types of Assessments

We find it useful to characterize assessments by the function they serve. This way of categorizing assessments is not always clear-cut since some assessments can serve more than one purpose, but it is crucial to understand what each measure contributes to the overall assessment system. Currently, describing assessment systems in terms of screening, diagnosis, progress monitoring, and outcome is very much part of federally funded initiatives such as Reading First (Kame'enui et al., 2006). The concept, however, is much older.

Useful assessment procedures go from broad to narrow; broad assessments are given to everyone, and more targeted ones go only to those students for whom more information is needed. The strategy recommended by McKenna and Stahl (2003) involves a series of questions, beginning with whether a child is comprehending at grade level. If not, the next questions are directed at determining the underlying causes of the problem. This is where screening measures prove useful.

Screening Measures

A screening measure assesses a broad area of reading proficiency, such as phonics or phonological awareness. The measure is typically brief and individually administered. Its sole purpose is to identify (or rule out) a particular area as a problem. Screening systems rest on assumptions about reading development; if a higher-order skill is in place, screenings assume lower-order ones to be in place as well. If the results of screening identify a trouble spot, screening with a more basic instrument might be needed to get to the root of the problem. For example, if a teacher screens Jimmy in the area of phonics and he does poorly, it would next be prudent to screen in the area of phonological awareness, which is a prerequisite area. The advantage of screening tests is that they enable a teacher to quickly develop a profile of a student's strengths and weaknesses. Many screening tests now categorize a child's performance in terms of risk—low, moderate, or high—determined through prediction studies. When a child's performance is low enough that the risk of future failure is projected to be moderate or high, diagnostic assessment is called for.

Diagnosis Measures

The limitation of screening tests, however, is that they do not go very far toward telling us what we need to teach. They are not specific enough. This is where diagnostic measures are needed. Once a problem area has been identified through screening, a diagnostic test identifies specific deficits that can be addressed instructionally. Jimmy's poor performance on the phonics screening test leads first to screening in phonological awareness. If this is not the basic problem, then a diagnostic test of phonics can identify specific phonics-skill needs and can help a teacher plan instruction accordingly. Diagnostic tests need not be the rigorous norm-referenced assessments that special educators give. A perfectly serviceable test of phonics, for example, is a progressive list of skills. Likewise, a good diagnostic sight word test is a list of high-frequency words administered in such a way that the time a child takes to pronounce them is measured. To determine if a test is truly diagnostic, ask yourself this question: *Are the results specific enough to plan tomorrow's lesson?*

A drawback of diagnostic measures is that they are not particularly useful in determining instructional needs in the areas of comprehension and vocabulary. In the case of comprehension, attempts to separate this process into discrete skills that can be assessed independently of each other have failed. In the case of vocabulary, no consensus curriculum exists that might provide a basis for determining deficits (i.e., words a child does not know but should). In both cases, the most practical path is to use curriculum-based assessments. For example, if several new words are introduced in a unit, then the assessment of those words becomes, in effect, diagnostic.

Progress-Monitoring Measures

Diagnostic measures can help teachers determine the instructional needs of a child who is at risk of failing to learn to read. Once that instruction begins, it is important to determine whether it is having a positive impact. One way to do this is by readministering the screening test, using different versions. The child's progress can be tracked over time, and the instruction provided can be maintained, modified, or discontinued as indicated by the results. The process of giving screening, diagnostic, and progress-monitoring tests is depicted in Figure 4.1.

Outcome Measures

A question that is important to many stakeholders, including a coach, is that of how well a reading program is working. For this we rely in part on testing that may be conducted exclusively to answer this question, such as nationally normed group-achievement tests or standards-based state tests. These are "high-stakes" measures

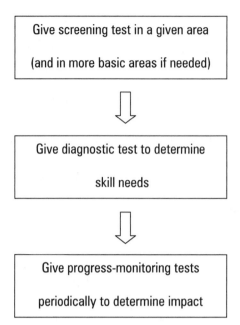

FIGURE 4.1. The sequence of screening, diagnostic, and progress-monitoring assessments.

that impact the inescapable realities of adequate yearly progress and other issues. They cannot, however, tell us very much that is helpful in planning instruction. At best, they can tentatively sort children with respect to a desired level of proficiency, such as a proficiency criterion or a national norm. A coach can learn to use these measures to track grade cohorts of children, charting average scores for the same group of children at successive points in time. Doing so can be helpful to teachers, administrators, and other stakeholders. We caution, however, against placing too much emphasis on these tests because of their inherent limitations (Popham, 2007).

It is far more prudent, in our view, to begin looking at screening tests as a form of outcome measure. In addition to their principal use in identifying areas of weakness, screening tests afford a window on how groups of children are progressing, and it is up to coaches to model their use. To be sure, a phonics screening test is not the kind of high-profile measure we read about in the newspaper, but the results of such a test, when administered at key points in kindergarten and first grade, can reveal much about the collective effectiveness of instruction in this area. The results can be available in time to make real improvements. Moreover, the results of a set of screening measures can provide a telling profile of the overall reading program, component by component and grade by grade.

Step 2: Conduct an Assessment Inventory of Your School

Which of these assessments are available in your school? Which are actually administered? All teachers can readily list the assessments they are required to give. Some can identify additional assessments they find useful in planning. Few can enumerate every measure available in the school, even at their own grade level.

These are items a literacy coach must know. It is not enough to recount them from memory or to rely on the recollections of others. It is necessary to go looking. Available assessments for teachers should be noted in written charts, organized by grade level, and a separate chart should exist for assessments given by reading specialists and special educators. We recommend organizing the charts in a grid, by area of instruction and by type of test. (We have not included qualitative measures, such as classroom observations and analyses of student work, but we acknowledge that these can be useful sources of information to help understand or confirm data produced by the four principal types of assessments.) Figure 4.2 presents a chart that can be reproduced for each grade. Many coaches may find it more convenient and flexible to recreate the grid in the form of a Microsoft Word table. Although we have accorded equal space to each type of test and each component of the reading program, the assessments will not be evenly distributed across grades—nor should they be.

Completing the chart will require legwork. Start with district- and state-required assessments as outcome measures. Core programs will contain many assessments, as will commercial intervention programs. Special educators and reading specialists are likely to have measures that classroom teachers will not use, but these should still be charted since they can be useful in determining the impact of intervention programs as a whole and for individual students.

Step 3: Judge Available Assessments Critically

Simply because a test is available does not mean it is a good one or that it is administered regularly and appropriately. Likewise, some tests are given almost by rote with little use made of the results. A good example is weekly comprehension checks for core selections in elementary school commercial reading programs, which actually measure children's memory for what has been discussed and/or read aloud by the teacher. Your chart will readily identify gaps in your available assessments. Other than the predictable dearth of assessments in vocabulary and comprehension, the remaining portions of the grid should not be empty. After you've completed the chart, consider coding it as follows:

+ Useful and routinely administered
− Administered but not very useful
± Useful but rarely administered

Grade:				
	Type of assessment			
Component assessed	**Screening**	**Diagnostic**	**Progress monitoring**	**Outcome**
Phonological awareness				
Phonics and alphabetics				
Sight word vocabulary				
Oral reading fluency				
Vocabulary				
Comprehension				
Composition				

FIGURE 4.2. Available reading assessments, categorized by type and program component.

From *The Literacy Coaching Challenge* by Michael C. McKenna and Sharon Walpole. Copyright 2008 by The Guilford Press. Permission to photocopy this figure is granted to purchasers of this book for personal use only (see copyright page for details).

Making these judgments will require talking with teachers about typical practice. There will be gaps where no assessments are available and filling these gaps will require a different endeavor. You will need to identify instruments that are reliable and convenient to administer. Fortunately, there are many sources of these, many in the public domain (e.g., McKenna, Stahl, & Stahl, in press). The charts will vary considerably by grade, and the following sections describe a typical process of compiling them. The completed charts will represent an inventory of assessment resources that can form the basis of gauging the needs of groups and individuals. Wisely interpreted, they can richly inform coaching by grounding it in student achievement data.

Primary Grades

From the beginning of kindergarten to the end of third grade, readers develop along several trajectories. They acquire phonemic awareness of the sounds that make up words; they learn the letters and combinations of letters that represent these component speech sounds; and they integrate and apply this knowledge by becoming increasingly fluent oral readers. Meanwhile, their vocabulary and comprehension abilities progress, their factual and experiential knowledge increases, and their recognition of important text structures develops. Comprehension of written text at grade level, the "bottom line" of our instructional efforts, is therefore the product of many interrelated factors, and determining where problems lie requires information about each of them. At each successive grade level, some problems are more likely than others. This means that the assessments of most use to classroom teachers will vary by grade level. For example, tests of phonemic awareness are more useful at kindergarten than third grade, not because phonemic awareness declines in importance but because the likelihood that it is a root cause of reading difficulty diminishes.

Our experience suggests that primary-grade teachers employ an assortment of assessments to obtain this information but that their use is not coordinated. Most teachers have access to, and tend to administer, end-of-theme tests that accompany their core reading program—most accurately described as a type of progress-monitoring measure. Core programs tend to lack the full array of assessments a first-grade teacher is likely to need, however, so a completed assessment chart is likely to reveal gaps that need to be filled. Once these gaps are revealed, screening and progress-monitoring assessments are required. A useful tool is available in the searchable, beginning-reading assessment database maintained by the Southwest Educational Development Center *www.sedl.org/reading/rad/* or Rathvon's (2004) *Early Reading Assessment: A Practitioner's Handbook*.

In grades 1 and higher, children can be screened with graded oral passages; others might benefit from a spelling inventory, which can be group administered and has the advantage of screening in several areas at once, such as phonemic awareness and phonics (e.g., Bear, Invernizzi, Templeton, & Johnston, 2007). Diagnostic tests are also needed for those children who do not pass the screening. Letter-name and letter-sound inventories, sight word lists, and phoneme segmentation tasks are examples of diagnostic tests that have most utility at kindergarten and grade 1 because they provide information that is detailed enough to plan instruction.

Screening in vocabulary and comprehension is problematic because inadequate decoding skills might skew the results on group measures and create the impression of weakness in these areas. For this reason, results of group-achievement tests should be interpreted with caution. Teachers can note responses to read-alouds to gain a better indication of a child's vocabulary and comprehension in listening contexts. Toward the end of first grade and beyond, when word recognition is more proficient, a child can be asked to read a grade-appropriate passage and either retell it or respond to probe questions (or both). There are many sources of such passages, such as core selections, trade books, and informal reading inventories. To prevent decoding problems from masking adequate comprehension and vocabulary, the passage should be read to the student orally, and it should be available for reference (look-backs) during retelling or questioning. A teacher can introduce the task directly, by cueing the student: "I want you to read along with me while I read to you. When I am done, I am going to ask you some questions. If you need to, you can look back to find answers."

Upper Elementary and Middle Grades

When children reach the upper elementary grades, the characteristics of strugglers continue to change. According to Chall's stage theory (1983/1996), children should progress successfully from acquiring the fundamentals of phonological awareness, print concepts, and foundational oral language (through learning the alphabetic code that is the basis of word recognition) to oral reading that is fluent. Oral fluency at grade level, she suggests, is a prerequisite for comprehension. Adequate fluency should be acquired in grades 2 and 3. In the upper grades, we try to determine how far a struggling student has progressed through these stages. At each successive grade, there are students who experience difficulties related to fluency but whose decoding skills are adequate. There are fewer students with inadequate decoding skills but acceptable phonological awareness, and there are still fewer students whose phonological awareness problems linger, preventing adequate decoding and fluency from developing. In Figure 4.3, we use a pyramid to display the likely proportions of these readers in upper-elementary and middle-grades classrooms.

These proportions suggest that screening to detect where a student's difficulties lie is different in the upper grades. Using a grade-level passage is an excellent first step. (See Chapter 5 for a detailed example at grade 7.) A measure of words correct per minute can be used to gauge oral reading fluency, and a few follow-up questions (with look-back options) can provide an idea of comprehension and vocabulary

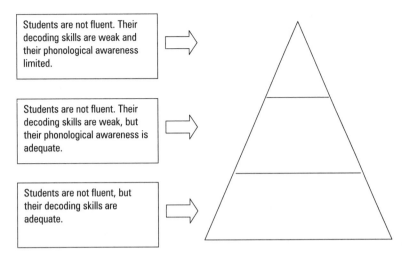

FIGURE 4.3. Proportions of struggling readers with fluency, decoding, and phonological awareness difficulties in the upper grades.

difficulties. Remember that some struggling readers in the upper grades possess adequate fluency, so they are not represented in the pyramid. In their case, vocabulary knowledge and comprehension strategies are the principal factors limiting their development. Remember also that some students have problems caused by both decoding and fluency and by limited vocabulary and comprehension. We advise that screening begin with a grade-level passage and is followed up with additional testing if fluency is a concern. Figure 4.4 outlines the process we recommend. It does not take long and can quickly result in a reliable profile for each student. This procedure follows the cognitive model of reading assessment (McKenna & Stahl, 2003).

Step 4: Develop Your Assessments into a System

Begin by remembering the chief reasons to assess. There are two, and a coach will need to draw on all four types of assessment to address them.

1. To guide instructional planning for all students.
2. To gauge the achievement of groups (by grade, classroom, subject, achievement level, or teacher) and to chart group trends over time.

These two reasons are represented in Figure 4.5. A coach's first priority must be to design and use an assessment system to guide instructional planning. This will enable teachers to make informed decisions that affect children, including the decision that an individual's needs can only be addressed in an intervention. The second priority, tracking group achievement, is broader in scope, and addressing

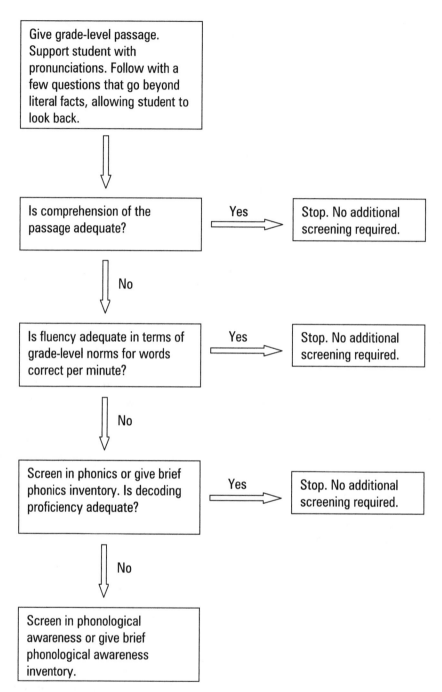

FIGURE 4.4. A screening process for struggling readers in the upper grades.

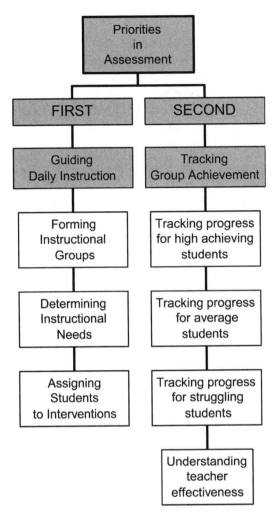

FIGURE 4.5. Priorities for a school's assessment system and how they are related.

it requires that data about individual children be combined to tell us about the bigger picture. This is a bit complex, we realize, but we want to underscore how the components of the assessment system work together. When you have organized the assessments in your charts to address these reasons, you will have established a viable system through which instruction is more likely to be informed by data and through which teachers will be better aware of the results of their efforts.

Guiding Daily Instruction

The process of administering screening, diagnostic, and progress-monitoring assessments is the backbone of an assessment system. It links planning for individual students to data. It ensures that the instruction students receive is targeted and that it is discontinued once its objectives are achieved. It also informs the creation of small groups in which children with similar needs are combined on a temporary basis to receive the instruction indicated by assessments. It provides the teacher with the information needed to periodically reform these groups so that children continue to receive instruction that is well matched to their needs.

Elsewhere (Walpole & McKenna, 2007) we have offered recommendations for small-group differentiated instruction in the primary grades. These suggestions are closely tied to assessments. We summarize them as follows:

1. Determine the needs of struggling students first through screening and then through diagnostic assessments.
2. Group students with similar needs together. For the sake of management, focus each group on two areas: (a) phonological awareness and phonics, (b) phonics and fluency, (c) fluency and comprehension, or (d) vocabulary and comprehension.
3. Plan instruction that is grounded in research-based approaches.
4. Conduct progress-monitoring assessments to determine the impact of small-group instruction and when to reform groups.

We believe this system will serve teachers in the upper grades, as well. The assessment process outlined in Figure 4.4 can be helpful in guiding these teachers as they move toward small-group differentiation.

Tracking Individual Students

Maintained over time, assessment results for individuals can reveal trajectories that are useful in planning. Many assessments now offer computer-generated reports that depict student progress over time. Because classroom teachers are understandably concerned with present data, they are not often inclined to look backward. This is where a coach can provide a powerful service by compiling past-performance data and bringing it to a conference. The history of a struggling reader represented in this way may offer a partial explanation of present data and can lead to insights about instructional approaches.

Tracking the progress of students most at risk can also help to inform the planning for students in intervention programs. Intervention teachers can be coached to build their own systems, incorporating the results of individually administered assessments unique to the intervention program. Not only can these results be aggregated to determine the effectiveness of the intervention across the students served, but they can also be used to gauge how well the approach is working for a specific student. The concept of response to intervention (RTI) uses assessment results kept over the interval during which a child is served. Whether the approach is having the desired effect entails an analysis of tracked data. This approach is an alternative to the older "discrepancy" model for identifying children for special education, based on comparing achievement with aptitude. Instead, children are tested for special education only if they do not make progress in very targeted, small-group instruction.

We believe that the future of RTI is promising, both because of the measurement difficulties of the older approach and because progress monitoring alerts specialists to the gains made by individuals. Where gains are modest or negligible, RTI calls the approach into question and causes teachers to rethink and to plan differently. Figure 4.6 displays how an RTI system might proceed if it is determined that a child requires a fluency intervention. Growth toward a benchmark is periodically measured, and the change over time is used to gauge the child's response to the particular intervention in use. (To read more about RTI, we suggest Fuchs & Fuchs, 2006; Gersten & Dimino, 2006; Klingner & Edwards, 2006; McEneaney, Lose, & Schwartz, 2006.)

Tracking Achievement Trends

We acknowledge that the principal goal of assessment is to plan instruction for individual students and to gauge its impact. However, viewing assessment data collectively can help a coach identify trends to address on a larger scale. What happens to achievement levels as students progress from grade to grade? Which groups of students experience the greatest difficulties? Which areas of reading development are associated with least growth? And, yes, which teachers can improve the most in meeting the instructional needs of their children? These are questions a coach can address by looking at assessment data collectively.

Let's begin with the results of a state proficiency test, administered yearly in grades 1 and above. In our example, we'll assume that this test battery provides

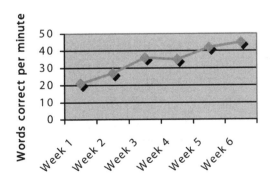

FIGURE 4.6. Example of a response-to-intervention tracking system.

a vocabulary and a comprehension score and a "total reading" score, which is a weighted combination of the two. Decisions regarding adequate yearly progress are made on the basis of total reading. Each subtest yields a scale score, the result of a statistical process through which items are assigned different weights. A scale score is impossible to interpret without a frame of reference. To meet this need, the state has set two criteria for interpreting the scale scores for each subtest. The more important criterion is the minimum score required to pass the test. A second criterion defines performance considered to be highly proficient. A coach will be concerned with both scores, but for different purposes; meeting the minimum requirement ensures progress for struggling readers, but a highly proficient status may be necessary to provide students choices and opportunities in later grades.

Figure 4.7 provides the achievement histories of Jefferson Elementary School. The numbers represent the percentage of children passing a specific subtest. Although the test changes at each grade, of course, the use of percentages ensures a constant referent to the mandated criterion. Note that a coach will probably need to create a multi-year chart of this type, by combining reports for successive years. A Microsoft Excel or Word table can be useful, and it is easy to add years once the chart is begun.

Jefferson Elementary's results represent an overwhelming array of numbers and we will need a strategy to make sense of them. The local newspaper reports that the achievement of this year's third graders is only up one percent from last year, from 72% to 73% passing. This is a relatively flat pattern and not particularly reassuring. But such a comparison involves different groups of third graders, and their characteristics may differ. It would be more sensible to track the same children from one grade to the next, which would allow us to compare apples with apples. The shaded cells in our table track what is called a *modified cohort of children*, from first to second, and finally to third grade. This approach is "modified" since we are not taking the time to ensure that exactly the same children are in each grade. We simply assume that most have remained in the school. This approach works well

Grade	Year 1			Year 2			Year 3		
	Vocab	Comp	Total	Vocab	Comp	Total	Vocab	Comp	Total
1	65	70	67	66	71	68	71	74	73
2	67	69	68	69	71	70	73	72	73
3	70	72	71	71	72	72	71	75	73
4	69	71	70	71	73	72	74	74	74
5	68	70	69	69	69	69	72	74	73

FIGURE 4.7. Jefferson Elementary's 3-year achievement history on the state proficiency test.

in schools where student turnover is not high. In high-turnover schools, it may be worth the trouble to limit the comparison to children who actually attended all three grades. This is the only reasonable way to gauge the school's impact on reading achievement. The shaded cells reveal a more encouraging pattern across the primary grades. The percentage of children passing the exam has increased three percent per year. If we examine the trends for the other two 3-year cohorts—those who began year 1 in second and third grade—we see similar upward tendencies.

Figure 4.8 displays a 3-year history for Joplin Middle School. For this example, we assume that the state proficiency test extends through eighth grade, which is typically the case. The process of interpreting Joplin's results is the same. We use a modified cohort analysis to look for important trends. Again, we find that same-grade comparisons reveal a stationary trend. Achievement appears to have plateaued. At eighth grade, which attracts the most attention because of its gateway status, the same percentage of children have passed the test in each of the 3 years. But a modified cohort analysis reveals a downward trend that is slightly alarming (note the shaded cells). Moreover, this trend is consistent for different cohorts. Although we do not have 3 years of data, we can observe that 65% of year 3's seventh graders passed compared with 70% of these same students when they attended sixth grade. Similar downward trajectories are evident if we make 2-year comparisons from year 1 to year 2.

In the case of both schools, the next step is to try to gain a better understanding of these patterns. One approach is to disaggregate the data by groups, creating similar charts for students from ethnic minorities, English language learners (ELLs), and students with learning disabilities. It may be that the patterns evident in the whole school can be explained in part by how these groups are performing. If so, it is important to consider allocating additional services for members of those groups and planning professional support for teachers to better identify and address their needs. For the state proficiency test, data needed to make such comparisons are usually available due to reporting requirements.

Another approach is to compile 2-year charts presenting results at the level of

Grade	Year 1			Year 2			Year 3		
	Vocab	Comp	Total	Vocab	Comp	Total	Vocab	Comp	Total
6	70	70	70	71	69	70	71	69	70
7	65	68	66	63	70	66	66	67	65
8	58	62	60	61	64	62	61	64	62

FIGURE 4.8. Joplin Middle's 3-year achievement history on the state proficiency test.

the teacher. Figure 4.9 presents a follow-up chart for the four third-grade teachers at Jefferson. We use it to compare year-end averages with the second-grade pass rates of the same students. The second-grade scores operate essentially as a pretest. In our example, we note nearly identical pass rates for the children who enter and leave the classrooms of Lee, Marks, and Wilson. In the case of Reed, the end-of-year pass rate differs from that of the other teachers, but this difference is related to the entering scores. Such a result raises questions about how children are assigned to homerooms. In the case of White, we note an alarming drop in both subtests and in the total reading score. This trend is worth pursuing and makes White a potential candidate for focused coaching.

When the coach observes White during the course of one-on-one coaching, a different type of data becomes available. Observations can be a means of explaining achievement trends and helping to direct a teacher's efforts into more productive channels. Although when we speak of assessment measures we think primarily of those designed to provide useful information about children, observation measures can give a coach useful insights concerning the type of instruction children receive. In Chapter 8, we describe how checklists, rating scales, and open-ended observation frames can be used to structure observations so that they yield information of this kind.

A third approach is to consider the results of additional measures that are administered individually. For example, a phonics screening and progress-monitoring assessment in the area of phonics can be charted by child, teacher, and grade. The increasingly popular use of online recordkeeping systems to house data and generate reports make this kind of analysis convenient. In addition, it has distinct advantages over the use of high-stakes achievement tests. One is the fact that these measures are administered individually. A good testing maxim is this: *Individually administered assessments produce better results than group assessments*. This is because a child's engagement can be assured. A second advantage is that charting component measures (e.g., phonics, fluency) permits a more fine-grained analysis

Teacher	Last year (Grade 2)			This year		
	Vocab	Comp	Total	Vocab	Comp	Total
Lee	64	69	67	66	71	68
Marks	67	69	68	69	71	70
Reed	58	51	55	54	53	54
White	74	80	76	61	60	61
Wilson	68	67	68	69	69	69

FIGURE 4.9. Cohort comparison of Jefferson Elementary's third-grade teachers.

of the reading program, permitting a coach to further isolate areas where (and teachers for whom) instructional improvements are needed. In order to understand the larger, more general trends, it is necessary to identify the smaller, more specific ones.

Finally, coaches might consider tracking the relative success of students who enter a grade level with different initial skills. Such an approach is particularly important if teachers are using a differentiated instruction model (e.g., Walpole & McKenna, 2007). In such a model, teachers have data that can be used to "sort" students into initial achievement categories (e.g., high-achieving, average-achieving, struggling). Later, they can gauge the relative success of each of the three groups. The model assumes that teachers plan and implement different instruction, at least part of the time, and that instruction allows all of them to make substantial progress. There are many possible outcomes in such a model. For example, consider the progress of high-achieving children (whose needs are too often neglected). Looking at their progress separate from the progress of their classmates answers questions about the effectiveness of the curriculum for them. If such tracking is applied to each teacher in a grade level, coaches can find teachers who are especially successful with specific types of students (and then they can study their work and learn from them). We have gained valuable insights about schools, grade levels, and individual teachers by tracking progress over time for groups of students sorted by their initial achievement.

USING ASSESSMENT DATA TO GUIDE YOUR COACHING

In Chapter 2, we spoke of three coaching contexts—working with individuals, with small groups, and with large groups. Data can richly inform a coach's work in all three contexts.

Individual Teachers

Using assessment results makes conferences more objectively focused and provides an opportunity for coplanning. Together a coach and teacher can use progress-monitoring results to chart the impact of differentiated instruction and to decide when to reconstitute group membership. Assessments can be tied to observations, which serve as a means of confirming, qualifying, or amplifying testing data. Madeline Hunter once asked whether a basketball coach would be likely to prefer all of the statistics related to a recent game or a video of the entire game. It was a trick question because in her view the coach would need both. Similarly, a literacy coach can make predictions and inferences based on data and can examine their validity through observations. Involving the teacher observed in the analysis can be beneficial to both the teacher and coach.

Small Groups

Working in small-group settings, a coach can use data to facilitate a discussion of trends and problem areas. Grade-level groups will benefit from the year-to-year trend analyses a coach can prepare. Together, faced with the evidence, teachers can craft solutions. The coach becomes the facilitator who leads teachers to try productive alternatives rather than the guru who prescribes and preaches. An important caveat is to be cautious about presenting assessment results that are broken down by teacher. Imagine the reaction of White, the Jefferson Elementary teacher, if confronted in a group setting with her negative trends. It is important to discuss these trends, but doing so in a group meeting is likely to evoke a defensive response that will be counterproductive.

Large Groups

Assessment results can be relevant to an entire school faculty, but the focus must be on cross-grade trends. Targeting results at a particular grade level is better situated within grade-level meetings, *unless* the results have lessons for adjacent grades. The coach's role as data analyst comes front and center on these occasions, and it is a challenging role that may surprise some teachers. More than a recitation of statistics, however, these "state-of-the-school" addresses must aim to build a team spirit among faculty, and they can have that effect only when schoolwide implications are presented. These addresses must also accentuate the positive as well as the problem areas. They are opportunities for reminding all teachers of the literacy goals of the program, and of signaling progress that teachers have made in addressing the needs of their most challenging students.

LESSONS FROM THE LARGEST GROUP

Because of coaches' understandable concerns with their own schools, it is easy to lose sight of how their assessments add a few brushstrokes to a much larger picture. School data are nested within district contexts, and school-to-school comparisons are inevitable and often frustrating. District results contribute to state trends, with the same inevitable comparisons. This is the end of the line for school data. They are not collected to chart national trends because the measures are too varied and the results would be difficult to collect.

This does not mean that national achievement results are unavailable, however. In 1969, the first National Assessment of Educational Progress (NAEP) was conducted, using assessments that were independently developed. Since then, periodic reports have been published in a range of subject areas for grades 4, 8, and 12. In the area of reading, the latest reports can be accessed easily by googling

"Reading Report Card," which is a part (we think the most important part) of *The nation's report card*. Here, the NAEP trends can be studied at a glance—for the nation as a whole, for the states, and for various categories of children.

It is unlikely that your school has taken part in the NAEP testing. This is because sampling theory is used to draw conclusions from a set of schools that reliably represent the national population. The same approach is used by those who conduct political polls, and you may recall that the results of these polls are always reported with a margin of error. The NAEP, too, has a margin of error, but it is not large enough that the results are in dispute. And those results are dismal, especially for the most disadvantaged children in our society. Figure 4.10 summarizes the overall results for 2005 (the most recent available at this writing) by comparing them with the results for 1992. Of particular interest is the percentage of students who do not read at a "basic" level, defined in terms of the proficiencies required to meet the reading demands at a given grade.

These proportions are nothing short of alarming. Disaggregating them by ethnicity and gender reveals that the achievement of girls, as a group, exceeds that of boys, and students from ethnic minorities do not read as well as their white peers. Disaggregating the results by state reveals that state performance is highly correlated with the percentage of minority population in each state. As the 13-year trend suggests, these are longstanding problems that have proved resistant to many of the reform efforts of the past. This is the national context in which the literacy coach must work, addressing local challenges that are part of national ones and achieving small successes that contribute to success on a grander scale.

CONCLUSION

Assessment is critical to the work of a literacy coach. Planned carefully, assessment directs instruction for students, as well as professional support for teachers. Over time, assessment also directs evaluation of the effectiveness of a coaching effort. Remember that we are asking you to wait to design your coaching effort until

Grade	1992	2005
4	38	36
8	31	27

FIGURE 4.10. Percentages of children reading below the basic level at grades 4 and 8. Data from National Assessment of Educational Progress, National Center for Educational Statistics.

you have considered the many choices that we present. Whatever you decide, an assessment system will be necessary to guide your work. An assessment system is different from a collection of assessments. A system is planned and efficient. It supposes an interconnected series of options, consistent with your curriculum goals and adapted to the changing achievement profiles of your students. The design of an effective assessment system is an ongoing task, and one that we hope coaches will lead.

CHAPTER 5

Providing Professional Support

Professional support is a *system* for enhancing knowledge, skills, and attitudes of teachers so that they can improve student achievement. It is purposeful and intentional, ongoing, and systemic. It has clear, worthwhile, and measurable goals. Those goals are appropriate for the school and supported by infrastructure and policy in the school. At its very best, professional support is both site-based and district-based, with integrated, coherent strategies that can be sustained (Guskey, 2000). The goal of this chapter is to describe a variety of strategies that coaches might employ in such a system.

In a call to action on the subject of staff development, Joyce and Showers (1996) begin:

> We have a vision of a comprehensive, job-embedded, staff development system, and we picture it as the most prominent feature of professional life. (p. 2)

They then describe an architecture for such a system, with interconnected initiatives at the individual, school, and district level. They call such a system "unusual" rather than difficult to initiate. Teachers link with one another in small teams; these small teams link with one another in larger collaboratives; and all participate in setting the district agenda for building professionalism, sometimes by using the expertise of existing personnel and sometimes by seeking outside consultation. Imagine how much easier their system would be with the services of a school-based coach! Given the resources devoted to making coaching happen, we have even more responsibility to make coaching work. Coaching can only work when it is a vehicle for coherent and responsive professional support.

HOW PROFESSIONAL DEVELOPMENT AFFECTS ACHIEVEMENT

None of the aspects of this model is optional for the coach. Guskey and Sparks (1996) navigate the distance between professional support and improvements in student achievement. The road is not a direct one; it is depicted in Figure 5.1. They start with high-quality professional support, guided, in part, by the same concepts that inform the NSDC standards we shared in Chapter 2. These standards stress the importance of content, process, and context. In order to plan professional support, content matters. The focus of the initiative must be research-based and realistic so that it can be reliably predicted to improve achievement and so that all teachers can actually adopt it. Once an appropriate focus has been chosen, the processes used to develop it matter. Think back to Chapter 2, in which we discussed adult learning and adult education; without attention to the needs of the learners, even the best idea will not yield improved achievement. Finally, the context matters. If an initiative does not intentionally adapt to the constraints of the setting (e.g., the time, personnel, and materials) it is unlikely to produce any change. In fact, it is unlikely to be adopted at all.

Guskey and Sparks point out that even high-quality professional support in these three areas does not yield direct benefits for students. This is because other factors are at work in any school setting, such as the administration. High-quality professional support builds administrator knowledge and influences administrator practice. Specifically, it encourages administrators to engage the support of professional developers and to tie their own teacher-evaluation processes to the school-level curriculum and instruction targets. This emphasis from the principal surely influences teacher buy-in. At the same time, though, teachers are also

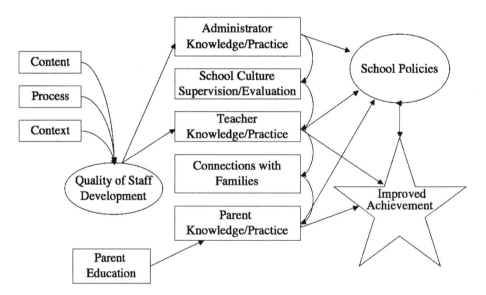

FIGURE 5.1. From staff development to student learning. Data from Guskey and Sparks (1996).

influenced directly by the professional development. Thus, they experience dual effects supporting implementation. Because of this, they are likely to engage in "translation," sharing what they are learning and doing in parent conferences, thus building parents' connection to the initiative. They are also likely to engage in effective conferences with students. These connections build parent knowledge, skills, and support.

In this system, principals, teachers, and parents are equipped to make policy improvements, influencing the real world of teaching and learning. They might make curriculum changes, organization and scheduling changes, or grading changes. These policy changes might improve student achievement, especially since they are paired with improvements in teachers' direct work with students and with parents' support. The road is long here, and winding. But this time, there is a coach to monitor progress. And that coach is a literacy coach, with specialized skills and knowledge about literacy, and with a mandate and professional responsibility to a particular set of teachers.

There has been a sea change in the literature of professional support to inform literacy coaches since we first entered the fray. Namely, there are more and more descriptions of professional development systems designed by literacy professionals to support literacy achievement. Federal support (e.g., Reading Excellence Act, Reading First, Striving Readers) surely has influenced this growing commitment, but there are loud calls for even more work (Doubek & Cooper, 2007). We are always on the lookout for models, and they are appearing more and more often. What we find (not surprisingly) is that they all seem to converge on and support the concepts from adult learning literature—they just apply them specifically to the area of literacy. We choose two to summarize below because they were both published in *The Reading Teacher;* you can read the full articles if you have back issues, or you can order the individual articles via the IRA's website.

Mesmer and Karchmer (2003) implemented a homegrown professional support system in two schools enacting Reading Excellence Act reform. They describe the staff development model they used as recursive, with traditional staff development followed by supported classroom implementation and then reflection sessions. In this 2-year initiative, they learned that they had to contextualize their work (even differentiating between the two schools). Their candor in reporting the ways in which they came to take their preplanned focus and make it more adaptive to the schools' and teachers' specific needs is helpful for those literacy coaches doing the same type of work.

Larger-scale efforts are also trickling into the professional literature. The state of Ohio has a well-articulated system for state-level professional support in literacy pedagogy (Kinnucan-Welsch, Rosemary, & Grogan, 2006). The domains that organize the content of the initiative are knowing, planning, teaching, and assessing. In addition, the following design principles, distilled from the literature of professional development, are inherent in the system:

1. The initiative is connected to student learning goals.
2. The sessions involve active learning for adults.
3. The work is embedded in real schools and classrooms.
4. The initiative is ongoing.
5. The initiative allows teachers to focus on their own learning, their students' learning, and the characteristics of instruction.
6. The initiative plans for coherence.

Those who are coaching without such state-level support and structure are on the front line already, constructing their own systems. We know that their work is complicated. Scaling up such work to the district or state level is even more complicated, and we are glad that the successful efforts of state and university partnerships to do such work are being included in our professional literature.

To say that high-quality professional support is complicated is not to say that it is impossible; in fact, once we share this potentially overwhelming orientation to the field of professional support, we advise coaches to "just get started." We rely on a cyclical process that we have adopted from the work of Joyce and Showers (2002). Cycles are helpful because they repeat. Figure 5.2 presents one way to think of the continuous cycle from theory, to demonstration, to practice, and to feedback. In this case, coaches can make different choices based on their experiences in each cycle. In the sections that follow, we provide very specific examples of those choices.

THEORY

We use Joyce and Shower's term, *theory*, to acknowledge the contribution that their work has made to our thinking. However, there are some ways that the

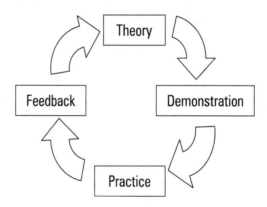

FIGURE 5.2. Professional support cycle, based on Joyce and Showers (2002).

term might be misleading. We looked it up and found definitions of *theory* to range widely: A theory might be a group of principles used to explain a complex phenomenon; it might be an unproven conjecture; it might be a system of rules or principles. When we think of professional support systems, we think of theory as the complex web of knowledge, developed *outside* the classroom, that informs the complex decision making required for teaching *inside* the classroom. Knowledge is at the heart of theory, but we think there are specific areas of knowledge building that together drive a well-articulated professional support system. These include knowledge of curriculum materials, research, and achievement. In Chapter 2, as we described the needs of adult learners and strategies for coaches to use in serving them individually, in small groups, and in large groups, we provided guidance for formal presentations. Formal presentations are one strategy that a coach likely uses to help teachers develop theory. In the sections that follow, we present other possibilities, each of which is more interactive than a formal presentation.

Understanding Curriculum Materials

We choose to begin with curriculum because, broadly speaking, it is the chief tool that teachers find when they enter their classrooms each fall. All teachers work within certain constraints; they are hired to teach a particular subject in a particular place with particular materials and goals. They are also charged with preparing students to meet standards, either immediate or long-term, regarding knowledge, skills, and strategies.

We also begin with curriculum because we find that many coaches assume that working directly with curriculum materials is not professional support but merely technical assistance. They are wrong. We think that this stance may come from their experience in graduate school, where they learned generic (hopefully research-validated) procedures and constructed lessons on their own to demonstrate their understanding. Such is not the work of real schools. Most teachers have (and use) core commercial programs in the language arts; most content-area teachers have (and use) textbooks. An important part of professional support is making time and establishing collaborative procedures for developing deep understanding of the tools that teachers are provided to accomplish their work. Teachers appreciate coaching that provides time and opportunity for them to accomplish tasks that are directly and immediately useful to them.

Understanding curriculum deeply also implies, for us, taking a critical stance. We recommend content analysis, which is simply a page-by-page examination. Teachers can work in groups to identify exactly what the curriculum designers expect them and their students. The most rigorous content analyses come from comparing the scope and sequence of knowledge and skills and the practice activities provided for students with an external set of standards (Walpole & Blamey, 2007b). This critical comparison allows teachers to work together to measure the overall quality of the tools they have, and it guides their decisions about how to use and supplement these tools. In *The Literacy Coach's Handbook: A Guide to Research-Based Practice*, we provide a set of external standards for curriculum examination for K–3 reading materials. There are other sources, though, to consider. State and district curriculum standards are especially important. Literacy coaches should consider this procedure, perhaps accomplished over two sessions:

1. Select an appropriate external metric (e.g., set of standards, curriculum framework, or research review).
2. Arrange a meeting of teachers who use the same curriculum materials.
3. Provide an overview of the external metric.
4. Divide the teachers into pairs.
5. Ask each pair to read the teacher's manual for one theme or unit and to report to the group anything from the metric that is not included or treated poorly.
6. Make a plan for how to supplement in areas not already included in the curriculum.

In *Differentiated Reading Instruction,* we argue that in core materials provided for the elementary school reading curriculum, the actual scope and sequence of knowledge and skills may be hidden among many potentially distracting activities. If coaches work with materials like that, they are well advised to work with grade-level teams to simply list the objectives for each target area (e.g., phonemic awareness, alphabet knowledge, spelling patterns, high-frequency word recognition, oral vocabulary development, comprehension skills and strategies) in order, week by week. This skeleton scope and sequence helps teachers to evaluate the design of the curriculum and to make informed choices about how to pace, differentiate, and enrich their instruction, and how to design practice and extension activities. It also helps them to integrate additional materials (e.g., trade books, read-alouds), because it helps them to know which ones would enhance other parts of the instructional plan.

Understanding Literacy Development and Pedagogy

Although we have presented strategies for understanding curriculum first, that is only because curriculum is immediate in the life of a teacher. Coaches starting their professional support system there are likely to earn appreciation from teachers anxious to complete their lesson planning for the start of the school year. The heart of the theory building in the professional support system, though, must come from selection and analysis of relevant research. In literacy, those findings include research on literacy development and on specific instructional materials and practices associated with positive outcomes for students.

The question for a coach is where to start. What research is relevant? Which books and articles are useful? One strategy is to begin with a research synthesis. We live in an era of such documents, and they have much to recommend them. First, good syntheses have a transparent strategy for how research was selected; literacy coaches can evaluate the match of the selection processes used with the characteristics of their school. For example, a synthesis that systematically excludes studies involving ELLs might not be highly relevant to a school that serves large numbers of children with limited English proficiency. Second, these syntheses are available for download on the Internet; they are free for coaches to examine and for distribution to teachers. And third, these syntheses are brief, appropriate for presentation in full faculty meetings or in grade-level team meetings. In addition, most begin with an executive summary so that a quick examination of the utility of a particular synthesis is possible. Figure 5.3 lists some current syntheses that we think could be useful. We have organized them by topic and provided their websites. You will see that visits to these websites open many additional avenues for choosing resources for professional support.

We recommend that a research synthesis be used to get the theory building

Elementary school instruction

Moats, L. C. (1999). *Teaching reading IS rocket science: What expert teachers of reading should know and be able to do.* Washington, DC: American Federation of Teachers. Retrieved from *www.aft.org.*

National Institute of Child Health and Human Development. (2000). Report of the National Reading Panel. *Teaching children to read: An evidence-based assessment of the scientific research literature on reading and its implications for reading instruction* (NIH Publication No. 00-4769). Washington, DC: U.S. Government Printing Office. Retrieved from *nationalreadingpanel.org.*

Partnership for Reading. (2001). *Put reading first: The research building blocks for teaching children to read.* Washington, DC: Author. Retrieved from *www.nifl.gov.*

Torgesen, J. K. (2006). *A comprehensive K–3 reading assessment plan: Guidance for school leaders.* Portsmouth, NH: RMC Research Corporation, Center on Instruction. Retrieved from *www.centeroninstruction.org.*

Middle and high school instruction

Biancarosa, C., & Snow, C. E. (2006). *Reading next—A vision for action and research in middle and high school literacy: A report to Carnegie Corporation of New York.* Washington, DC: Alliance for Excellent Education. Retrieved from *www.all4ed.org.*

Graham, S., & Perin, D. (2007). *Writing next: Effective strategies to improve writing of adolescents in middle and high school—A report to Carnegie Corporation of New York.* Washington, DC: Alliance for Excellent Education. Retrieved from *www.all4ed.org.*

(cont.)

FIGURE 5.3. Recent research syntheses.

Heller, R., & Greenleaf, C. (2007). *Literacy instruction in the content areas: Getting to the core of middle and high school improvement.* Washington, DC: Alliance for Excellent Education. Retrieved from *www.all4ed.org.*

Kamil, M. L. (2003). *Adolescents and literacy: Reading for the 21st century.* Washington, DC: Alliance for Excellent Education. Retrieved from *www.all4ed.org.*

Lewis, K., McColskey, W., Anderson, K., Bowling, T., Dufford-Melendez, K., & Wynn, L. (2007). *Evidence-based decision making: Assessing reading across the curriculum interventions* (Issues & Answers Report, REL 2007—No. 003). Washington DC: U.S. Department of Education, Institute of Education Sciences, National Center for Education Evaluation and Regional Assistance, Regional Educational Laboratory Southeast. Retrieved from *ies.ed.gov/ncee.*

English language learners

Gersten, R., Baker, S. K., Shanahan, T., Linan-Thompson, S., Collins, P., & Scarcella, R. (2007). *Effective literacy and English language instruction for English learners in the elementary grades: A practice guide* (NCEE 2007-4011). Washington, DC: National Center for Education Evaluation and Regional Assistance, Institute of Education Sciences, U.S. Department of Education. Retrieved from *ies.ed.gov/ncee.*

Short, D. J., & Fitzsimmons, S. (2007). *Double the work: Challenges and solutions to acquiring language and academic literacy for adolescent English language learners—A report to Carnegie Corporation of New York.* Washington, DC: Alliance for Excellent Education. Retrieved from *www. all4ed.org.*

Struggling readers

Francis, D. J., Rivera, M., Lesaux, N., Kieffer, M., & Rivera, H. (2006). *Research-based recommendations for instruction and academic interventions.* Portsmouth, NH: RMC Research Corporation, Center on Instruction. Retrieved from *www.centeroninstruction.org.*

Scammacca, N., Roberts, G., Vaughn, S., Edmonds, M., Wexler, J., Reutebuch, C. K., et al. (2007). *Interventions for adolescent struggling readers: A meta-analysis with implications for practice.* Portsmouth, NH: RMC Research Corporation, Center on Instruction. Retrieved from *www. centeroninstruction.org.*

FIGURE 5.3. *(cont.)*

rolling; it can guide in the selection of additional resources, and it can also be one external source used in the curriculum examination described above.

Once a coach has chosen a general focus for this theory-building work, the coach has to accept two challenges: the first is to be willing to engage, over time, in deep technical reading, either alone or with other leaders. In doing that, the coach is trying to stay a step ahead, modeling the personal commitment to go the extra mile as a learner. In addition, taking on such a challenge builds the coach's professional library so that those resources can be used to provide answers to teachers' questions. We may be old-fashioned, but we recommend that the library begin with books. Journal articles are also useful, but they are sometimes harder for coaches to get their hands on. In Figure 5.4 we have provided a starter set from which a coach might begin to build a professional library. We think our list has something for everyone, and these texts are ones that we have actually used in our own efforts to coach coaches. Having texts to consult keeps coaches from simply imposing their own theories on teachers. Instead, coaches can serve as reference librarians.

Theory building in the area of research and development through the coach's own study is important, but it is not the actual stuff of the professional support system. The second challenge lies in providing texts for teachers to read, as well as time and structure. The first step for a coach in this area is to select texts that are appropriate. They must be written well, in a voice that is accessible to teachers, and with a focus on issues that are actually timely in the school. For that reason, we

Baumann, J. F. & Kame'enui, E. J. (2002). *Vocabulary instruction: Research to practice*. New York: Guilford Press.

Bean, R. M. (2004). *The reading specialist: Leadership for the classroom, school, and community*. New York: Guilford Press.

Block, C. C., & Pressley, M. (2002). *Comprehension instruction: Research-based best practices*. New York: Guilford Press.

Breznitz, Z. (2006). *Fluency in reading: Synchronization of processes*. Mahwah, NJ: Erlbaum.

Gambrell, L. B., Morrow, L. M., & Pressley, M. (Eds.). (2006). *Best practices in literacy instruction* (3rd ed.). New York: Guilford Press.

Gillon, G. T., (2004). *Phonological awareness: From research to practice*. New York: Guilford Press.

Moats, L. C. (2000). *Speech to print: Language essentials for teachers*. Baltimore: Brookes.

Pressley, M. (2006). *Reading instruction that works: The case for balanced teaching*. New York: Guilford Press.

RAND Reading Study Group. (2002). *Reading for understanding: Toward an R&D program in reading comprehension*. Santa Monica CA: RAND. (Available at *www. rand.org/pubs/ monograph_reports/MR1465/*)

Rathvon, N. (2004). *Early reading assessment: A practitioner's handbook*. New York: Guilford Press.

Stahl, K. A. D., & McKenna, M. C. (Eds.). (2006). *Reading research at work: Foundations of effective practice*. New York: Guilford Press.

Strickland, D. S., & Kamil, M. L. (Eds.). (2004). *Improving reading achievement through professional development*. Norwood, MA: Christopher-Gordon.

Sweet, A. P., & Snow, C. E. (Eds.). (2003). *Rethinking reading comprehension*. New York: Guilford Press.

Wagner, R. K., Muse, A. E., & Tannenbaum, K. R. (2006). *Vocabulary acquisition: Implications for reading comprehension*. New York: Guilford Press.

Walpole, S., & McKenna, M. C. (2004). *The literacy coach's handbook*. New York: Guilford Press.

FIGURE 5.4. Books for coaches.

recommend that coaches gather several books on the same topic and ask teachers to select the one they would most like to study. In addition, we recommend that coaches facilitate more than one specific book club at a time, on two different topics, allowing teachers to join a club matched to their own interests. This combination of selection within and between study groups allows coaches to adjust to the needs of their adult learners for choice and voice in the professional support system, and still maintain its focus on the school's plan. Figure 5.5 provides a list of texts that we have found to be appropriate in work with teachers; of course, it is not exhaustive, but it might give coaches a starting point.

Once you have formed a study group and selected a book for study, the next

General sources on elementary instruction

Bear, D. R., Invernizzi, M., Templeton, S., & Johnston, F. (2007). *Words their way: Word study for phonics, vocabulary, and spelling instruction* (4th ed.). Upper Saddle River, NJ: Pearson.

Diller, D. (2003). *Literacy work stations: Making centers work*. Portland, ME: Stenhouse.

McKenna, M. C. (2002). *Help for struggling readers: Strategies for grades 3–8*. New York: Guilford Press.

Tyner, B. (2004). *Small-group reading instruction: A differentiated teaching model for beginning and struggling readers*. Newark, DE: International Reading Association.

Tyner, B., & Green, S. E. (2005). *Small-group reading instruction: A differentiated teaching model for intermediate readers, grades 3–8*. Newark, DE: International Reading Association.

Walpole, S., & McKenna, M. C. (2007). *Differentiated reading instruction: Strategies for the primary grades*. New York: Guilford Press.

Phonological awareness

Ericson, L., & Juliebo, M. (1998). *The phonological awareness handbook for kindergarten and primary teachers*. Newark, DE: International Reading Association.

Lane, H. B., & Pullen, P. C. (2003). *Phonological awareness assessment and instruction: A sound beginning*. Boston: Allyn & Bacon.

Phonics

Beck, I. L. (2005). *Making sense of phonics: The hows and whys*. New York: Guilford Press.

Fox, B. J. (2007). *Word identification strategies: Building phonics into a classroom reading program* (4th ed.). Upper Saddle River, NJ: Prentice Hall.

O'Connor, R. E. (2007). *Teaching word recognition*. New York: Guilford Press.

Fluency

Rasinski, T. V. (2003). *The fluent reader: Oral reading strategies for building word recognition, fluency, and comprehension*. New York: Scholastic.

Rasinski, T. V., Blachowicz, C., & Lems, K. (Eds.). (2003). *Fluency instruction: Research-based best practices*. New York: Guilford Press.

FIGURE 5.5. Books for teachers.

Rasinski, T. V., & Padak, N. D. (2007). *From phonics to fluency: Effective teaching of decoding and reading fluency in the elementary school* (2nd ed.). Boston: Allyn & Bacon.

Vocabulary

Beck, I. L., McKeown, M. G., & Kucan, L. (2002). *Bringing words to life: Robust vocabulary instruction.* New York: Guilford Press.

Stahl, S. A. (1999). *Vocabulary development.* Cambridge, MA: Brookline Books.

Stahl, S. A., & Nagy, W. E. (2005). *Teaching word meanings.* Mahwah, NJ: Erlbaum.

Comprehension

Duffy, G. G. (2003). *Explaining reading: A resource for teaching concepts, skills, and strategies.* New York: Guilford Press.

Klingner, J. K., Vaughn, S., & Boardman, A. (2007). *Teaching reading comprehension to students with learning disabilities.* New York: Guilford Press.

Assessment

Hosp, M. K., Hosp, J. L., & Howell, K. V. (2007). *The ABCs of CBM: A practical guide to curriculum-based measurement.* New York: Guilford Press.

McKenna, M. C., & Stahl, S. A. (2003). *Assessment for reading instruction.* New York: Guilford Press.

Writing

Buss, K., & Karnowski, L. (2000). *Reading and writing literary genres.* Newark, DE: International Reading Association.

Buss, K., & Karnowski, L. (2002). *Reading and writing nonfiction genres.* Newark, DE: International Reading Association.

Graham, S., MacArthur, C. A., & Fitzgerald, J. (Eds.). (2007). *Best practices in writing instruction.* New York: Guilford Press.

FIGURE 5.5. *(cont.)*

step is to facilitate and focus the group work. This entails making a schedule, or syllabus, collaboratively to allow your adult learners to participate in decisions about the time they are committing to read and the time they are committing to discussion. We have consistently tried to plan for the "reading" to happen during the study group session (by actually handing out the texts and asking participants to read the day's portion immediately). We have done this for two reasons: (1) it demonstrates our commitment to professional support *during the school day*, and (2) it ensures that everyone has done the reading before the discussion. Some of our colleagues, though, resist this approach, mainly because there is not enough time to accommodate the reading preferences of all; some would prefer to read much more slowly, taking time to digest ideas, contending that their needs are not met in the time allotted. Coaches have to weigh their decisions in this area and be flexible when they are not successful.

The second step is to set procedures for discussion. Study groups for the purpose of theory building in professional support systems are not the same as book clubs formed to engage adults in collaborative responses to literature; they simply must have more structure than that. Remember that adult learners filter new ideas through their personal experience. Sometimes this means that they will gloss over ideas from professional readings, taking the stance that they already do all of the things that are recommended. Our goal is first to facilitate deep discussion and understanding of what the author means. Only after that can we move to discussion of ways in which the ideas are consistent and inconsistent with current practice, and to use the author's ideas to improve it.

We have used three specific formats for guiding study-group discussions after participants have read. As you read about each, you will see that they offer choices that may help you fit the format to the nature of the group and the structure of the book.

Discussion Starters

With *discussion starters,* the coach identifies key passages directly from the text, distributes them to individuals or pairs, provides a short time for discussion, and then asks each group to summarize the concept that they were assigned and describe how it fits into the broad argument that the author makes. Presentation of these ideas by the participants keeps discussion focused on text ideas and prevents the coach from taking on a didactic role.

Reading Guides

The second strategy used for study groups is formal reading guides. For groups with substantial background knowledge about the ideas in the text, reading guides speed their work. *Reading guides* are simply questions designed to direct participant attention to specific concepts and to ask them to summarize, respond, or react. The guides can be used in small groups, and they allow teachers to work through important text ideas with their peers. These are not to be confused with the reading guides sometimes used to support students as they make their way through challenging text (e.g., Wood, Lapp, & Flood, 1992). They are simply tools for helping busy professionals focus as they read and for organizing discussions that follow.

Jigsaw

The last study group format that we have used combines the reading guide format with a *jigsaw* discussion. In this case, participants read in advance, are divided into groups, and complete reading guides for a specific chapter or portion of the text. After time for discussion, they present their shared understanding to the other groups. In this format, then, all participants discuss one chapter deeply with peers and then get an overview of the discussion in which the other groups took part. We have chosen this strategy in an effort to nurture teacher leaders, not just to facilitate the processing of new content. Our hope is that teachers choose to read additional chapters later, their interest piqued by their colleagues' presentations.

Whichever strategy is chosen for engaging in comprehension of the text, the coach must build in time to consider ways to use new knowledge to make improvements. This work can take place individually, as the coach guides specific teachers to commit to specific goals, or collectively, as the study-group team commits to collaborative work. The research in the text, though, has to begin to make its way into classroom practice.

Understanding Achievement Data

We have encouraged you to focus on building theory by formal presentation, by critical examination of curriculum materials, and by book study. Those are not your only choices. In fact, as we mentioned in Chapter 4, we cannot imagine any coaching efforts to be effective without the use of data to identify concerns and evaluate the success of efforts to address them, and there are many different ways to go about it. Data examination is another form of theory building. It takes place outside the classroom, and it provides guidance for work inside the classroom. We see data as a tool in individual coaching, in small-group coaching, and in large-group coaching.

Given the demands of the NCLB Act that schools make adequate yearly progress on state-designed measures, most schools now engage in school-level data analysis. Such sessions are useful to guide thinking about the success of the previous year's plan; they are also useful for identifying groups of students for special attention. We support the use of disaggregated data to accomplish such tasks, and we have seen principals and coaches working together to depict data in ways that are understandable. In large-group theory-building sessions, visual depictions are especially important. We see these sessions as useful in garnering support for new initiatives and in providing public recognition of the collective efforts of a group of teachers striving to improve achievement.

In small groups, data-based discussions are even more powerful. Our best efforts have been guided first by sharing data with the grade level as a whole, combining all data as if students were in one classroom. This procedure communicates collective responsibility for achievement and avoids singling out specific teachers whose students may be making less progress. Such data can be easily summarized with three specific, simple, mathematical procedures: frequencies, percentages, or averages. *Frequencies* (sometimes called *counts*) tell how many and what kind. They are appropriate for reporting numbers of children meeting benchmarks, for example. *Percentages* sometimes make frequencies come alive; they help display the relative progress of the group and can be represented through pie charts or colored bar graphs. We tend to use both frequencies and percentages together because, when the sample is small, percentages can be misleading—in a group of 15, three individuals constitute 20%. Figure 5.6 presents two depictions of the same grade-level data.

The data constitute state-level fall achievement in basic alphabet and phoneme awareness skills on Dynamic Indicators of Basic Early Literacy Skills (DIBELS) subtests: Letter-Name Fluency (LNF), Phoneme Segmentation Fluency (PSF), and Nonsense Word Fluency (NWF). Each subtest is interpreted by placing children in categories of risk, based on prediction studies (low risk, some risk, and high risk). In the left panel, counts are given. In the right panel, frequencies and percentages are reported with the support of a visual. Numbers of individuals in each of the three categories are large, so the percentages, depicted in the right-hand panel, are meaningful.

Figure 5.7 depicts averages. These averages come from curriculum-based measures of oral reading fluency. They are average words per minute for students in four second-grade classrooms. By the end of the year, on average, students had met the goal; that is not to say that all students met the goal. Remember that when you consider average performance, very high-scoring students (or very low-scoring students) can skew the results.

Both of these charts were actually used by literacy coaches to build theory through data examination. In both cases, the coach was working with groups of teachers, and the data that were shared publicly were summarized. In both cases, though, individuals had copies of their own data. In the first case, literacy coaches could compare percentages of their own first graders meeting the fall benchmark to the state data; this helped them to reflect on the relative success of kindergarten instruction. In the second case, individual teachers could look at the mean words

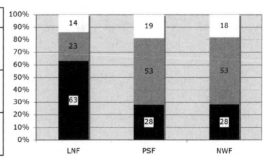

	LNF	PSF	NWF
Low Risk	5407	2416	2418
Some Risk	1981	4555	4555
At Risk	1160	1575	1558

FIGURE 5.6. Sharing percentages and frequencies.

Reading rate: grade 2				
1st 9 weeks	2nd 9 weeks	3rd 9 weeks	4th 9 weeks	Goal
58 wpm	79 wpm	85 wpm	96 wpm	90 wpm

FIGURE 5.7. Sharing averages.

per minute for their own class, compared with the status of the grade level as a whole.

A teacher knowing how his or her students are doing compared with others does not necessarily influence achievement directly in any way. In our experience, though, it does foster discussion of what is working well and what is not. Coaches must be cautious of not singling out teachers whose data stand out. Teachers with lower achievement than their peers will be embarrassed by such treatment, and, surprisingly, so will teachers with high achievement. Instead, coaches can share data and ask general questions to the group.

Our experience has been that small-group data sharing sessions lead to individual ones; namely, teachers whose students are struggling come to the coach for help. These can be the most productive theory-building sessions that a coach facilitates. They play into the adult learning literature because they are entirely problems-based and immediate. They also allow for collaboration because there are other settings in the same school environment where achievement profiles are different. Coaches can either describe instructional strategies they have seen used in other classrooms, or, if teachers are willing, they can arrange for peer observations.

Another way to share data is to take a case-study approach. In such a session, teachers can bring data for a student whose achievement is troubling them. Together, with the coach and with peers, they can brainstorm new ideas, specifically suited to their examination of the data. Student-focused coaching (Hasbrouck & Denton, 2007) is an individual coaching model that has been used to address literacy achievement and also behavior concerns in this way. Data are used first to identify and specify the concern, then to plan a solution, and finally to measure the success of the teacher's efforts. As students respond (or fail to respond) to efforts to improve instruction, both teachers and coaches build their understanding of teaching and learning.

To sum up, theory can be built through formal presentations, curriculum examinations, book study, or examination of data; such sessions can be large group, small group, or individual. The important issue here is that the coach begins by building theory, but the theory-building effort is not followed by another one. Instead, theory must be followed by demonstration.

DEMONSTRATION

When we speak with coaches about demonstration, they automatically consider classroom modeling. In fact, classroom modeling is a very powerful form of demonstration, but there are others. What they have in common is that they all take the theory into the classroom, as close to actual practice as possible.

Modeling

If you are constructing your own vision of coaching as you read, you may have just made a simple calculation. You may be working with 20 teachers at four different grade levels. You would have to spend at least several hours with each group in theory-building sessions; perhaps you could accomplish that in a week's time. But then, if you were to model next (and do nothing else) you would be planning at least four different lessons and implementing them five times each. Given the realities of schools, that would take at least 2 weeks to accomplish.

There are ways to make modeling more efficient. One way is to use lesson planning as a proxy for modeling. After theory-building sessions (or at the end of the sessions), you can make a direct connection to practice by facilitating creation of a specific lesson plan, embodying the characteristics of the theory. You can further ensure success by having a planning template and materials ready for teachers to use. That way, teachers will leave their session with a concrete idea to try in their classroom.

Another possibility is to use role-playing as a proxy for modeling. At the end of theory building sessions, you can role-play instruction. If you are careful about your time and planning, you can first model the lesson or strategy yourself, with the teachers acting as students. Then you can let them model for one another. These two forms of modeling make a direct connection to practice, but not the powerful connection that one-on-one modeling affords.

Finally, coaches can simply model in individual classrooms. The power of such efforts comes from the fact that they directly challenge the claim that "this will not work with my class." The class in question *is* the teacher's class, so that challenge can be answered directly. Coaches must remember that they should think through the needs and personalities of individual children before modeling, and that they should be prepared not to be perfect. Our caution about one-on-one modeling comes not because we think it won't be effective; we just worry that it won't be feasible. There are organized ways to include direct modeling with children, though, in group formats. In the sections that follow we examine some possibilities.

Lesson Study

An interesting model for instructional improvement has been developed in Japan. The approach is called *lesson study* (Lewis, 2002). It assumes that instructional improvement comes from deep analysis of instruction. Modeling is an important part of the cycle. In a lesson-study cycle, a group of teachers meets together to identify goals and then construct a lesson plan to enact the goals. One member of the planning team volunteers to implement the lesson, while the rest of the team watches the lesson, collecting evidence of its effectiveness in addressing the goal. The team meets to discuss the evidence and to improve the lesson, sometimes reteaching the revised one and returning through the steps in the cycle.

American coaching models have used versions of this team-based modeling cycle effectively. In Collaborative Coaching and Learning (CCL), a model used in Boston public schools, teachers work in teams to study aspects of reader's and writer's workshop (Schwartz, McCarthy, Gould, Politziner, & Enyeart, 2003). They establish a lab site, a classroom where team members demonstrate workshop lessons for the rest of their cohort, meeting afterwards to debrief. Although all members of a CCL course take turns modeling at some point, the system also provides continuous direct application of theory, witnessed by the entire team.

Model Classrooms

An even more intensive modeling approach is used in the reform program, America's Choice (Poglinco, Bach, Hovde, Rosenblum, Saunders, & Supovitz, 2003). Interestingly, as in CCL, the goal of this reform model is to implement reader's and writer's workshops. In this case, though, the coach begins by borrowing a classroom for 6 or 8 weeks and teaching the workshops directly. Once the coach is comfortable, teachers at that grade level can come and watch the coach teach. This procedure ensures that the coach has direct expertise in teaching the curriculum at each grade level, and provides a running model of implementation that is accessible to teachers. It means, though, that the coach can only serve one grade level at a time.

Using Video

All of the approaches to demonstration that we have described can be enhanced and made more efficient through the use of video. In fact, whenever coaches model, they should consider collecting video evidence, because those videos can bring work inside the classroom to sessions outside the classroom. We find adults somewhat reluctant to be taped, so we make the following commitment to them: We will only use the tape if they approve afterward. We view this kind of virtual modeling as a reasonable choice for coaches who work with multiple teachers and want to bring theory into real classrooms with real children. Advances in digital camcorders have made it relatively inexpensive to capture clear footage with good acoustic quality.

PRACTICE

After theory building and modeling, teachers need time to mull over new ideas and practice new techniques. This simply makes good sense; if you ask teachers to do something as complex as improving instruction in an environment as complicated as real classrooms, with their own specific climates and procedures, they need time to get comfortable. It is somewhat embarrassing for us to report that we neglected this fact; we often expected our adult learners to build theory with us, watch demonstrations of its utility, and then enact it for us immediately back in their schools. Besides the general tension such a system engenders, it is unlikely that any products (assessments, work samples, observations, or reflections) collected in such a system represent the true potential of the adults to internalize and use the new ideas. Rather, such a system is only a test of wills, and is likely to provide only shallow implementations.

We have learned to avoid such mistakes. Our general strategy is to be more interactive at all levels of the cycle. We build time and strategies for checking understanding during theory building. We construct various demonstrations and allow for our participants to ask questions after watching them or participating in them. And then we ask them if they are ready to try the new ideas. If they say *no*, we return to theory and demonstration. If they say *yes*, we ask them how long they would like us to wait before providing feedback.

FEEDBACK

Feedback is essential to a professional support cycle. At first, coaches must acknowledge that although they are very excited to watch teachers teach, and although they have strong relationships with their teachers, teachers might be anxious. This anxiety has many sources. First, teachers might be anxious to please coaches, anxious to show that they are competent. Second, they might be afraid that the opposite is true, that someone will "catch them" and uncover their inadequacies. They might be anxious that they could be embarrassed in front of their peers, that the coach will tell other teachers about their weaknesses. Finally, they might be anxious that the coach will report information to the principal, influencing their formal evaluations. Coaches must anticipate each of these anxieties and make overt efforts to relieve them.

Feedback about teaching should take a before–during–after structure. Coaches should interact with teachers *before* providing feedback, telling them exactly when, why, and how they will observe them. They should elicit input from a teacher, inviting the teacher to indicate specific areas of concern that the coach should attend to. And the coach should review procedures that will be used both *during* and *after* the observation.

We conduct many observations of teaching, and we have learned to use formulaic language beforehand to attempt to reduce anxiety. Here is an example:

"I am excited about my observation time tomorrow. Remember that I am observing so that I can evaluate the success of my own professional development in _____. I know that you are working hard to implement the ideas, and I am interested to see how they work in your classroom. I am really only going to be looking for _____. Are there any specifics that you want me to focus on? While I am in your room, I will be taking notes. I will try to stay out of your way; I won't talk to you or to the children. I will stay for _____. I will give you feedback about what I saw _____. Then we can plan next steps together. If this lesson is going well, we can work on something new. If not, I will help you by modeling, coplanning, or arranging for you to visit another teacher. Either way, the only person that I will talk to about this observation is you."

This preobservation meeting can be very brief, perhaps lasting only 5 minutes, but it is not optional. It serves the important purpose of reviewing and specifying the contract the coach has with the adult learner; it cements and focuses procedures; it provides the teacher a chance to participate. It directly addresses, out loud, all of the anxieties that the teacher might have.

"Getting into classrooms to observe more" is one of the concerns that we hear from the coaches with whom we work. While some schools and districts must negotiate the specifics of observations with their teachers' collective bargaining units, we tend to answer that professional support is impossible without feedback—both to the adult learners and to the coach. We also contend that observations must be conducted for every teacher, at regular intervals, and only later repeated for those who request or need additional feedback.

Observations

While we see the preobservation meeting as essential for all observations, coaches have choices to consider for what they do *during* the observation. In order to plan professional support in meaningful ways, coaches must have feedback on the relative success and failures of their work. They must receive that feedback, though, as measures of the quality of their own work rather than of the work their teachers are doing.

To go beyond our own experiences with observations, we have examined formal observation tools used in early childhood settings (Walpole & Blamey, 2007b). This work has identified several common strategies that coaches can adopt to make their observations more focused. They include checklists, scales, quality rubrics, and open-ended procedures. If a coach is designing and implementing a reflexive professional support system, each of these tools can actually be designed collaboratively, with teachers contributing dimensions of teaching they think are important. Such a construction helps to focus the coach and also communicates to the teachers that the purpose of the observation is specifically linked to the content of the theory and demonstration.

Checklists are relatively low-stakes observation tools. They document the presence or absence of specific characteristics of the classroom environment (e.g., children's literature is displayed; leveled texts are organized; centers are present) or instructional procedure (e.g., the teacher names and models the strategy; the teacher provides guided practice; the students engage in independent application). Checklists might be an early strategy for observation; if they are constructed with and given to teachers in advance, all teachers can feel empowered to earn a perfect score. The problem, though, is that checklists are not useful for capturing or reflecting on quality.

Scales go a step further than checklists, but they are still fairly safe, controlled tools. Scales can identify specific areas of focus and then provide documentation of how often they are observed. For example, in a professional support cycle focused on increasing explicitness in teacher-directed instruction, a scale might include individual items targeting modeling, use of manipulatives, use of physical gestures, every-pupil-response techniques, and paired-practice techniques. Each of those could be identified as present *never, somewhat,* or *often* during the observation period. Slightly more information is provided, but that information is still more about surface-level implementation than real instructional quality.

More open-ended tools and procedures are necessary to focus attention on instructional quality, but totally open-ended observation procedures are not advisable. They demand incredible skills on the part of the coach and provoke unfocused feedback to the teacher. Rather, an open-ended observation can be more focused; it can be derived directly from the lesson plan that was developed from theory and used for demonstration. For example, if teachers are learning to implement Tier-Two vocabulary instruction (Beck, McKeown, & Kucan, 2002), they can use the characteristics of that instruction to make an observation framework. Figure 5.8 provides an example.

During observation with such a frame, the coach simply collects evidence in each of the categories in the frame. The trick here is for the coach to be entirely present and attentive to what *is* happening rather than concerned about what *could be or should be* happening. Later, just after the observation, the coach can reflect on the quality, taking care to be constructive and to offer assistance.

After conducting any type of focused classroom observation, coaches must provide feedback to their learners. Teachers might worry about what the coach observed, so we think that timing is important. In fact, the sooner the feedback can come, the better. Otherwise, we find coaches spending too much time on the form (rather than the content) of the feedback and teachers forgetting too much about the instruction to really benefit. The important thing is for coaches to be honest, specific, and supportive, both of the teacher's efforts and about next steps.

Observation frame: Teaching Tier-Two words
The strategy requires teachers to choose 3 to 4 Tier-Two words from a children's literature read-aloud. I noticed
The strategy requires that you say the word, and children repeat. I noticed
The strategy requires that you tell how the word was used in the text. I noticed
The strategy requires that you tell a child-friendly definition. I noticed
The strategy requires that you give examples of the word used in multiple, unrelated contexts. I noticed
The strategy requires that you invite children to construct an example. I noticed
The strategy requires that you have children repeat the word. I noticed
Overall, I noticed
Here are some questions that I had:

FIGURE 5.8. An example of a focused, open-ended observation template.

Over time, a coach can develop many focused observation frames, specifically tied to work accomplished outside the classroom. The coach can use multiple frames, observing gradually longer and longer portions of instruction, once many different instructional strategies have been attended to in professional support cycles. To maintain momentum, it is important to communicate to teachers that items from previous cycles continue. A first observation might include only one instructional procedure. A second observation might include the first one and a new one. Gradually, a coach can develop frames and even choices of frames that together constitute full, quality implementation of the entire initiative.

School Walkthroughs

The observation strategies we have described are time intensive. There are times when coaches might need to initiate some changes more quickly; there are also times when coaches need to gather insights about the relative quality of the entire curriculum as it is currently being enacted across classrooms. We recommend school walkthroughs as strategies to accomplish this. School walkthroughs, like checklists used to guide observations, are opportunities to reflect on the presence or absence of items, or the general quality of the instructional environment. They are not appropriate avenues for directing intensive personal feedback to teachers.

One strategy we believe to be especially useful, when applied at periodic intervals in an instructional-improvement initiative, is the *standards-based walkthough* (Roberts & Pruitt, 2003). A standards-based walkthrough builds community and collaboration, and, although it involves every single classroom and teacher in a school, it is quick and relatively low-stakes. The reason for this is that the walkthough itself happens when children are not in the building and no one is teaching—it happens after school or on a building-level professional development day. The purpose of the walkthrough is for teachers to visit classrooms to look for evidence that the curriculum is being implemented there. Coaches (or principals) form cross-grade teams and provide them a checklist or format to focus their attention. These teams take a tour of the school, all at the same time, and come to a consensus of the many ways that the curriculum is visible. Since the teams comprise teachers from different grade levels or content areas, each has specific insights to offer the others about why certain classrooms might be organized differently. After the walkthrough, each member of the school faculty can commit to improving his or her classroom environment in specific ways.

Other walkthroughs take other specific forms. We have been developing a specific walkthrough form using a procedure called *innovation configuration* (Roy & Hord, 2003, 2004). An innovation configuration is a type of rubric, designed for a specific setting, where individuals implement a complex innovation in different ways. What better way to describe a coaching model! The designer of the innovation first describes its components implemented in an ideal fashion. Then the designer visits real settings where the innovation is being tried (in this case, classrooms) and collects information in the form of actual descriptions. Finally, those descriptions are ordered, from least-like the ideal to most-like the ideal, and they constitute a realistic road from very-weak implementation to very-strong implementation. For example, the "ideals" column for an innovation configuration that we are using to guide our own walkthroughs in Reading First schools is provided in Figure 5.9. When we use it, we get feedback on the extent to which our professional support system for these schools is working, and we use that feedback to consider our next steps.

MAINTAINING COHERENCE

Unfortunately for coaches, the proof of professional development is in the pudding. That pudding is made from an untested recipe, stirred by multiple chefs, and cooked on a stove with an unpredictable heating element. Struggling schools, especially, get feedback about whether their efforts are effective, and that feedback comes with state-mandated test results and reports of adequate yearly progress. The likelihood of success is greatly improved when the professional development system is coherent, pooling time and talents rather than dissipating them. Cobb (2005) contrasted a failed initiative with a successful one. The real difference was coherence. In the unsuccessful school, the services of a consultant and a new curriculum were hastily contracted; in the successful one, a school-level leadership team examined data, chose a focus, arranged for support on their own terms, and coordinated the support so that all professional learning for the staff was coherent and linked directly to the needs of the school evidenced in its data.

This is not always the case, especially for teachers working in high-risk, high-needs schools. In fact, those schools are very likely to suffer multiple externally controlled initiatives, some from the federal government, some from the state, and some from the district. Teacher time might be fragmented among many required professional learning sessions—perhaps about science, technology, literacy, and safety all in the same week. Coaches work with principals and district and state staff to protect teacher time and allow for a coherent focus on the school's professional support goals in order for teachers to really benefit from a professional support system. Figure 5.10 is an innovation configuration that we have used to document the collective efforts of principals and coaches working in reform-oriented elementary school initiatives.

This issue of coherence applies very specifically to the coach's own choices about using time. Reports that coaches spend a large amount of time on administrative tasks (e.g., Deussen et al., 2007) trouble us; if a coach is to enact a coherent professional support system with attention to theory, demonstration, modeling,

Physical environment
The classroom is neat, clean, and organized so that the teacher can monitor all children and accomplish whole-group and needs-based instruction and so that children can get the materials they need. Wall space is used to display student work and curriculum-related materials that children need to accomplish tasks.
Curriculum materials
There is one core reading program in active use. There is physical evidence of text-level and word-level skills and strategies targeted in the classroom environment. Texts and manipulatives for whole group, small group, and independent practice are organized and available.
Children's literature
There is a large classroom collection of high-quality children's literature deliberately organized and in active use that includes narratives, information texts, and multicultural texts.
Instructional schedule
There is a posted schedule inside and outside the classroom to define a diet of whole-group and needs-based instruction; teacher and student activities correspond to the schedule.
Whole-group instruction
Whole-group instruction is used to introduce new concepts and to model strategies. Children have multiple opportunities to participate and respond during instruction.
Small-group instruction
Small-group instruction is used to reinforce, reteach, review, or extend. Each child spends some time in a small group each day; small-group instruction is clearly differentiated. Children have multiple opportunities to participate and respond during instruction.
Independent practice
Children work alone, in small groups, or in pairs to practice skills and strategies that have been previously introduced. They read and write during independent practice. They do this with a high level of success because the teacher organizes independent practice so that it is linked to whole-group and small-group instruction.
Management
The classroom is busy and active, but focused on reading. Classroom talk is positive and academic, including challenging vocabulary. Children know how to interact during whole-class, small-group, and independent work time. Very little time is spent teaching new procedures.

FIGURE 5.9. Ideal descriptions of components of a specific elementary school initiative.

Instructional materials			
4	3	2	1
There is clear evidence that the leaders in this building made thoughtful choices to purchase commercial curriculum materials to meet school-level needs.	There is evidence that the leaders this building are in the process of choosing commercial instructional materials to meet school-level needs.	There is evidence that commercial materials were purchased, but no evidence that these decisions were made based on school-level needs.	There is no evidence that new commercial materials were purchased for this project.
Word identification and fluency strategies			
4	3	2	1
There is evidence that the leaders have chosen noncommercial instructional strategies and implemented them fully.	There is evidence that the leaders have chosen noncommercial instructional strategies, but they were not fully implemented.	There is evidence that the leaders are considering noncommercial instructional strategies.	There is no evidence that new noncommercial instructional strategies were used in this project.
Oral vocabulary and comprehension strategies			
4	3	2	1
There is evidence that the leaders have chosen noncommercial instructional strategies and implemented them fully.	There is evidence that the leaders have chosen noncommercial instructional strategies, but they were not fully implemented.	There is evidence that the leaders are considering noncommercial instructional strategies.	There is no evidence that new noncommercial instructional strategies were used in this project.
Study groups			
4	3	2	1
The leaders in this project reflectively designed professional development to include both formal knowledge building and collaborative study groups.	The leaders in this project reflectively designed professional development, and it is partially implemented.	The leaders in this project have conceptualized a comprehensive professional development system, but it is not implemented.	The leaders in this project delivered professional development, but there is no evidence that it was comprehensive or adapted to the school's needs.

(cont.)

FIGURE 5.10. Innovation configuration sample for principals and coaches.

From *The Literacy Coaching Challenge* by Michael C. McKenna and Sharon Walpole. Copyright 2008 by The Guilford Press. Permission to photocopy this figure is granted to purchasers of this book for personal use only (see copyright page for details).

In-class support			
4	3	2	1
The leaders in this project provide systematic and regular support to all teachers, based on their level of expertise, through modeling and observation.	The leaders in this project are implementing a system to support most teachers through modeling and observation.	The leaders in this project are implementing a system to support some teachers through modeling and observation.	There is no evidence that the leaders in this project provide systematic and regular support to teachers through modeling and observation.
Use of assessment to drive instruction			
4	3	2	1
The leaders of this project have designed a comprehensive assessment system that teachers use to differentiate instruction.	The leaders of this project have designed a comprehensive assessment system, but teachers do not yet use it to differentiate instruction.	The leaders of this project have designed a partial assessment system that teachers use to differentiate instruction.	There is no evidence that the leaders of this project have designed a comprehensive assessment system that teachers use to differentiate instruction.
Leadership support			
4	3	2	1
There is clear evidence of cohesive support for this initiative as the only one guiding literacy instruction.	There is some evidence of cohesive support for this initiative as the only one guiding literacy instruction.	There are competing reforms that specific leaders support.	There is evidence that building- or district-level leaders actively hinder this initiative.

FIGURE 5.10. *(cont.)*

and feedback, there is no time to lose. Dole and Donaldson (2006) urge new coaches to employ three standards as they think about how to use time: focus all of your attention on your goal, spend the majority of your time inside classrooms, and build the confidence of your teachers that you can help them to improve. Such a laser focus is necessary if coaches are to realize their potential to manage high-quality professional support systems.

MAINTAINING YOUR SANITY

This chapter is long and complicated. We wrote it that way to demonstrate that you have many choices, and you can make different choices over time. Professional development systems that work are actually elegant solutions to problems in the real life of teachers; they are informed and reformed by real life. Remember the big idea: Professional development systems progress through multiple cycles of theory, demonstration, practice, and feedback. Coaches have choices to make in each of those areas. The important thing is to make a choice, live it out, and evaluate it before making another one.

CHAPTER 6

Classroom-Level Coaching

Regardless of the coaching model that a school chooses or develops, the coach has to work with teachers to set goals for their classrooms. This goal-setting work is not a one-time event. It entails periodic checks of progress and revisions of the goals based on new data. In this chapter, we introduce you to three classrooms, constructed to represent differences, both in the procedures for goal setting and in the actual choices that coaches and teachers make together. Although the classrooms are at different grade levels, we are not suggesting that the choices are necessarily more appropriate for that grade. In fact, we think that coaches should consider all of the strategies as potentially useful for any given classroom goal-setting initiative. The goals themselves start with student achievement and progress to apportioning instructional time, negotiating content coverage, exploring grouping formats, and increasing engagement. We end each section with an extreme makeover idea, one that would drastically change the entire environment and be consistent with a reform-oriented approach to coaching.

To make matters easier, we assign one coach to all three of these situations. It is unlikely, of course, that a single person would actually serve such a wide range of grade levels; our intent is to allow the coach's background to remain the same while we change the instructional setting. Sara Martin is an experienced teacher who spent most of her time in fifth grade, where she employed a successful reading and writing workshop format; she is also experienced at conducting guided reading lessons (Fountas & Pinnell, 1996) and at managing book clubs (McMahon & Raphael, 1997). She has a master's degree and is a certified reading specialist. She spent 2 years outside the classroom as a curriculum supervisor for the district's English language arts curriculum, and she worked with the design team to draft the state standards in that area. In addition, she served on a state-level planning committee to draft an initial RTI protocol, an experience that taught her much about meeting the needs of struggling readers. Perhaps her greatest gift, however, is her interpersonal skills. Sara never gets rattled. She has an easy, nonthreatening manner, excellent technology skills, and extensive positive experience with classroom management.

She is worried, though, that her experience is not broad enough to guide her as she begins her new job as a school-based coach.

FIRST GRADE

The first teacher Sara will coach is Mrs. Thurston. She is an experienced first-grade teacher with a flexible approach to instruction; her entire curriculum is organized around literacy and math instruction. She has core programs for both subjects, and she is accustomed to using them as resources for curriculum design. She also has a large and eclectic collection of children's literature, including beginning reading texts that children read on their own and more difficult texts that she reads aloud. Parents of high-achievers have long requested that their children be placed with her, but a new principal, Mr. Henderson, has decided to end this practice by assigning all kindergarteners to first-grade classrooms based on achievement. This year Mrs. Thurston must contend with a much broader range of needs; she has 21 children, seven of whom did not learn all of their letter names in kindergarten.

Sara's initial meetings with the first-grade team, during preplanning, are surprising. She asks them to share their assessment system with her so that she can get a better sense of the inner workings of beginning reading classrooms; what she expected was a plan for establishing instructional reading levels by measuring oral reading accuracy and comprehension. What she learns is that the team uses a hodgepodge of assessments, most of which come from commercial materials. She also learns that they report the results of these assessments to parents on report cards, and that all of the teachers believe that to be a district requirement. She knows, from her work at the district, that this is not true, but she keeps that to herself, choosing instead to listen.

Setting Goals for Achievement

Sara's first task, setting goals for achievement in each classroom, is stalled by the lack of a first-grade assessment framework from which to work. She takes advantage of the situation, viewing it as an opportunity to shore up her own knowledge of assessment systems in beginning reading. She first reviews the conceptual framework in the state's RTI plan; it requires that schools document the quality of whole-class instruction and set measurable goals for all struggling readers, to be met in their intact elementary classrooms through differentiated instruction. She then uses the search engine on the IRA's website to search for articles on assessment in *The Reading Teacher*, because she has a subscription. After reading several articles, she finds a short piece that would be especially relevant to the first-grade team (McKenna & Walpole, 2005). That article proposes a system for using assessments to inform instruction (see Figure 6.1). The first step is to

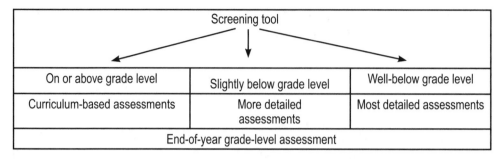

FIGURE 6.1. Assessment frame for first grade.

choose a screening tool that would identify children who were on or above grade level, somewhat below grade level, and well-below grade level. The next step is to plan different assessments for different groups: The children with at least grade-level achievement would profit from monitoring via the end-of-theme tests that teachers already used in the reading program. Those not quite at grade level would use assessments associated with a classroom-based small-group intervention. Sara thinks that a guided reading assessment, based on reading accuracy in a series of leveled books, would be appropriate there. Finally, the children whose achievement is well-below grade level would need more assessments to adequately document their needs; those assessments would come from an intervention program.

Sara takes her ideas to Mrs. Thurston, and together, they work through the ideas. Because Sara is new to the school and to first grade, she approaches Mrs. Thurston as an expert, able to advise Sara on how to proceed with the rest of the team. Mrs. Thurston is adamant that all of her children will achieve at least grade-level standards by the end of the year, but she is less clear about how she will know.

Sara begins with the curriculum-embedded assessments that Mrs. Thurston is comfortable using. Together, they examine the very last test for each of the weekly basal units, or themes, a multiple-choice comprehension test about the content of the stories in that theme; Sara asks Mrs. Thurston to help her understand what it measures. Together, they realize that the test measures two things—children's understanding of the week's discussions about the story (*not* their reading comprehension of the story) and children's ability to read the questions. Both agree that that standard is not rigorous enough to constitute evidence of grade-level achievement.

Further searching locates other assessments, presented in separate stand-alone teacher's editions of the reading program. These assessments include a set of new stories, never read together with the class, and comprehension questions. Those seem a better candidate for measuring whether children are reaching independence by the end of first grade, whether they can read and understand, at least at a basic level.

The next task is to choose a screening tool that would be useful for initial screening. Given end-of-year data from the kindergarten, Sara knows that some of Mrs. Thurston's children do not know their letters. This means that screening would need to begin at a very basic level, and she gathers a variety of professional books that include assessments of early literacy skills. They decide that a screening should be quick to administer, easy to interpret, and that all children will take the same assessment. They consider a reading passage, but conclude that too few of the children have enough skills for that. They consider a writing sample, but conclude that it would be difficult to know what the children actually know because, among other things, their choice of a topic would influence them. Finally, they select a developmental spelling inventory (Bear et al., 2007). The inventory is a set of words carefully selected to represent spelling concepts of progressive complexity. The children will have never studied the words and will spell them as best they can. The spellings will be scored and interpreted to represent the children's level of knowledge about the alphabetic system. Sara and Mrs. Thurston choose a spelling inventory because they can interpret it both conceptually and practically. Asked to spell a word like *map*, children with little or no alphabet knowledge might respond with random marks or letter-like forms; children just-below grade level might represent only one sound (e.g., *m*); children on or above grade level at the beginning of first grade might represent more than one sound (e.g., /m/-/p/).

Now that they have chosen a screening, they have to select additional assessments for those just-below and well-below grade level. They choose a phoneme segmentation task (Yopp, 1995) and a letter-sound inventory from the core series for just-below-grade children and a letter-name inventory from the core series for those well-below grade level, with the option of progressing to the phoneme segmentation task for those who have at least some letter knowledge. Figure 6.2 shows how these specific choices fit into the general plan suggested by McKenna and Walpole (2005).

Now that they have measures to guide them, they set goals for the three groups. Because Mrs. Thurston agrees that all of her first-grade children should achieve independent comprehension of the passage that they have selected for the end of the year, she realizes that the lowest-achieving children will have to make very rapid progress in acquiring alphabet knowledge. She sets goals for the first 6 weeks of school, to correspond with the first marking period for report cards, but she is looking forward to end-of-year goals, as well. She wants *all* children to grow, and the weakest students' growth will have to be rapid enough to predict success by the end of the year. She decides that, at this first checkpoint, all children will know all of their letters and half their sounds. In addition, children in her middle group will be able to segment words for spelling. Her high group will be able to read and retell a new text, selected from the set of additional ones found in the core series.

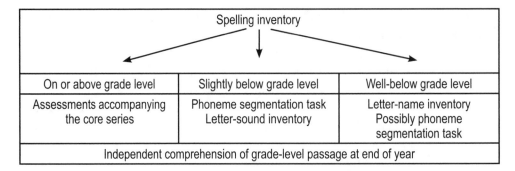

FIGURE 6.2. First-grade assessment frame reflecting specific choices of assessments.

Setting Goals for Instructional Time

The next set of discussions between Sara and Mrs. Thurston concern instructional time; Sara's experience in upper elementary does not prepare her for Mrs. Thurston's description of her day. As with her approach to the assessment decisions, she listens first, and then begins to ask questions to help her to understand and to encourage Mrs. Thurston to be reflective. Mrs. Thurston describes a free-flowing plan, with all decisions about instructional time presented to the children during morning calendar in response to the work of the previous day. Sara's specific questions about lesson planning do not receive clear answers. Mrs. Thurston thinks it obvious that planning is ongoing and responsive to the children's needs. Planning simply means that they study math together, read and write with a variety of purposes, and integrate science and social studies into the classroom via explorations. It also means following the outline of commercial programs as closely as possible.

Sara is able to draw upon their previous conversations, when they established an initial assessment plan, to redirect the conversation. She asks how Mrs. Thurston would serve the needs of the three groups of children. Mrs. Thurston's initial response is that she has always served all of her children in the past, but then she wonders whether these children are different and whether this assessment system will be difficult to manage once the differences came to light.

Sara guides Mrs. Thurston to plan for whole- and small-group time, anticipating three small groups each day. They negotiate 1 hour of instructional time for the core lessons, provided in whole group, and 1 hour for small-group time. Mrs. Thurston is immediately skeptical; she has not experienced a rotation like this, with some of the children working independently while she works with others. Sara offers two supports: She will design an initial set of center tasks, and she will come into the classroom and teach the children how to move through the centers.

Figure 6.3 displays the schedule they agree to follow. Sara makes her initial

1. Whole-group lesson from reading series, shared reading of a big book, phonemic awareness instruction, direct instruction in letter names, sounds, and patterns, and supported reading of a very simple little book		
2. Whole-group, interactive read-aloud from a children's literature selection; introduction of the daily response to reading (which would progress over time from a draw-and-label activity, to a written personal connection, to a story mapping or graphic organizer activity, to a written retelling)		
Lowest group	Middle group	Highest group
Complete the response activity	Meet with Mrs. Thurston to work on letter sounds, segmentation, and spelling	Complete the response activity
Lowest group	Middle group	Highest group
Meet with Mrs. Thurston to work on letter names, letter sounds, and phonemic segmentation	Work in pairs to practice the tasks from the day's small group	Work in pairs to read or reread a text from a set selected for them
Lowest group	Middle group	Highest group
Work in pairs to practice the tasks from the day's small group	Complete the response activity	Meet with Mrs. Thurston to reread the little book from the day's whole-group lesson; if they are fluent with it, read a new, more difficult little book with support
Whole-group genre-based writing instruction		

FIGURE 6.3. Instructional time frame for first grade.

instructional time frame quite broad, with the hope of teaching the children how to move through a cycle of whole-group, small-group, and independent or paired work. It is her hope that she can make the frame more and more specific over time. Eventually, she will help Mrs. Thurston plan which letters and sounds to teach and generate lists of words and instructional strategies to teach segmentation. She will also collect a series of graphic organizers that Mrs. Thurston can use to guide responses to the read-alouds.

Setting Goals for Content Coverage

Now that Sara has collaborated with Mrs. Thurston to select assessments and make a general instructional plan, she wants to make her actual instructional goals each day more specific. Sara carefully reads the first volume of the first-grade basal teacher's edition; she sees that there are many activities suggested and that, to her eyes, some of them are very loosely tied to actual instructional goals. It appears that the reading lesson in the core program targets several specific areas of literacy development: phonemic awareness (segmenting and blending of syllables, onsets and rimes, and phonemes), word study (letter names, letter sounds, letter formation, spelling patterns, high-frequency words), fluency (automatic word recognition in the context of specially selected stories), and comprehension strategies (prediction, making inferences, and using prior knowledge). She makes a lesson-planning template (Figure 6.4) to help direct Mrs. Thurston's attention to these core instructional objectives.

Sara brings the chart to her meeting with Mrs. Thurston. Filling in the first week's data proves difficult. But eventually they achieve a rhythm for separating the wheat from the chaff in the basal lessons. Mrs. Thurston admits that this exercise helps her see how the program designers conceptualized connections among the various strands. She finds that she agrees with most of their decisions, but disagrees with some. Her previous experience with the program and with first graders tells her that children will likely struggle with some aspects of the progression. Sara indicates that knowing this up front is very helpful. Mrs. Thurston can either anticipate these hurdles herself and plan for more intensive teaching when she reaches them, or

	Phonemic awareness	Word study	Fluency	Comprehension strategies
Week 1				
Week 2				
Week 3				
Week 4				
Week 5				
Week 6				

FIGURE 6.4. Content-coverage frame for first grade.

From *The Literacy Coaching Challenge* by Michael C. McKenna and Sharon Walpole. Copyright 2008 by The Guilford Press. Permission to photocopy this figure is granted to purchasers of this book for personal use only (see copyright page for details).

she can build in simpler tasks along the way to better prepare the children for the upcoming demands. For example, when the program introduces consonant blends (e.g., *bl-*, *cl-*, *pl-*) the children might have trouble. Mrs. Thurston decides that she will plan much more intensive modeling, guided practice, and independent practice with four-phoneme words.

Sara believes that this is enough commitment to content coverage at first. Later, she hopes to build a focus for the writing curriculum and to map the science and social studies standards onto this chart so that they can be reinforced through reading as much as possible. In her mind, those mappings will be useful to help guide Mrs. Thurston's selection of read-aloud texts and to integrate the instructional day for the children.

Strategies for Flexible Grouping

Given an assessment plan, a basic plan for whole- and small-group instructional time, a curriculum map of the core materials, and a few weeks of experience with the children, Sara is ready to help Mrs. Thurston begin to internalize a flexible grouping strategy. The children have not been regrouped since their initial meeting. Sara brings to the meeting a list of that first grouping. She begins by going through the list quickly, asking Mrs. Thurston about each of the children. She is not surprised to hear her say that almost one-third of the children would probably be better served (in the next round) by a different placement.

Sara draws again on her interpersonal skills to make Mrs. Thurston comfortable. Sara suggests that she herself probably recommended inaccurate groupings for some of the children because she had never before used developmental spelling data for first graders. She also wonders aloud whether some of the children simply came back from the summer "rusty" and did not really show what they actually knew. Both of these reasons free Mrs. Thurston to suggest that she might regroup them immediately. Sara supports this decision and reminds Mrs. Thurston that if she uses a variety of groupings during the school day, and is willing to reevaluate group placement as soon as it appears not to be serving the children, no one grouping decision is high-stakes. They review some basic concepts about grouping.

Homogeneous Groups

Homogeneous groups in the early elementary grades are designed to make a teacher's instruction more targeted. They are formed and reformed based on formal and informal assessments of children's skills. Thinking of these groups as targeted, temporary skills groups might remind teachers not to form them based on convenience. For example, some teachers might be tempted to form groups based on personalities or behavior traits. Others might want to be sure that the groups are of equal size. Either decision could lead to groupings that are not created to allow a specific skill to be addressed directly.

Cooperative Groups

There are other times during the day when issues such as managing group size and linking children who work together well can be addressed. *Cooperative groups*, formed for purposes other than explicit instruction from the teacher, can be used during a skills-based rotation (by grouping children not working with the teacher in a way that allows them to work cooperatively, and then calling homogeneous groups out of that collaborative format). They can also be formed for writing instruction and for content-area investigations. In beginning reading, a hybrid grouping of a strong reader with a weaker one has been used successfully for fluency-building activities in an instructional framework called *peer-assisted learning strategies* (Fuchs & Fuchs, 2005). This is one example of how collaborative work might occur among children at a range of skill levels while the teacher instructs a homogeneous group.

Sara is able to encourage Mrs. Thurston to try one unit of social studies in a collaborative grouping format. She offers to help her form the groups and then to gather information on whether the grouping is useful. As Mrs. Thornton begins to see that she can use different grouping configurations for different purposes throughout the day, she becomes more comfortable with regrouping. When she chooses to use homogeneous groupings, she is quick to form them and even quicker to reform them once the students' specific needs have been met.

Increasing Engagement

As Mrs. Thurston becomes more comfortable, Sara begins to focus on specific instructional strategies for ensuring higher levels of student engagement. She begins with read-alouds, an activity Sara regards as crucially important. Mrs. Thurston's read-alouds are not very interactive. She does ask questions, but she tends to call on only one child among the many with raised hands, and then she moves on. Sara notices that some of the children are first antsy and then distracted during read-aloud time because they rarely get a chance to speak. She wants to increase engagement for all children during this time, because it is an important opportunity for language and vocabulary development.

Sara models an interactive read-aloud for Mrs. Thurston in which she asks questions but also has the children share with a partner rather than answer her. She pairs the children as listening partners in advance, and they sit together. Then she explains that during the read-aloud, she wants to be sure that everyone has a chance to share ideas. The children are able to share with one another, and it significantly increases engagement, especially for the children most likely to be left out.

Extreme Makeover

Sara employed fairly soft coaching strategies with Mrs. Thurston. These strategies built their relationship, helped Sara gain entry into the world of first grade, and ensured that changes were paced so as not to overwhelm Mrs. Thurston. Sara also made decisions to build on what Mrs. Thurston was already comfortable doing. These are all benefits, but they come with a cost. We calculated their meeting times to require 11 full hours, spread over at least 7 school days. In the real world of schools, this series of meetings and tasks may have taken a whole month to accomplish—with one teacher. Most coaches work with at least 20 teachers in at least four grade levels. And, in some schools, there is not a second of instructional time to waste.

A faster-paced reform-oriented series of goal-setting meetings might look very different, with some of the up front decision making done in advance by the coach or by a literacy leadership team. For example, the coach could meet with the grade-level team to share an assessment system created in advance and including a calendar and a set of reporting forms. That assessment system could be designed based on the conceptual framework for assessment (screening, diagnosis, progress monitoring, and outcome) and on empirical criteria for selecting valid and reliable measures. It might require the use of new measures with which teachers would need to become familiar. It could include much stricter goals, gathered from research (e.g., norms for words read correctly in 1 minute).

The coach, or a small team, could also make the schoolwide instructional schedule in advance. This type of planning, including decisions about when core subjects will be taught and for how long, is essential for using support staff (e.g., paraprofessionals, reading specialists, special educators) wisely in a time of increased need for service and decreased funding for additional staff. This type of scheduling might require all reading instruction to take place at the same time or, alternatively, it might stagger instructional blocks so that one grade level is teaching reading while another is not.

Likewise, curriculum-mapping projects completed during the school year mean that the year's instruction may be fairly haphazard; such efforts are akin to designing the plane while flying in it. Summer is a more appropriate time for such work, because it means that teachers can begin the year with a clear roadmap (or flyable plane). Again, such projects might be accomplished by individuals or groups contracted for summer tasks. Given new instructional materials often associated with reform-oriented coaching, it is imperative that at least some individuals in the school develop deep understanding of the core scope and sequence before school starts. This understanding, combined with program-specific coaching during preplanning (often jump-started by individuals associated with the commercial enterprise), can lead to at least partial implementation of the new plan in the first week of school.

Finally, well-articulated assessment systems make specific grouping decisions more transparent. If progress-monitoring assessments are conducted for students, their differences are visible soon after they emerge, and regrouping needs are easier to recognize and accommodate. If progress-monitoring data are shared with the coach and principal, the impetus to use them immediately is even stronger.

Keep in mind that Sara accomplished a set of tasks collaboratively, but it was costly in terms of time. She based her decisions on what was already happening, and she tried to help Mrs. Thurston make new decisions she was comfortable making. Our reform-oriented approach, described in Chapter 1, is more top-down, more intrusive, and less responsive to what teachers have been comfortable doing. This is because reform-oriented coaching is designed for settings where what teachers have been comfortable doing yields unacceptable outcomes in terms of student achievement. The reform-oriented coach must be prepared for more resistance than the coach who works in a softer model. In fact, Sara's strong interpersonal skills would be even more essential had she taken a reform-oriented stance.

FOURTH GRADE

Our second teacher is Ms. Rogers. She is a new teacher, in her second year. She works in a school with a history of high achievement on state tests of reading and math, but relatively lower achievement on the state writing assessment. She teaches 26 students in a self-contained fourth-grade classroom. There are two other fourth-grade teachers, and the three tend to work independently in math and reading and to plan together for science and social studies; Ms. Rogers works mainly on the state history units. The state standards have changed drastically since the last textbook adoption, so Ms. Rogers gathers a hodgepodge of materials, mainly from the Internet, to address the content standards.

Ms. Rogers has 45 minutes of planning each day, but, according to her collective bargaining agreement, only one planning period per week can be used for professional development. In addition, there are 2 contract hours after school each month—one for professional development and one for a faculty meeting. The principal has assigned Ms. Rogers (and her two colleagues) the goal of increasing achievement for her students on the writing portion of the state assessment. That assessment includes one extended writing task. The students read a passage to start their thinking. They then are assigned a particular response to that reading, based on a prompt—that is, to take an expressive, persuasive, or informative format. The written product is judged with rubrics for specific traits: development, organization, style, word choice, sentence formation, and conventions (Spandel, 2004). Moore (2007) points out that the advent of rubrics has occasioned debate concerning their reliability but that most writing educators view them as a significant advance over the multiple-choice tests of the past. The state tests in high-stakes format in third and fifth grade, but in low-stakes format in the fourth and sixth grade.

Setting Goals for Achievement

Sara's first meeting with Ms. Rogers is organized and business-like; it lasts 40 minutes. They look at the state scores for all of her students from the previous year. Although 90% of them made at least a passing score on the criterion-referenced tests in reading and math, only 40% achieved passing scores for writing, with no students earning the highest rating. They find that none of the students who passed in writing failed in reading. Next, they look at the scores of her entering students. The situation is slightly better, in that 65% of them passed the third-grade test. Together, they set the goal of achieving at least an 80% passing rate in writing for the classroom; that means that at least 21 of her 26 students would have to pass. Ms. Rogers tells Sara that she thinks the prompts for third and fifth grade are much simpler than those used in the off years, and the test itself is unfair. Sara tells her she will try to investigate this claim.

Sara prepares for her next meeting with Ms. Rogers. She uses the state website to examine released prompts, but she cannot find a pattern. What is clear, though, is that the prompts encompass very specific genres (e.g., letters, essays, speeches) and are more likely to be persuasive or informative than expressive. Sara downloads and prints her evidence of this interpretation, along with a set of the fourth-grade standards for writing. Although in many cases the standards reflect the same competencies listed at the third- and fifth-grade levels, they also identify the genres that students must be able to produce. For persuasive writing, these include letters and advertisements; for informative writing, they include letters, summaries, essays, articles, messages, notices, autobiographies, and biographies. Expressive writing includes stories, poems, journals, and personal essays, but these are infrequent on the fourth-grade state assessment.

Sara wonders whether it makes sense for her to gather more assessment data until she knows more about the instruction that Ms. Rogers provided. Given that the children were good fourth-grade readers, Sara assumes that they had basic skills related to spelling and grammar. One additional explanation merits investigation: The children may not have had adequate opportunity to learn the characteristics of the genres that they were called on to produce. Figure 6.5 represents Sara's thinking. The outcome measure is influenced both by students' individual skills and by their opportunity to learn the material. In addition, individual skills and opportunity to learn influence one another.

At Sara's next meeting with Ms. Rogers, again lasting only 40 minutes, she brings her standards and assessment documents, and she asks her to describe her approach to teaching writing. She learns that Ms. Rogers uses a grammar workbook to teach the parts of speech and punctuation rules, and dialog journals

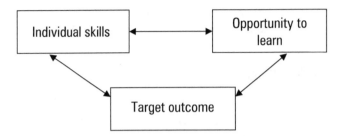

FIGURE 6.5. Assessment frame for upper elementary.

to engage the children in self-selected or prompted writing tasks. She admits that the content of the writing is often shallow, sometimes because the children do not have adequate knowledge about the topics in the prompts. In addition, as they examine the standards, Ms. Rogers admits that she has not taught the text types directly; rather, she follows the sequence in her core reading materials, which does not distinguish between persuasive and informative texts, and focuses most of its time on narratives. Sara concludes (privately) that it does not make sense to try to assess whether the students know these text structures or not. In general, last year's students simply did not have ample opportunity to learn them. It does make sense to ensure that this year's students have good instruction in the content of the curriculum before conducting more assessments to try to pinpoint their needs.

Setting Goals for Instructional Time

Given that the principal has noticed the poor writing performance of her students, Ms. Rogers is willing to rethink instructional time; Sara takes on this task next. Ms. Rogers is worried that she is not spending adequate time on writing, but she is also worried about how allocating any additional time to writing instruction might hurt achievement in the other content areas. Sara addresses this concern first by helping her plan her instructional day, and then by building in a cycle for writing instruction.

There are 6.5 hours, or 390 minutes, in the school day; 95 minutes are already taken for specials classes, lunch, and recess. Ms. Rogers begins to describe her usual schedule for the rest of those minutes; it is filled with transitions and breaks that, all told, leave little instructional time. Together they total the allocated time for a typical day, assuming, for the moment, that every minute could be used. Their work, which we believe is fairly typical, is represented in Figure 6.6. Keep in mind that this is not a chronological schedule, but an accounting for how much time is apportioned to the demands of the day. On the basis of this breakdown, Sara and Ms. Rogers realize that the time available for teaching writing is still very brief—

Category	Time (in minutes)
Lunch	30
Art/music/physical education/library/computer lab	45
Recess	20
Math	60
Reading	90
Science	40
Social studies	40
Writing	30
Class meeting	15

FIGURE 6.6. Preliminary fourth-grade time allocations.

barely enough to do a teacher-directed lesson without any guided or independent practice.

Sara and Ms. Rogers decide to consider pairing writing with social studies. That way they can have over an hour each day for the two subjects combined, and that will provide time across the week for knowledge-building; introduction of the characteristics of the types of writing addressed in the standards; and planning, drafting, and revision of multiple pieces across the year.

Ms. Rogers commits to planning for one full piece of writing each week. She will generally begin the week with a writing lesson, in which she will set the task for the week. She will teach the characteristics of each type of writing directly and create a graphic organizer that children can use to plan their own piece; given the time available, she can engage in a shared writing exercise, based on recent social studies content, to demonstrate how to use the graphic organizer. Doing so combines writing instruction with content review. She will then turn to new content; this will help the children meet their social studies objectives and will give them something to write about. She has many materials to use to build background knowledge, including Internet-based sources and videos. Once she has taught important ideas and terms, she will have the children read from the variety of sources that she has gathered, ending Wednesday's lesson by supporting the children as they use their graphic organizer to plan their writing. Thursday, students will draft, with support from her. Friday will be reserved for editing and revising. She will be able to model punctuation rules with which the children are struggling and to introduce new sentence structures. This weekly plan is outlined in Figure 6.7.

Setting Goals for Content Coverage

Now that they have developed a plan for integrating writing and social studies, and for apportioning instructional time, Sara must help Ms. Rogers make a curriculum map. Sara examines the history and social science standards for fourth grade. They comprise a rigorous and comprehensive picture of life in the state, with 10 themes, including the geography of the state, the state's role in the American Revolution and the Civil War, and a description of the current state government. Given the chronological organization, it does not make sense to reorganize the standards. Instead, Sara will begin with a rough roadmap for the social studies curriculum, and then map the writing genres onto it.

Ms. Rogers's interest in history makes this task simpler; she already has a curriculum map from the previous year. Sara's meeting time, then, is used to make logical connections between that map and the writing genres. For example, the standards target the roles of George Washington, Thomas Jefferson, and Patrick Henry in the American Revolution, so Sara encourages Ms. Rogers to teach biography that week. When Ms. Rogers is teaching about the effects of segregation, she will teach poems; when she is teaching about state transportation and communications systems, she will teach the characteristics of newspaper stories.

Sara leaves her meeting with the promise of gathering a set of graphic organizers that Ms. Rogers can use to guide her writing introductions. This task will take Sara some time, both in her professional books and on the Internet. She will have to be sure that the organizers she chooses encompass the characteristics defined in the state standards documents and tested in the state assessment, and also are of appropriate complexity for fourth-grade students. She imagines that she will make some of them on her own, and that she will have to view her choices as pilot documents, gathering information on the utility of each one from Ms. Rogers and the rest of the fourth-grade team. The first order of business is to determine whether the state website offers supporting guidance and resources. She will also need to inspect the school's language arts core and inventory the resources available there.

Monday	Tuesday	Wednesday	Thursday	Friday
Introduce a type of writing	Build background knowledge; review previous content	Read to learn more; make a writing plan	Draft	Edit and/or revise

FIGURE 6.7. Weekly plan for linking writing instruction to social studies in fourth grade.

Strategies for Flexible Grouping

What Sara has accomplished thus far is substantial. She has supported Ms. Rogers in organizing her plan by helping her decide what to teach and when. That is a good start, but it does not prove totally successful in practice. As Sara walks through the school on a Friday, the day reserved for editing and revising drafts, she finds Ms. Rogers showing a movie during the time scheduled for social studies and writing. Ms. Rogers comes to Sara after school, knowing that she will wonder why. She readily admits that despite a good attitude and a good start, she cannot keep pace with the plan. In particular, she is unable to provide written feedback to all students for Friday's editing; in fact, she cannot respond to more than half each week. On Friday, then, when children are scheduled to work on their revisions, only half have enough guidance to make any improvements. She has already twice canceled the revisions. Because Ms. Rogers feels unsuccessful, she wants to purchase a state-produced assessment practice workbook.

Sara asks Ms. Rogers to try a strategy—cooperative learning—that might be more effective than a workbook (Slavin, 1995). *Cooperative learning* is an instruction and grouping strategy in which students are assigned to teams to work together to accomplish tasks. Real cooperative learning is much more than "group work." It entails a plan for recognition of the efforts of the entire team and individual team members, as well as a system for making sure that all members of the team can contribute. In this case, cooperative learning will enable Ms. Rogers to keep up with her responses to individual students by working with fewer students each week; the strategy will also enable her to help the others work productively together.

Sara and Ms. Rogers work after school to generate a rank-ordered list of students, in rough order of achievement in writing. They then take the list and generate six heterogeneous groups of four or five. The group tasks (planning, composing, drafting, and revising a specific written piece) are already set. Sara and Ms. Rogers must create a system for individual accountability. Revision is the simplest target; the students can work in cooperative groups in the classroom to plan their pieces using the graphic organizers, then at classroom and library computers to draft them. Each Thursday, Sara can take the six drafts and make comments. On Fridays, she can return individual copies of the group drafts, using a highlighter to assign specific revisions to individual students, partially based on what she knows about their skills. Because all students will be working at once, most will have to revise their sections by hand. Six students, though, one member of each team, can be assigned a total individual revision each week, on a rotating basis, using the classroom computers.

Sara has helped Ms. Rogers plan a true cooperative learning format for writing. After her introduction of the writing form and her knowledge-building lessons, the students will work collaboratively every week to compose a draft, and every student will do some revisions; every 6 weeks, every student will have done a complete revision. Every week, she will have a system for recognizing the efforts of the group and of each individual student; she will also be able to tailor the individual work to the specific needs and abilities of the student.

Increasing Engagement

Sara visits Ms. Rogers' classroom many times over the next weeks. Although cumbersome at first, the cooperative learning strategy becomes easier to implement over time. Students learn strategies for working together and for working productively. Ms. Rogers is more and more comfortable with short, targeted grammar lessons on Fridays. She reflects on the errors that she sees in her group essays each Thursday and chooses lessons to teach from the grammar textbook she has used previously. Sara encourages her to link grammar instruction closely to writing applications and to avoid the misconception that extensive grammar study somehow leads to better writing (Moore, 2007).

Sara's concern, though, is what happens on Wednesdays, the day set aside for students to read to learn more about the social studies topic prior to their writing. What she notices is that Ms. Rogers uses her original set of cobbled-together resources, downloaded from the Internet and copied. These packets do contain information about the topic, but, taken as a whole (like the Internet itself), the materials are not coherently organized and vary widely in difficulty. Weaker students are disengaged, and Sara wonders whether this is because the information is too difficult for them to read. Ms. Rogers appears disengaged, too, in that she is serving more as a monitor than a teacher, trying to keep students on task when the task itself is ill-defined (and possibly ill-advised).

Sara meets with Ms. Rogers about her progress. She is willing to continue cooperative learning, but it still entails some stress. She is also more and more comfortable with targeted direct instruction in grammar rather than workbook or textbook pages. She, too, is concerned about Wednesday's time. She is frustrated that the students are not as excited about poring over the history resources as she is. Sara considers that the texts themselves are not particularly engaging. She promises Ms. Rogers that she will investigate resources for enlarging and diversifying the types of texts that children are reading during their research.

Sara's first thought is that the reproduced Internet texts are visually dull; she considers whether individual children or even pairs of children would be more engaged if they could see the resources in color on the computer screen and scroll through the information. She realizes, though, that not all students could see the available computer screens at once. She will also have to locate other resources, and she prefers that they be trade books. The IRA's website search engine is helpful again. Sara searches text and motivation and finds a piece on engaging readers that describes several resources for selecting texts (Opitz & Lee, 2005). Criteria include reading level, but these are not the only criteria used. Sara begins to assemble a text set for an upcoming unit; when she delivers them to the classroom, both the students and Ms. Rogers are immediately thrilled by their choices.

Extreme Makeover

Now we have eavesdropped on Sara providing coaching to two classroom teachers. In both cases, Sara engaged teachers in setting goals about achievement, instructional time, content coverage, grouping strategies, and engagement. She was careful to listen, to suggest rather than insist, and to avoid seeming heavy-handed and overly prescriptive. As was the case with Mrs. Thurston, Sara's strategies with Ms. Rogers are comprehensive and responsive, but slow.

The general strategy that Sara adopted with Ms. Rogers over time is curriculum mapping. Poor test scores were not easily explained by poor basic skills, so they focused on providing more organized and systematic access to the curriculum. Basically, they returned to the characteristics of the state assessment and to the standards themselves, and they made better use of the instructional day. They combined time for two subject areas and planned content-knowledge building and demonstration of that knowledge through writing. Over time, they constructed a cooperative learning plan, which encouraged social interaction and reduced the demands of grading. Finally, they began to address issues of engagement by reconsidering their text selections.

Consider a more intrusive, faster-paced road to this same place. What if all of the teachers had poor performance on the state writing test? Given additional knowledge that the writing curriculum was not well organized, Sara might have organized it in advance of the school year.

In such a reform-oriented context, Sara might have done the curriculum mapping herself or, better yet, with a team, during the summer. She might have created grade-level pacing guides to link social studies and writing, and to coordinate the schedule with the school's calendar for reporting progress to parents. She might have purchased text sets in advance for each unit. In order to cut costs, she might have had to stagger the instruction, with half the teachers in each grade-level team teaching before lunch and half after lunch, moving the books between two classrooms.

Such decisions would likely be viewed very differently by different teachers. Some would welcome the support and view Sara's planning as a great opportunity for them to focus more of their attention on responding to their students rather than on designing the entire curriculum. Others, though, would see this as a violation of their rights to teach the curriculum in their own way. The two sets of respondents would not constitute "effective" and "ineffective" teachers, as effective and ineffective teachers would be in each camp. Sara's interpersonal skills would again be important here. Equally important, though, would be the principal's support of the implementation of the curriculum. Reform-oriented coaching strategies are not effective unless they are implemented in a reform-oriented system, at the request and with the support of the principal. In that case, top-down decisions can streamline the changes and allow the coach to actually have time to work one-on-one with more teachers.

SEVENTH GRADE

Let's move Sara to one more classroom. Our last teacher is Mr. Waterman. He teaches seventh and eighth grade English in a school with a fairly fractured curriculum and a struggling student body. He meets with five large sections of 35 to 40 students, three at seventh grade and two at eighth grade, for 50 minutes each day. Although other teachers on the seventh- and eighth-grade team complain about the students' attitudes toward school, Mr. Waterman tends to have strong relationships with his students. Consequently, he has strained relationships with his more negative peers, and he prefers to work alone.

Setting Goals for Achievement

Sara comes to this school and finds data everywhere, and the data management system is virtually paperless. There are smart boards and multiple computers in every classroom. The school uses computerized systems for tracking reading outside of school, computerized adaptive systems for measuring reading and math achievement every month, and computer-based student practice programs for all of the state tests. The first day of preplanning is taken entirely by presentations about data: representatives from each commercial system use multimedia resources to show teachers how to engage the system, migrate (or "reroster") students from last year into their new class lists, view student progress represented in multiple ways, and troubleshoot technology problems. All claim that their tests are not designed merely for evaluating progress but for targeting and organizing instruction.

Initially, Sara is impressed with this data collection scheme. She can envision her work in the area of assessment vastly simplified by the reports produced by the system. She decides to start by generating a classroom-level profile for each teacher to use in her first meeting. She is quickly confused, though. Each teacher has a profile on each assessment. All profiles in the area of reading claim to report some numerical reading level. In various places, she finds a grade-level equivalent, an instructional reading level, a categorical label related to the state test, and other metrics, not readily interpretable. Sara asks her principal to explain the system to her. He directs her to confer with Mr. Waterman, a teacher whom the principal says is an expert.

Sara feels very uncomfortable taking Mr. Waterman's time, and she is even more uncomfortable once she begins the meeting. Sara shows him the reports she has generated based on one of his sections from last year; she asks him to interpret them for her. Matter-of-factly, he tells her that the data show that all of his students grew in their skills in the past year. He does this by indicating the data column called "gain," in which the computer has subtracted the beginning-of-year score from the end-of-year score to yield a remainder. Those remainders ranged from 5 to 118. When Sara asks why a particular student made a large gain, Mr. Waterman indicates that that student was very talented and motivated, read extensively outside of school, and came from a family with enough resources to provide many educational opportunities. A student with poor gains has the opposite profile. When Sara turns to the next set of results, Mr. Waterman informs her that all the tests have the same pre–post format. Sara thanks Mr. Waterman for his time.

Needless to say, Sara's concerns over the assessment system are not allayed. There are two reasons. First, multiple tests (each taking time during the day to administer and each involving high financial costs) are used for tracking progress in the area of reading. In addition, they generate numbers on various scales that could be interpreted to show growth, but there is no clear indication of how much growth actually is meaningful.

Sara considers her options, and she has to study. She decides to refer to a text on curriculum-based measurement (Hosp, Hosp, & Howell, 2007) that the state team had consulted in its RTI protocol. She remembers that text because it includes multiple examples of *aim lines*, which are simply graphic displays of the rate of growth necessary across multiple points in time in order to reach a goal.

Aim lines show how quickly an individual would have to grow in order to meet a specific goal. In Figure 6.8, the student starting in September at the preprimer level must grow more quickly than the student starting at the early first-grade level; the student starting first grade well-above grade level can have a much more aggressive goal. These lines are constructed by choosing an end goal, measuring initial achievement, and then drawing a line to represent growth over time. Then, as students progress, progress-monitoring measures indicate their status with regard to the goal, either above, on, or below the aim line; these scores can be superimposed on the aim-line chart. Such measures can be used to judge whether the instruction currently being provided is likely to yield the desired outcome.

Sara decides to ask Mr. Waterman whether he would be willing to select one test and pilot an aim-line system. His initial response is that the tests already include aim lines; they calculate a goal—1 year's growth—for each student based on the first score. Sara shows Mr. Waterman that 1 year's growth for a student 4 years below grade level would only maintain his critically weak achievement gap. Mr. Waterman reminds Sara that he teaches 190 students each day and can not make up for the range of deficits he inherits at the start of the year. Sara tells him that she understands and that she would be working with all of the intervention teachers to

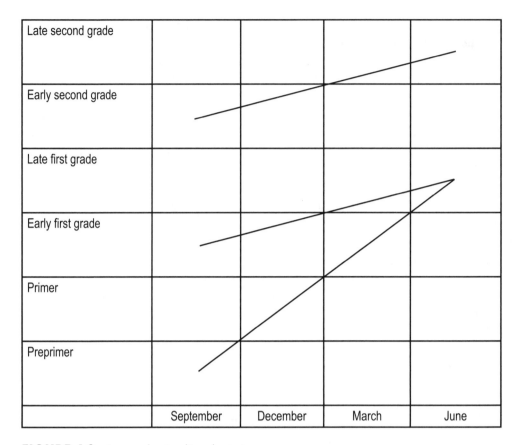

FIGURE 6.8. A sample aim-line depiction.

make their services more effective. She convinces him to help her create aim lines, on an exploratory basis.

This procedure is useful. Both Sara and Mr. Waterman have good technology skills, so they are easily able to construct aim-line charts and even to automate them so that they can be generated quickly after each assessment. They agree to start with the goal that all children should make at least 1 year's progress, and, given additional resources and support outside of the English classroom, that children below grade level should make enough progress to end the year on grade level. Mr. Waterman is skeptical about the latter goal but agrees to go along in principle.

When Sara sees the profiles, she is astounded at the range. In every section, most students are clustered fairly close to their grade level, but a large group, at least 10 in each classroom, are far below, some even with comprehension scores corresponding to second-grade achievement. Sara quickly realizes that she will have to learn more about those students.

She wants to sort the students into at least three groups, and she has to do it quickly. She choose a fifth-grade nonfiction passage from a core program and marks off the first 240 words. By making sure that the excerpt she is asking the students to read is exactly 240 words long, she avoids having to calculate reading rate; if she sets her watch to beep after 2 minutes, she will be able to tell whether students can read 120 words per minute or not (approximately mid-fifth grade, according to Hasbrouck and Tindal, 2006); if she also tallies their errors, she can tell whether they read with greater than 90% accuracy (the minimum typically required to avoid outright frustration), by simply setting the cut point at 24 errors.

In order to administer these assessments, Sara comes to Mr. Waterman's classes. First, Mr. Waterman assigns all of the students a feature article about a former student of his who has won a college writing award; they are to read the article and then write either a congratulatory note to send to the student, or a note to Mr. Waterman about their own goals for the year. That assignment provides Mr. Waterman and Sara the opportunity to do their quick assessment, both working at the same time. With a class list of all scores on the comprehension test, they first know all students for whom extra information was needed. In order not to single out the struggling students, they actually query the stronger students on what they had read or written over the summer, jotting down the information on their clipboards. They are able to conduct the quick oral reading samples discreetly, and to finish the entire process in one regular class period.

When the testing is done, Sara and Mr. Waterman have found that a majority of the newly tested students have adequate fluency and need to work on comprehension and vocabulary; they can be served by rich instruction along with their much stronger peers. A smaller number have adequate decoding but weak fluency; they need to try to build their reading rate to make reading an easier process and to allow more of their efforts to be directed at comprehension. And a small number in each section of the classes have decoding skills totally inadequate for the demands of grade-level texts; those children certainly need decoding interventions outside of the seventh-grade English curriculum, and they need access to taped or computer-assisted versions of the class texts. These three problem categories are summarized in Figure 6.9.

Setting Goals for Instructional Time

Both Sara and Mr. Waterman feel they have accomplished a great deal in a short time. Now they have to decide what to do with their knowledge. Single-period English classes in seventh and eighth grade leave very few choices about time. Mr. Waterman is surprised when Sara asks him how he uses instructional time. He simply replies that they study the themes of the six novels selected for seventh grade, write one five-paragraph essay about each one, and complete a vocabulary workshop book and a series of grammar exercises. Sara asks about the collection of individual copies of novels that ring the classroom; Mr. Waterman explains

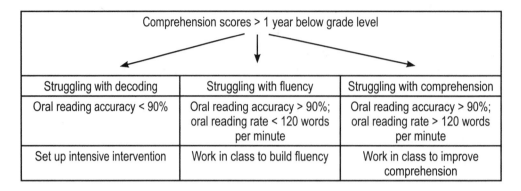

FIGURE 6.9. Assessment frame for seventh grade.

that she is referring to his classroom lending library, and that he allows children to borrow books to read at home in order to participate in the school's reading motivation system. Sara asks about homework, and Mr. Waterman is surprised again; students, he explains, read chapters from the novels and do vocabulary and grammar exercises each night for homework. In class, the students check one another's work and discuss questions that they struggled with. End-of-book exams comprise questions from the reading guides, so students who did not understand them at home could fix their answers to prepare for the test. Tests have multiple-choice items about the plot and characters in the novels, short-answer items that mirror the discussions the class has had about themes in the texts, and one longer essay in which students choose from several possibilities, each designed to make a connection between the novel's theme and a personal experience.

In essence, then, even students well-below grade level can pass the novel tests; they simply have to copy and study the answers to the reading guides. Sara asks Mr. Waterman what his goals are; he reports that the state standards target connections with prior knowledge and critical thinking about literature. He is engaging students in that critical thinking, even those who cannot or would not read the novels. Unfortunately, though, students (especially struggling students) are doing almost no actual reading.

Sara asks Mr. Waterman to consider a 1-week break from the novel routine each month. To do that, he will have to compress his curriculum plan, but he agrees to try it. During that week, students will choose to enter into book clubs designed to increase the sheer volume of their reading. She selects texts, including magazines, from which the students can choose. Some texts are deliberately chosen to be much easier to read, so those have to be particularly engaging. Others are even more complex than the novels being read in class.

This time, though, all of the time in class is spent reading. Students can read silently, with a partner, or they can listen to a taped version and read along. At night, instead of reading, they write a short response to that day's text. These responses are kept in a journal that Mr. Waterman can check and respond to during the other 3 weeks, when the class is studying the novels. On Friday of the book club weeks, members of the club get together to discuss the book. Some are finished with it, but many are not; they can keep the book and finish reading it if they wish.

Setting Goals for Content Coverage

The pressures of single-period classes make it challenging for teachers to plan, content coverage that goes beyond the actual story line of a series of novels. The state standards are modeled on *Understanding by Design* (Wiggins & McTighe, 2005) to encourage a particular three-stage type of unit planning. At first, teachers identify their desired results. Teachers examine standards and performance indicators, such as this one from Delaware: "Students will demonstrate an overall understanding of printed texts by making connections within and between texts." Then, they select from among a series of essential questions to guide unit planning: "What's new and what's old here?" "Have we encountered this idea before?" Then, they work through the planning process, committing their time to supporting enduring understandings, knowledge, and skills.

The next stage in planning is determining what evidence will be collected. Multiple sources are identified. Evidence includes performance tasks, tests and quizzes, and work samples. Unprompted evidence can also be gathered, as teachers observe students. Finally, student self-assessments are included as they help students to increase control over their own learning. Only after those two stages are complete can the actual learning be planned, as a series of experiences and instruction. This is the last stage in the planning process. This type of planning is very different from the planning that Mr. Waterman has described, during which he chooses novels, assigns them, discusses them, tests the students, and has the students write about them.

Sara decides to ask Mr. Waterman to plan two units with her in this format. He examines the state standards, which are useful in persuading him that she is on the right path, and chooses to begin with a standard targeting self-monitoring during reading. It is associated with the enduring understanding that good readers use many strategies, and they try new ones if the ones they are using are unsuccessful. The essential question tagged to the standard is "What do good readers do when they don't understand?" Mr. Waterman is hard-pressed to match his current content-coverage plan to this standard. Instead, he realizes that he will have to identify a set of strategies to teach, and then he will need a plan for gathering evidence that students know and use the strategies. This changes his thinking. He will want to devote more class time to reading.

He starts to think in terms of a 3-week unit, shorter than the time he usually spends on one novel. This encourages him to consider shorter selections, including classic short stories, which provide him an opportunity to model the strategies in action. He can then assign the students selections to read, and prompt them to find places to use the strategies. Finally, he can select a short final text to use in an assessment, one that provides the students another chance to use strategies to construct understanding, demonstrated either in a summary or on a quiz or test. Sara is surprised at how much the planning process is engaging Mr. Waterman to consider adding more reading to the school day.

Strategies for Flexible Grouping

Considering this new general frame, including flexible strategy instruction and more texts, Mr. Waterman is forced to contend with the fact that assessments indicate that many of his students are well-below grade level and will have difficulty with the reading. Sara pushes him to consider that his new plan provides him more chances to work with students in smaller groups. In effect, if he simply uses 20 minutes each day for actual reading or writing, he can do it in three regular groups. Some students can read on their own, and others can read in pairs, either orally or silently but requesting help on difficult words. The weakest students (or a combination of the weakest and others who choose to join) can read with him. He can read the text aloud and then have them reread what he has just read; then, they can discuss the test briefly. Such a system will add no planning time to his load and will be a flexible strategy for grouping to give students the support they need.

Increasing Engagement

Mr. Waterman has already done two things to increase engagement. He has initiated week-long book clubs, and he has initiated flexible groupings during in-class reading periods. Both of them have one thing in common: They increase time for students to be engaged in the actual act of reading during school. This is an important way to increase engagement generally—there is nothing like a group of students lost in books.

There are other ways that Mr. Waterman might increase engagement. Instead of keeping hundreds of individual texts as outside-the-curriculum rewards, they could become integrated into daily life and work, with increasing reading volume an integral goal. For example, Mr. Waterman could replace his grammar workbook with a sentence-composing approach (e.g., Killgallon, 1997). He could use teach a particular sentence type and then have students read selections from the class library to find additional examples.

In addition, Mr. Waterman is not teaching anything but "the novel." Many early adolescent readers would prefer more information text, and they could easily work in cooperative groups to read to learn background information that would help them to better understand novels set in different times and places.

Extreme Makeover

Mr. Waterman's initial plan was not really a sound one for his students. Too often, young adolescent readers stop reading in school and instead learn about the themes in very difficult books from the canon based solely on class discussion. There are many more intrusive ways that a coach might work with him. In fact, the first thing that a reform-oriented coach might do is initiate a different scheduling plan to increase instructional time. Two possibilities include *block scheduling* (where the course would meet in a double session every other day) or replacing both English and social studies with a course called *humanities*, covering the standards for both. Neither one of those solutions would require additional personnel, and both would provide extended time for teaching and learning. Both would involve extensive school-level planning on the part of the principal. Both would allow Mr. Waterman to engage in meaningful teacher-directed instruction, reading time during school hours, and small-group interactions.

CONCLUSION

Setting goals for classrooms is absolutely essential for literacy coaches. It is not easy work. In all coaching models, such goal setting assumes that coaches guide and support teachers to consider making changes. That means that they must confront evidence about the extent to which what they are doing is consistent with achievement goals. They must consider data. Unfortunately, many schools have not yet established meaningful assessment systems. Such systems provide for screening, diagnosis, progress monitoring, and evaluation; they include protocols for gathering data on all students in some cases and for gathering additional data on some students. They provide real direction to instruction during the school year and real opportunity to reflect on the year's level of success after the school year.

Reevaluating how teachers use instructional time is tricky business. It is a strategy likely to yield large dividends, though, because many struggling teachers simply do not use time efficiently. Regardless of the model a coach uses, helping teachers to consider a plan to use their time to serve the needs of the students they have is essential.

Making plans for curriculum coverage is, in our experience, less stressful. State standards must guide such work, but state standards do not do the work. Teachers tend to respond positively to such tasks, because they are (or, at least, should be) directly associated with success on state-mandated assessments. We see standards as opportunities. Most are specific enough to provide direction and vague enough to provide choice.

Instructional groupings are, again, tricky. Improvements come at a cost. All grouping formats besides whole-group, teacher-directed instruction entail more careful planning and better management skills. All improvements must be revisited, particularly when they involve homogeneous skills groups. Coaches must help teachers to know that grouping is ongoing and temporary, but, again, that means that teachers and coaches must work at it together.

Finally, the opportunity to help teachers to increase engagement is really at the heart of instructional improvement. It is also the most individual and costly work a coach must accomplish. Real improvement means real knowledge of the inner workings of the classroom. Real improvement in some classrooms will mean modeling. Fortunately, though, real improvement in this area will be lasting. We favor a reform-oriented coaching model because it hastens progress in these areas, and it creates more time for the coach to work one-on-one with teachers, learning about them and about the students.

Remember that in Chapter 1 we asked you not to commit to any one coaching model. That charge remains. Consider all of the strategies that our coach, Sara, employed. None is actually specific to any one grade level; none is actually specific to any one coaching model. All may be useful to you as you consider (or reconsider) your role as a coach.

CHAPTER 7

Grade-Level Coaching

In the last chapter, we explored several important coaching goals. We focused coaching efforts in individual classrooms, with teachers at different grade levels. In each instance, we explored specific achievement profiles, and Sara worked with teachers to adjust their instructional time, make more systematic plans for content coverage, and use a variety of grouping formats to meet individual needs. Once initial changes had been made, we illustrated efforts to increase engagement. The work of the coach with individual teachers was intense and very time-consuming, but it provided a comfortable rate of change for the teachers. Finally, in our extreme makeovers, we provided a faster-paced route, more consistent with reform-oriented coaching. In this chapter, we again illustrate coaching cycles, this time at three different grade levels. Coaches whose charge is to work with grade levels rather than individual teachers already assume a certain level of collaboration. Given that, in this chapter, we depict choices in the professional development cycle that we introduced in Chapter 5. We also attend to opportunities to enhance and increase collaboration.

Since Sara was so successful with individual teachers, we bring her into this chapter, as well. Remember that her teaching experience is at fifth grade. She is expert in facilitating reading and writing workshops. She is a reading specialist, and she has worked in district and state curriculum and assessment initiatives. We again bring her into new situations so that we can encourage new coaches, but we also expect more experienced coaches to consider ways to improve their craft by taking Sara's lead. We consider different grade levels this time because, frankly, expert teaching at different grades is different (see Block et al., 2002, if you are interested in research documenting the differences).

KINDERGARTEN

In all schools around the country, the kindergarten team begins each year with a new group of children and families, and that group reflects changes in the community.

Although, historically, Madison Elementary has served children entering school with rich preschool literacy experiences, times have changed. A combination of factors, including redistricting and increased economic opportunities for immigrant families, has vastly changed the literacy achievement profiles of incoming kindergarteners. This is the second year of schoolwide Title I status for the school; 55% of the families qualify for federal lunch subsidies. Given the federal requirements for Title I, average class size is 21 children. This year, though, fully one-third of the new kindergarten children are ELLs.

The four kindergarten teachers have an eclectic set of experiences. Two have taught kindergarten successfully for over 20 years. One is an experienced teacher, but had a very difficult year in third grade and was reassigned to kindergarten. The final teacher is in her second year at the school. She is the youngest, with a master's degree in reading, but she was unable to secure a job as a reading specialist in the district this year. She is waiting for an opening, teaching kindergarten in the meantime. She is very close-mouthed about her instructional practice and unwilling to showcase the success of her students. Both of the experienced teachers are skeptical about the other two, but for very different reasons.

Each teacher has a paraprofessional partner. The expectations for paraprofessionals vary considerably from classroom to classroom, as do their own backgrounds. One is actually a former teacher who prefers not to have the added expectations and hours. The others have some college experience, but none has a 4-year degree. No one on the kindergarten team speaks Spanish, the home language of the ELLs.

Creating Time for Professional Collaboration

State-level testing indicates that changes are necessary; the school, always fully accredited in the past, did not make adequate yearly progress (AYP) last year. Students from low socioeconomic status homes and ELLs, on average, did not perform well on the state reading test. In addition, demographic projections indicate that more and more students in each group will be served at the school in the years ahead. The principal at Madison Elementary has allocated substantial resources from the Title I budget and the professional development budget to support Sara's position. He is expecting that all professional development be planned by her and accomplished within the existing grade-level teams. He is also committed to protecting Sara's time so that she is able to work directly in classrooms. He sets the following expectations for Sara:

1. She will work with each of the six grade-level teams (K–5) in small-group sessions 2 hours each month.
2. She will observe all 24 teachers for the full language arts block once each marking period.

Sara begins by sketching her general schedule in broad strokes. She wants to stagger her theory building and her observations so that teachers have time to practice the new applications they learn about. She realizes that her work will be much more productive if she does all of her outside-the-classroom work on the same day each week, facilitating three 1-hour sessions and spending the remainder of the day planning for the next week. The rest of the week, then, can be used for observation and feedback. She anticipates that she will spend the first week of each marking period assisting with and interpreting student achievement data. She will have 8 weeks left, and she thinks about them in 2-week cycles. In order to answer the principal's mandate, she will have to be able to observe at least three individual teachers each week. Her activities for the first 4 weeks are outlined in Figure 7.1.

The kindergarten team has had a tradition of meeting for collaborative work 1 hour each week, on Mondays. That hour has been created by scheduling recess back-to-back with a *special* (physical education, music, computer lab, library, and art). The general schedule for kindergarten instruction is represented in Figure 7.2. Traditionally, kindergarten teachers have relied on paraprofessionals to supervise recess and lunch, and paraprofessionals eat lunch during specials. Given the schedule they have established, kindergarten teachers could work together any day during the week for 1 hour (and still have time for lunch). If the teachers rethink their responsibilities, the paraprofessionals could have the same opportunity. They could engage in professional development with Sara for 1 hour each week while the teachers supervise the children during recess and lunch.

Choosing a Focus

Midway through the first week of school, the most salient focus for kindergarten is clearly shared: The teachers need to learn about literacy instruction for ELLs. There are already significant rumblings, especially among the two experienced teachers, that these children will simply need 2 years of kindergarten. Sara knows that this is not a viable plan, and she needs to head it off quickly.

	Outside the classroom	Inside the classroom
Week 1	Theory building with K, 1, 2	Observations with 2, 3, 4
Week 2	Theory building with 2, 3, 4	Observations with K, 1, 2
Week 3	Theory building with K, 1, 2	Observations with 2, 3, 4
Week 4	Theory building with 2, 3, 4	Observations with K, 1, 2

FIGURE 7.1. Basic plan for the coach.

Monday	
8:30–9:00	Calendar, morning meeting
9:00–9:30	Work with words and shared reading
9:30–10:00	Literacy centers
10:00–10:30	Shared writing
10:30–11:30	Read-aloud
11:30–12:00	Recess
12:00–12:30	Lunch
12:30–1:00	Specials
1:00–1:30	Math
1:30–2:00	Math
2:00–2:30	Science or social studies theme

FIGURE 7.2. General schedule for the kindergarten team.

Building Theory

Sara quickly locates a practice guide for ELLs in elementary school (Gersten et al., 2007) that will help them to begin. After reading the executive summary, she sees that the guide is organized to support five recommendations:

1. Screen for reading problems and monitor progress.
2. Provide intensive small-group reading interventions.
3. Provide extensive and varied vocabulary instruction.
4. Develop academic English.
5. Schedule regular peer-assisted learning opportunities. (Gersten et al., 2007, pp. 3–4)

She decides that she will work on the first recommendation, and then she will invite each teacher to take on one of the other recommendations. She will use a jigsaw format. She makes a graphic organizer to represent her plan (see Figure 7.3). In Sara's first kindergarten meeting, she distributes the guide, facilitates the division of the recommendations, and sets the team to work. As the teachers read their portion and take notes for the team, Sara works on her own contribution. She also circulates and answers individual teacher's questions.

At the end of the hour, team members agree that they will polish their work and also come up with a very specific demonstration for how to implement it. Their goal, then, for their next meeting, is to be able to demonstrate specific instructional applications. Sara plans a brief check-in with each teacher, after school, so that she

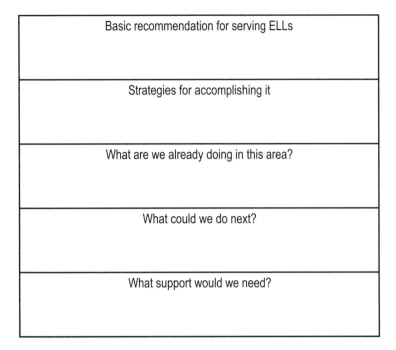

FIGURE 7.3. Jigsaw plan for the kindergarten team.

From *The Literacy Coaching Challenge* by Michael C. McKenna and Sharon Walpole. Copyright 2008 by The Guilford Press. Permission to photocopy this figure is granted to purchasers of this book for personal use only (see copyright page for details).

can see the teachers' work and help them if necessary before their next planning meeting.

Planning Demonstrations

Given the teachers' lack of optimism about the potential success of their ELLs, Sara is particularly concerned about two things: She wants each teacher to be excited about the instructional changes she is presenting, and she wants to be sure that the changes are sufficiently targeted and rigorous to be effective. She completes her own work (with the first recommendation) quickly, and distributes it, so that it can serve as a model. She then meets with each teacher to check in. Figure 7.4 summarizes what she learns from the teachers. Each is willing to construct an initial checklist for planning and implementing this particular change. Sara also tells the teachers that she will use the checklists when she visits their rooms to observe.

All of the recommendations that the teachers have generated are reasonable—except one. They can all be implemented with the current staff resources, and they are all improvements targeted in the research review and shaped for the school. But one teacher is struggling. The teacher who wants the team to purchase grammar workbooks is the teacher reassigned from third grade. Sara suspects (but does not know for sure) that she may be on a professional improvement plan. She is trying to adjust to kindergarten but having little success so far.

Sara reviews the guide (Gersten et al., 2007) that this teacher has read and sees just where her recommendation comes from. The guide does recommend that teachers adopt a scope and sequence for building academic language. In the earliest grades, though, it also suggests contrasting formal and informal language and building understanding of the meanings of prepositions. Sara knows that this teacher does not have the professional experience that would guide her toward appropriate language development activities for young children—let alone for young ELLs. She also knows that this teacher is not well received by the rest of the team. She cannot let her fail in this first collaborative activity, so she asks her to stay after school to work on it.

Sara decides to help the teacher design a retelling center, with puppets and story board manipulatives, for a series of simple narratives containing dialogue. They work together to read a stack of picture books (a good exercise for this teacher in itself) and choose the best examples. Then, they gather materials that the children can use to prompt the retellings. They also decide to tape-record the stories so the

Recommendation	Implementation ideas
Screen for reading problems and monitor progress.	• Conduct a Spanish-language vocabulary screening to establish that the children are not at-risk in their native language. • Monitor progress in letter-name and letter-sound acquisition every week for ELLs.
Provide intensive small-group reading interventions.	• During literacy centers every day, establish a three-group rotation: one group working with the teacher, one with the paraprofessional, and one in the literacy centers.
Provide extensive and varied vocabulary instruction.	• Have paraprofessionals spend calendar time every day doing an interactive, repeated read-aloud with one ELL. • Display oral vocabulary words from read-alouds supported by picture cues.
Develop academic English.	• Purchase a grammar workbook.
Schedule regular peer-assisted learning opportunities.	• Establish classroom buddies, always pairing an ELL with a native English speaker, for shared reading, shared writing, and math.

FIGURE 7.4. Teacher-generated ideas.

children can listen to them again at the center until the language becomes familiar enough for imitation.

Supported Practice

In their second team session, the kindergarten teachers each present their own instructional idea, together with an implementation checklist. The format is somewhat rushed, and Sara is reluctant to hold all team members accountable for all four of the new ideas. She asks each teacher to commit to two (her own and one other) for the rest of the week, and she schedules observations for the following week. She explains that she will be using the checklists generated by team members and that she will be thinking about how well these particular ideas work in their classrooms.

Teachers respond to this plan in different ways. The two experienced teachers quickly commit to each other's strategies. That way, they can collaborate to "get them right" in the same way in their two classrooms. Their concern, above all, is not to be compared to each other. In fact, they plan their weeks together so that when Sara visits each of them, she will see the exact same lesson repeated.

The reading specialist, as always, chooses to keep a very low profile. She can easily incorporate all five of the new ideas, but she only commits to two of them. When Sara visits, then, there is only evidence of a few changes. The struggling teacher, too, keeps a low profile. She is obviously uncomfortable with the flow of the kindergarten day, and her manner is not yet adapted to the needs of young learners for flexible, constant feedback. She focuses on classroom procedures, but many of them are the same ones that she had used fairly unsuccessfully in third grade. Her classroom is quiet, but not very focused.

Formative Feedback

In Sara's first set of observations, she is doing more than simply monitoring implementation of new ideas. She is also establishing her own confidential relationships with each teacher and learning more about how each team member is different from the others. She visits each teacher the afternoon before her observation to review the time and focus. She shows the teacher the checklist she will use and asks where she would like her to sit. She asks for permission to take a short break, and then she promises that she will leave the checklist for each teacher. She reviews her role as observer and reminds each teacher that no records will be kept for their personnel files.

Sara also wants to have the professional learning cycle start off successfully, so she decides that she will provide specific evidence of every item on the checklist being implemented and then provide only one question and one suggestion. This process is fairly simple because there are only five potential strategies to observe and only two in each classroom. Sara soon recognizes that all of the instructional strategies are viable. She also learns two other important things: There are vast differences in the quality of language used in the classrooms, and only the reading specialist uses her paraprofessional as an instructional partner. These two observations lead Sara to think about next steps in the professional support cycle for this team.

One classroom, predictably, is not working well. The paraprofessional is relegated to doing paperwork and setting up projects. The teacher is struggling with basic management. Sara asks to meet with her. Sara tells her that teaching kindergarten is different in terms of management, and that she is sorry not to have offered support in that area to aid the transition to the new team. Sara offers the teacher two possible choices: Sara can come in and help the paraprofessional to participate more in the instruction, or she can cover the class so the teacher can visit the reading specialist. Sara deliberately offers the choice of visiting the reading specialist because she knows that the reading specialist will keep these visits confidential.

Summary

Sara is pleased with her accomplishments in this first professional support cycle. She was able to choose a focus area in response to real needs. Her study group strategy, a jigsaw, allowed for both choice and accountability. When she went to visit, she only addressed issues that were on the checklist that team members generated. She was able to differentiate her support so that the teacher who needed more got more. In addition, she gained insights into the needs of each team member. Her next professional support cycle will focus on planning and managing small-group instruction. This time, she hopes to include both the kindergarten teachers and the paraprofessionals in the cycle.

THIRD GRADE

Let's move into third grade, in a different school with a very different environment. This large school has a history of core reading programs and of central-office mandates for instructional consistency. There are 12 sections of third grade in the school; third-grade children are served by two reading specialists and one special educator for part of the day. The school experiences high student turnover, but relatively low teacher turnover. There is a districtwide mentoring program for new teachers. It consists of training sessions for each of the district-selected commercial programs and distribution of the district pacing guides to direct instructional planning.

A new superintendent has abandoned the centralized professional development tradition and asked principals to plan building-level initiatives. When Sara was hired as coach, she was asked to focus her attention on third grade—the first high-stakes testing year. Although the school is still fully accredited, having earned AYP for 7 consecutive years, the stakes are getting higher and higher. Data indicate that third-grade performance has been stable, yielding about 75% passing rates each year. Fourth and fifth graders, though, who are housed in an upper elementary school, have demonstrated steadily declining performance. The new superintendent can see that the decline begins by third grade, continues in fourth grade, and then the principal of the upper elementary school has only 1 year to make a difference before the high-stakes testing.

Creating Time for Professional Collaboration

With such large grade-level teams, professional development during the school day is very difficult to schedule. Collective bargaining agreements prevent the coach from using building-level professional development days. During those days, teachers must be allowed to choose activities at state-sponsored conferences. Planning days cannot be used for any scheduled meetings. There is no way to actually schedule professional support for the entire team at once without additional resources.

Sara and the principal consider two options. They could take paraprofessionals out of kindergarten to cover classes in third grade. This would be a no-cost solution, but it would be very unpopular both with the kindergarten teachers and the paraprofessionals. An alternative would be to use Title I funds to schedule regular substitutes. They decide that 12 substitutes would be difficult to find, so they settle on six. They will come every Monday, and spend half their time in each of two third-grade classrooms. The plan, then, provides for 3 hours of professional development each week for each third-grade teacher, either in the morning or in the afternoon. Sara volunteers to make plans for the substitutes and to host a training; since they will always come on a Monday, the general focus in reading (to introduce and discuss the week's selection) will always be the same. She will also prepare an interactive read-aloud activity and a writing activity. This allows Sara to plan her professional support for the teachers without sacrificing the learning of the students. The reading program is actually more repetitive than the programs in the other content areas, and Sara is confident that she can teach the substitutes how to do the Monday lessons. When each group of teachers returns to the classroom, then, they will teach social studies, science, and math.

Choosing a Focus

The principal has already charged Sara with instituting differentiated instruction in the third grade. He tells her that they have ample evidence that whole-class implementation of the core reading program has not yielded acceptable results. Because of the longstanding central-office mandate, teachers in the third grade teach reading and language arts for 2½ hours each day, following their core reading program manual exactly. While the program is not actually scripted, the teachers' instruction is still closely coordinated because of the district policy. Teachers are on the same lesson each day; they use core program practice books and core program assessments. The principal asks Sara to revise their plan so that teachers use the core program materials but teach at least one small group each day.

Sara asks for time to examine the core program in third grade. She conducts a content analysis using the teacher's manual. She can see a general structure for teaching comprehension skills and strategies in the context of a set of fairly challenging selections. Amid a sea of choices for extension activities, connections to content-area instruction, and ideas to support struggling readers, the program designers plan for the range of skills in the classroom by using a very supportive general lesson plan. Students listen to and discuss the basal story on Monday. They are exposed to new vocabulary words, along with definitions and examples. They review a comprehension strategy. They are assigned a series of fairly low-level worksheets to practice the new word meanings. On Tuesday and Wednesday, they go back to teacher-directed reading of that very same story, this time reading specific portions with extensive comprehension scaffolding written into the manual. They also analyze some words in isolation for their syllable patterns. On Thursday, students read the story independently, and there are workbook pages to target the comprehension skills and strategies associated with the story. Friday is used for testing, with students reading short passages from the story and writing responses, as well as answering forced-choice questions about the vocabulary items.

Sara then examines the district's pacing guide. She can see, listed for each day in the school calendar, a list of the core program instruction, activities, and extensions that must be done. She cannot really tell why specific activities are included or excluded. They are not organized by type or focus. Conceptually, she cannot see how to make choices to eliminate specific tasks. She will have to, though, in order to make time for targeted small-group instruction.

Next, she visits the state curriculum website. There she finds a curriculum framework that she can use to plan. In third grade, for reading, students are encouraged to make the transition from learning to read to reading to learn. To accomplish this, students learn about words, reading with fluency and expression, and learning comprehension strategies. This framework can help Sara to better understand the strengths and weaknesses in the district's curriculum plan. Figure 7.5 captures Sara's analysis. Sara is still not sure what to do. There are clear items in each week's lessons that link to the standards. She imagines two potential explanations for why they are not working: Either the lessons themselves are too difficult given the knowledge and skills of the children, or they simply don't provide enough meaningful practice and application.

Sara meets with the third-grade team leader and the principal to share what she has learned. Together, they discuss possible explanations. It turns out that

Learning about words	Fluency	Comprehension strategies
Prefixes, suffixes, root word meanings; vocabulary words from the story; syllable types	Repeated reading (four times) of grade-level story, with gradually less support from the teacher	Modeling of comprehension strategies during rereadings of story; practice in workbook pages

FIGURE 7.5. Reading standards captured in basal plan.

the team leader supports both of Sara's explanations at the same time. For some children, the lessons are too difficult altogether. They have lingering decoding problems, especially with long vowel patterns and multisyllabic words. For others, the problem is a lack of reading practice. The team leader indicates that few of the struggling children read outside of school. She also cautions that the team is not going to respond well to mandates for more planning for small groups.

Sara meets finally with the principal to propose a plan, mindful that she will need his support to initiate it. Namely, she will need to initiate a new assessment to identify children with decoding problems and those with fluency problems. She has found an assessment that is relatively quick to give and can be purchased in classroom sets. The assessment, Phonological Awareness Literacy Screening: Grades 1 to 3 (PALS 1–3), (Invernizzi & Meier, 2000) has two basic parts for third graders: There is a developmental spelling inventory and a passage to read aloud with comprehension questions. If teachers time the passage, they will have a measure of word knowledge, a measure of fluency, and a measure of comprehension. They will have addressed the three areas in the state standards and the team leader's concerns about the students.

What to do once the teachers understand more about the students is another matter altogether. Sara will work within the grade-level materials. She will plan 1 hour of whole-group instruction in reading, reducing and refining the instructional lesson to include more fluency work. In addition, she will plan for 45 minutes of writer's workshop, and one small group each day, meeting for 45 minutes. She will stagger the schedule so that half of her team teaches small groups first, and 15 minutes later, the other half does. This structure, represented in Figure 7.6, will allow Sara to accomplish an important goal. She will be able to use two reading teachers and a special educator to provide instruction for small groups during the reading block. Not only will this strategy make the best use of these specialists, it will also make the idea of differentiation more palatable to the third-grade teachers.

What Sara envisions is called *within-grade-level regrouping*. Six heterogeneous classrooms will be regrouped for reading into nine skills-based groups, with the three weakest groups served by staff members with specialized training. Figure 7.7 represents the regrouping of one classroom for the small-group reading time; those students will be joined by students from the other homerooms. In the end,

Team A	Team B
Small-group reading (45 minutes)	Whole-group reading (1 hour)
Whole-group reading (1 hour)	Small-group reading (45 minutes)
Writer's workshop (45 minutes)	Writer's workshop (45 minutes)

FIGURE 7.6. Staggered schedule for small-group instruction.

the groups will be smaller than the homeroom groups because three additional teachers are added to the mix. In addition, the differences in the needs of students in each group will be smaller.

Sara will use the results of the PALS testing to rank the students from weakest to strongest. Then, she will form groups of similar skills, with those struggling with very basic decoding making up one (hopefully very small) group served by a special educator using an intensive intervention program for decoding. Two more-skilled groups will be served by the reading specialists. Sara imagines that they will work on high-frequency words, long vowel patterns, and fluency. Then six groups, ranging in fluency and comprehension skills, will work with the six classroom teachers. They will need additional materials for fluency work. Sara prices text sets from several publishers and chooses materials that range from early second-grade level to late fourth grade.

The principal endorses the plan, secures funds for the tests and texts, and hires substitutes to cover the third-grade classes. He has Sara draft a rationale that he can use to describe the changes to parents. He is able to describe the plan as flexible, differentiated, and targeted. He assures parents that the third-grade team will work together to support all of the children's growth. Once he does this, the third-grade

Homeroom A (25 students)								
Special educator	Reading teacher	Reading teacher	Teacher A	Teacher B	Teacher C	Teacher D	Teacher E	Teacher F
1	2	1	0	2	4	5	4	6

FIGURE 7.7. Regrouping for one homeroom.

teachers begin implementation quickly. The special educator and reading specialists administer the PALS assessment.

Building Theory

In order to initiate the plan, Sara must accomplish several things. She must gather the assessment data with the PALS assessment, form instructional groups, and establish reasonable, responsive lesson-plan frames for the third-grade teachers to use, in both whole- and small-group instruction. As she searches for texts to use in a book club, she considers what the major stumbling blocks might be. Teachers on the team are inexperienced with the reasoning behind and the management of differentiated instruction. In addition, they also have no resources, other than the third-grade core program materials, to teach word recognition; she imagines, too, that they might vary in their knowledge of phonics and spelling patterns. She decides that a text about the development of word-level skills across ages and stages of reading development will be the best choice, and she orders a set of *Words Their Way: Word Study for Phonics, Vocabulary, and Spelling Instruction* (Bear et al., 2007).

In order to establish the need for intervention, she starts by planning for the assessments. The spelling inventory, administered in whole group, can be collected very quickly; the oral reading samples, however, will take more time. Sara schedules the specialists to collect the assessment data to minimize the need for training and so that she can use them at the first 3-hour Monday session.

She plans a professional development cycle with the goal of initiating the new plan. In the first hour, she gives a formal presentation, based on content from the first chapter of *Words Their Way*. In that presentation, she lays the groundwork for examining and scoring the PALS spellings.

In the second hour, teachers score the spelling portion of the PALS assessment. That task involves identification of a series of specific spelling features that are either absent, partially understood, or fully understood by children. There is a spelling score that can be used to rank-order the students. The first response of the teachers is that the spellings cannot be scored this way because the children have not studied the words. Sara revisits the concept of assessing whether children have firm underlying word knowledge to bring to bear in new readings.

In the third hour, Sara guides the teachers to examine the connection between the spellings and fluency scores (oral reading accuracy and oral reading rate) for their students. They examine the students' scores, rank ordered in each area, and look for patterns. While the relationship is not one-to-one, strong patterns emerge. There is a large number of students with strong word knowledge and strong fluency, a fairly large number with strong word knowledge but weak fluency, and several groups with weak word knowledge and weak fluency. Comprehension scores vary. Except for the weakest spellers, some of the children have strong comprehension scores despite weaknesses in word knowledge, while others have strong word knowledge and fluency but weak comprehension. The team agrees that comprehension remains a general need for the group. Sara presents them the new pacing guide that she has constructed for the whole-group lessons. In order to save time, she has eliminated the extension activities. To increase engagement, she has also built in many more opportunities for paired and independent readings. These changes are not very drastic.

Because of the principal's mandate, the team must begin their regroupings quickly. They agree on the membership of each of the nine groups, grudgingly. In the end, in order to prevent teachers from keeping their own students and surreptitiously avoiding the grade-level regrouping, teachers agree that they will have a group comprising none of their homeroom students. In this way, too, they will minimize the stigma that could be associated with assignment to the three lowest-achieving groups. They also agree on procedures for moving the children from whole-group instruction in their own homerooms to small-group instruction in another room. For the first week's instruction, small-group time will be used for a read-aloud and a written response. The focus, then, will be on teachers learning to manage the new plan, rather than on implementing the new instruction.

Sara's theory-building day is a long one, as she must repeat this very intense cycle with the other half of the third-grade teachers. At the end of the day, though, she is pleased at least to have shared the rationale and made the grouping decisions. Improving instruction is another matter altogether.

Planning Demonstrations

In spite of the size of the group, Sara decides that classroom-based demonstrations will be the only effective medium for initiating the changes she envisions. Because the children with the greatest needs in the area of word knowledge will be served by the reading specialists and the special educator, she does not plan for them. She focuses her attention on the classroom teachers. Given their group compositions, there are really only two types of lessons to develop. Three of the teachers will be focusing entirely on fluency, vocabulary, and comprehension; three will need to address word recognition, especially for long vowel patterns and for multisyllabic decoding. She plans, then, two repetitive lesson frames, presented in Figure 7.8. She demonstrates the appropriate frame for each teacher; given the schedule, she can demonstrate in two different classrooms each day. As Sara teaches the small group, she gives the teacher a copy of her lesson plan with spaces to make comments or ask questions.

Supported Practice

After each demonstration lesson, Sara makes a visit to the teacher during her writer's workshop. She answers questions about the lesson and gives the teacher

	Frame 1 Word recognition	Frame 2 Fluency, vocabulary, comprehension
15 minutes	New reading with the teacher	Paired rereadings and easy readings
20 minutes	Paired rereadings; word study	New reading with the teacher
10 minutes	Written response	Written response

FIGURE 7.8. Third-grade lesson frames reflecting different emphases.

materials for 1 full week on her own. She expects that initial implementation will still be only surface-level, but simply engaging children in more reading may be an improvement. The very controlled culture of the school suggests that teachers will comply with the new plan, but that they will not engage readily in the kind of deep knowledge building that will be needed for expert implementation.

Since Sara's mandate from the principal is to work intensely with the third-grade team, she continues to plan lessons for the regrouped time. She sets herself the task, over time, of planning lessons for each of the texts in the sets she has purchased. This means that she will construct a large series of word study lessons and that she will read each text and select vocabulary items to introduce before reading and written responses for after reading. At first, she can only make the lessons needed for the next week, but she quickly becomes more adept. She keeps the lessons organized with the texts in order of relative difficulty.

Formative Feedback

While the teachers have accepted the lesson plans and the new structure, they are not ready to accept formative feedback. Sara is surprised by this. She asks for permission to visit so that she can monitor the effectiveness of her own lesson planning. A few of the 12 teachers agree to this, but they suggest that she model the lessons rather than observe them. In the end, she does this, but it is not a substitute for observations of the teachers themselves.

The principal's walkthroughs for the month always focus on a specific goal. He announces that he will be looking for evidence of high-quality, targeted instruction based on data. For the third-grade team, this will mean instruction during the regrouped block. He will be using the lesson plans that Sara has made to guide his walkthroughs. As soon as he makes his announcement, Sara extends the offer of observation and feedback again, this time to provide formative support *before* the principal's evaluative visits. More of the teachers agree; this time Sara is able to begin to build the trusting relationships that will allow her to provide more individual support.

Summary

Sara is more relieved than pleased with her initial attempts with this team; she does not yet feel she has been accepted on the team. What she has accomplished, though, is impressive. She has chosen and used a new assessment; she has revised the instructional schedule; she has provided targeted instruction for all children for 45 minutes each day. In addition, she has begun the relationship building that will allow her to really partner with the third-grade teachers. Because she helped some of them to be better prepared for their evaluations from the principal, she is beginning to win the teachers over to the notion of comprehensive professional support.

Sara knows that she has a long way to go. Teachers engage in book-study activities with her without really engaging in the content. They are unwilling, as yet, to ask substantive questions of her or of one another. The culture of centralized curricular control has made them wary, and Sara will have to empower them to trust one another and her.

SIXTH GRADE

Sara's final coaching opportunity is with a sixth-grade team at Martin Luther King, Jr., Middle School. This middle school is one of five large middle schools in the urban district, none of which has made AYP, and many of the problems are systemic. Dropout rates in the district are high, as is unemployment. On the other hand, considerable resources have been assembled for the schools. School-improvement initiatives are supported by the city's Urban League and funded by federal, state, and private grants.

As in many middle schools, the core organizational structure is interdisciplinary teaming. Teams include one teacher from within each of the content areas: English, math, social studies, and science, as well as one special educator and one bilingual teacher. King has three teams in each grade level (sixth, seventh, and eighth); each team serves approximately 120 students. The goal of the teams is to make the large school smaller for the students and their parents and to promote flexible curriculum planning and collaborative initiatives. One member of each team is appointed team leader by the principal and serves on the school's leadership team, which meets monthly. Each grade level has the services of a counselor and a social worker.

Creating Time for Professional Collaboration

Grant funds are used to provide students with access to art, music, and foreign language instruction during the regular school day and participation in fitness, sports, and clubs in extended time after school 4 days each week. For the academic teams, this organization means that they have 1 hour of planning at the same time each day. This time is used for professional development, for addressing concerns about specific students with the counselor and the social worker, and for IEP meetings for special education students. Individual planning is accomplished in the required contract hours before and after school.

There are 5 full days of professional development reserved for building-level initiatives in the district each year. These days are created by extending the contracts of all teachers by 1 week; they do not replace planning days before the school year begins or teacher conference days at the end the of each grading period. The professional development days are scheduled so that two occur together early in the fall, one is scheduled in the middle of the winter, and two are scheduled together after students leave for summer vacation.

One coach is assigned to each of the district's five middle schools. Each coach has a 12-month contract to allow for extensive summer planning. The coaches meet every other Friday for a full day of professional collaboration. Sara's individual charge, as coach, is to plan 5 days of professional development for the entire teaching staff in her school. Then, she will work extensively with each grade level for one of the three 12-week marking periods. This year, she will work first with the sixth-grade teams, then with the seventh, and finally with the eighth.

Choosing a Focus

Sara's focus for professional support is the collaborative decision of the school's leadership team. The focus each year comes from analysis of data from state testing; it must represent a shared concern that can be addressed school wide, but also by each member of each team. This year, it is vocabulary. Although student comprehension scores have risen slightly each year, vocabulary scores indicate a deep and compelling weakness in student achievement. In addition, a focus on building vocabulary provides opportunities for Sara to work across all content areas and to integrate the work of the bilingual teacher and the special educator into content-area work.

Sara's summer work is to plan the 5 building-level professional development days. These days are structured (and budgeted) to allow for an invited speaker and extensive group processing and application of new ideas. The district has experimented with several different approaches; what seems to work best is to invite the same speaker(s) for all 5 days. Often, with a contract this large, the district is able to find one main consultant who drafts a plan that includes partnerships with other researchers across the school year. The district protocol for these engagements includes a conflict-of-interest agreement. The speaker must be qualified and willing to provide professional education in the area of interest without recommending any commercial products. He or she must be willing to design all 5 days' professional learning in advance, with a specific format that the district has developed. Each day, 2 hours are devoted to large-group lecture, 2 hours to cross-grade- book club work, and 2 hours to same-grade guided discussions. Generally, the speakers have been university researchers with extensive school-level experience.

This year, Sara has been able to contract with a university-based researcher who studies the development of subject-matter concept knowledge. The professor will coteach each day with a middle school content-area teacher with whom he has worked extensively. Given his extensive work around the country, he can bring an English language arts teacher, a science teacher, a social studies teacher, a math teacher, and a special educator. The consultant proposes a structure for the entire year's reading. He will use the text *Building Background Knowledge for Academic Achievement: Research on What Works in Schools* (Marzano, 2004) during the first 2 days' training, combining his formal presentation time with reading guides and jigsaw activities for the cross-grade and same-grade teams. This text will start the teams' work to select content-specific words and concepts to teach from their own individual standards and curriculum. When he returns in the winter and at the end of the year, he will use a section of *Teaching word meanings* (Stahl & Nagy, 2005) to fine-tune their strategies for teaching those terms; the last sessions will use that same text to develop understanding of independent word learning strategies that can be incorporated the next year.

Building Theory

Sara's work with each of her grade-level teams complements this overall plan. She begins by reading the texts the consultant will use. Next, she searches for additional resources that she can use in her work. She locates three: *Semantic Mapping: Classroom Applications* (Heimlich & Pittelman, 1986); *Semantic Feature Analysis: Classroom Applications* (Pittelman, Heimlich, Berglund, & French, 1991); and *Vocabulary Development* (Stahl, 1999). Each is brief (in pamphlet format) and provides very specific examples.

Sara has 12 weeks to work with the three sixth grade teams. She uses the first 4 weeks for intensive theory building, meeting with every team for the full hour of team planning 4 days each week. They are able to review concepts from the consultant's session and complete tasks that stem directly from the Marzano book to select the specific concepts that each team member will teach. By the end of 4 weeks of intense work, each team has committed to a set of concepts to teach in each academic area. That set is consistent with state standards and paced with the curriculum plan. The combination of the consultant's sessions and Sara's follow-up has encouraged teachers to answer two important questions: "why to teach" and "what to teach." Sara can move to "how to teach."

Planning Demonstrations

Sara has selected three specific instructional strategies from which each team member may choose: semantic mapping, semantic feature analysis, and concept of definition mapping. Each is flexible. Each is research-based. Each is described in the resources she has gathered. She takes the words that the teachers have chosen and develops demonstration lessons for each of the three strategies across 1 week. Her schedule appears in Figure 7.9.

She has deliberately neglected the English teacher, knowing that direct instruction techniques will be more likely to resonate in that content area. The teachers respond well to the fact that Sara's demonstrations are specific to the terms they have chosen; in fact, in each case, the teacher in that content area asks if he or she can use the demonstration lesson Sara has prepared. Thursday's discussion is lively. Teachers on the team find particular strategies appealing and tend to dislike at least one, but Sara cannot detect a pattern other than personal preference.

Supported Practice

Sara plans supported practice in two ways. First, she reserves the next week's hourly meetings for teacher planning. The team will meet together, but all will be actually planning to use one or more of the strategies in upcoming lessons. Sara is there to support them, and she brings resources that they can use. She also formats and saves their work, sending it to them electronically to show that they are really accomplishing their tasks.

The next week is reserved for problem solving. Team members are implementing their lessons with their students, and when they come together, they share successes and challenges. Sara responds when she has ideas, and she refers them to the professional texts she has assembled, but by now the teams have also gained collaborative momentum to support one another.

Monday	Tuesday	Wednesday	Thursday
Demonstrate semantic feature analysis with math terms.	Demonstrate semantic mapping with social studies terms.	Demonstrate the concept of definition mapping with science terms.	Prepare a compare–contrast exercise to engage team members in an intensive discussion of the three techniques.

FIGURE 7.9. Sara's schedule of vocabulary demonstration lessons across content areas.

Formative Feedback

For the remainder of the professional support cycle, Sara observes each team member using two of the strategies and provides formative feedback. Because of the schedule, she can always meet with every teacher she observes either that day or the next day. She is surprised by her observations. Some teachers have been planning with facility but struggle with implementation; others seemed not to understand as deeply during planning but are expert in their actual classrooms. In each case, Sara learns more about her teams, and they learn more about her.

Summary

In this case, district structures have made Sara's work much easier. By the end of the 12-week cycle, Sara is confident that she has made targeted progress in the goals that the leadership team identified, and that her work has been entirely consistent with the work of the expert she identified. What she worries about, though, is that they have not really addressed issues in assessment. She has changed teacher practice, at least for the sixth-grade teams, but she has no real evidence that the strategies have changed word knowledge for the students. As she prepares to move to the seventh-grade team, she brings her concerns to the attention of her coaching colleagues in the other schools and begins to brainstorm improvements to her cycle.

REFLECTIONS

Coaching grade-level teams is surely more efficient than coaching individual classrooms. However, it assumes a level of support that some coaches we know do not have. In all cases, grade-level coaching can only be accomplished with a certain level of commitment to shared goals and with time to accomplish it. It will be best accomplished in a series of professional support cycles, with theory, demonstration, practice, and feedback (see Figure 5.2), but these cycles can be accomplished with vastly different strategies. In every case, Sara accomplishes much of what she planned, but she also has significant concerns and doubts. These can help her to plan a new cycle.

   We have neglected a very important component of coaching, both here and in our discussion of classroom coaching in Chapter 6. It is such an important issue that we have decided to save it for our final chapter. Although Sara's personal skills are impressive, we know of no coach who is not plagued with concerns about particularly reluctant teachers. Some teachers simply do not respond well to coaching—even Sara's coaching.

CHAPTER 8

Literacy Coaching in the Middle Grades

How does coaching in the middle grades differ from the primary grades? It is tempting to say that "coaching is coaching," and indeed there are many common responsibilities of literacy coaches regardless of the age of students, but there are also important differences. These differences, described in Figure 8.1, suggest that middle school literacy coaches have a job that differs considerably from their counterparts in the elementary grades. Moreover, the middle-grades coach faces challenges that either do not exist at the elementary level or are considerably easier to tackle in the lower grades. After reviewing the key differences between the two coaching contexts, you might feel that the deck is stacked against the middle-grades coach. Unlike his or her elementary-level counterpart, the middle school coach may well serve more teachers, many of whom tend to resist the idea of being coached in literacy. These teachers in turn typically have less time to serve more students with a broader range of abilities and worsening attitudes toward school and reading! Snow, Ippolito, and Schwartz (2006) comment on this negative contrast:

> We do not mean to suggest that the situation is hopeless, nor that primary-grade coaches lead luxurious, stress-free lives while secondary coaches are unsung heroes toiling away to little effect. Coaches at all levels are more similar than different, working in difficult "in-between" jobs that require interpersonal skills, teaching skills, and a great deal of literacy knowledge. (p. 43)

THE ROLE AND QUALIFICATIONS OF A MIDDLE-GRADES COACH

What should a middle-grades literacy coach be able to do to meet these challenges? While the answer to this question depends in part on the school context, the potential of coaching "in the middle" has led professional organizations to propose new standards that define the role of the literacy coach at the middle level. Because middle schools are organized around content learning, these organizations include

Elementary-grades coaching contexts	Middle-grades coaching contexts
Based on Snow, Ippolito, and Schwartz (2006):	
• Fewer teachers	• Usually more teachers
• Fewer students per teacher	• More students per teacher
• Teachers organized by grade level	• Teachers organized by discipline
• Fewer time constraints due to prolonged literacy block	• Greater time constraints due to short periods
• Literacy seen as central goal of teaching in all classrooms	• Literacy seen as tangential or irrelevant in content areas
• Support for literacy professional development	• Resistance to literacy professional development
• More teacher awareness of literacy needs of students	• Less teacher awareness of literacy needs of students
• Narrower range of student skills and proficiencies	• Broader range of student skills and proficiencies
• Lack of departmentalization makes it harder for students to slip through the cracks	• Departmentalization makes it easier for students to slip through the cracks
• Less sense of isolation from colleagues	• Greater sense of isolation from colleagues
• Extensive research on effective instructional strategies	• Limited research on effective instructional strategies
• Fewer competing social pressures	• More competing social pressures
• Adequate attitudes toward school and reading	• Worsening attitudes toward school and reading
• General recognition by teachers and administrators of need for differentiation and intervention	• Teachers and administrators may lack awareness of the need for differentiation and intervention
Based on Sturtevant (2003):	
• Curriculum is more flexible and reflects broad consensus	• Curriculum is less flexible and reflects traditions
• Some pressure to "cover" content standards permits varied approaches	• Heavy pressure to "cover" content standards leads to reliance on lecture

FIGURE 8.1. Key differences between elementary-grades and middle-grades coaching.

not only the principal literacy organizations (the IRA and the National Council of Teachers of English [NCTE]) but also the professional organizations for teachers of core subjects (the National Council of Teachers of Mathematics [NCTM], the National Science Teachers Association [NSTA], and the National Council for the Social Studies [NCSS]). The standards (IRA, 2006) paint an ambitious picture of coaching in the middle school, one that we summarize in the following paragraphs. The first section of the standards targets the areas of leadership, professional development, and assessment; the second section specifies the demands of the curriculum areas.

Leadership, Professional Development, and Assessment

To begin with, coaches are effective school leaders, and the standards identify examples of leadership skills and strategies that are consistent with our definition of coaching, maintaining their distance from the evaluative role of the principal. Middle-grades coaches are skilled at collaborating with other educators to effect change. For example, they work with the principal to build a literacy team and to supervise a schoolwide needs assessment to identify areas on which to focus. They communicate needs-assessment findings and facilitate problem-focused discussions in order to develop a literacy improvement action plan. They help align curricula to ensure that this plan will work, and they periodically evaluate the school's progress in making the plan a reality.

Once they have a clear plan, middle-grades coaches skillfully manage time and resources. They promote productive relationships with and among staff. Toward this end, they showcase content-area teaching strategies. They listen to the concerns of teachers and are nonjudgmental. They build trust by maintaining confidences, and they make a clear distinction between coaching and evaluating. They respond promptly to requests for help. They keep administrators informed and elicit their support. If their school or district has more than one coach, they collaborate with those other coaches.

Middle-grades coaches lead with a deep understanding of the needs of their learners—both child and adult. Coaches facilitate team meetings regarding adolescent literacy issues. They understand the school culture and appreciate the social stressors that act on middle schoolers. They demonstrate positive expectations for students (including ELLs). They apply concepts of adult learning in their interactions with teachers, and they encourage language specialists to serve as resources to content teachers.

This leadership strand in the standards is a tall order, and it demands constant learning on the part of the coach. Coaches endeavor to stay current and to strengthen their own professional teaching knowledge, skills, and strategies. To do so, they routinely examine best practices and materials. They demonstrate openness to new ideas, and they take part in professional development opportunities.

The second set of skills and strategies targeted in the standards is job-embedded coaching. The standards imply that job-embeddedness sets the work of coaches squarely within their content-area goals, with coaches supporting teachers to understand the needs of their students and to improve the effectiveness of their content-area instruction by infusing it with reading and writing. Middle-grades coaches work with teachers individually, in teams, and/or in departments. They help teachers select diverse, multi-level content-area texts and other materials. They provide assistance in planning instruction around content objectives, and they suggest strategies, identify potential comprehension barriers, and offer suggestions for students who "don't get it" the first time; such suggestions include scaffolding strategies for ELLs.

A large part of this job-embedded coaching targets specific instructional strategies effective for middle-grade learners. Coaches provide content teachers with professional development on effective before–during–after reading strategies and on research-based instructional models (e.g., modeling think-alouds, explaining gradual release of responsibility). They explore with content teachers cross-cultural communication patterns, and they can model effective instructional strategies for comprehension (e.g., reciprocal teaching, directed reading-thinking activities) and for vocabulary (e.g., the use of context to infer word meaning, morphology, cognates, derivatives and variants, and signal words). They also assist content teachers in increasing the amount of content- appropriate writing that students do. They acquaint teachers with useful Internet sources, including links to evidence-based research, which might be stored in a "strategy binder" for easy access.

The final area of job-embedded coaching is observation of instruction. Middle-grades coaches observe teachers and provide feedback, making clear that this process is not evaluative. A major goal of regular observing in content classes is to collect data about which instructional strategies are being used. This knowledge guides coaches in stimulating reflective dialogue before and after observations. Such dialogue helps to clarify objectives, determine assessments, identify successes and challenges, and focus on next steps. It also enables coaches to know when to demonstrate instructional strategies and provide follow-up support.

The final area in the standards is termed *evaluation*, which may have unfortunate connotations for coaching. Deep reading of the standards, though, clarifies the term and still separates the coach from the principal; we choose to stay strictly within the language of the standards to illustrate this point. Middle-grades coaches are skillful evaluators of literacy needs. They lead faculty in the selection and use of a range of assessment tools, and with these tools they develop a comprehensive assessment program. This might include formal measures such as standardized assessments in content subjects to track groups, literacy pre–post tests, ELL tests, content-area reading inventories, and authentic content-area knowledge assessments, and informal assessments such as journals and student surveys of outside literacy practices. Coaches schedule formative and summative assessments, help content-area teachers evaluate writing and assess whether new strategies are effective, and they stay current regarding assessment research and trends.

Choosing and scheduling assessments is not enough. Coaches conduct regular meetings with content-area teachers to examine student work and to monitor progress. They introduce content-area teachers to ways to observe student X, and they hold periodic meetings (monthly, or at the end of each marking period) to examine student work and assessment data. Coaches help teachers analyze trends in achievement. Doing so requires analysis by skill area (e.g., composition, vocabulary, comprehension) and by team or department. It also entails analysis of disaggregated progress data, especially for ELLs. Finally, coaches help teachers use assessment results to determine the best strategies to implement.

We have worked with this area of the standards and conducted a pilot survey of coaches (Blamey, Meyer, & Walpole, 2007). Our first impressions indicate that coaches currently working in the middle grades are more likely to focus attention on the leadership and professional development aspects of their work than on the areas termed *evaluation*. Given the comprehensiveness of the demands on middle-grades coaches, all need to engage in continuous professional development. An excerpt from the survey used in this study, included as Figure 8.2, could help coaches determine their own areas of strength and weakness and target their own professional learning.

Roles and responsibilities

1. As a *collaborator,* check all the activities that you have participated in during the most recent school year.
   - Assisted the principal in developing a literacy team.
   - Collaborated to conduct an initial schoolwide literacy assessment.
   - Facilitated small- and large-group discussions with teachers about students' skills.
   - Communicated the findings of the initial schoolwide literacy assessment to staff and other stakeholders.
   - Developed and implemented a literacy improvement plan.
   - Helped align curriculum to state and district requirements.
   - Conducted ongoing evaluations of literacy improvement action plan (or school improvement plan).
   - Managed time and/or resources in support of literacy instruction.
   - Showcased effective strategies employed by content-area teachers.
   - Listened and responded to the needs of students.
   - Listened and responded to the needs of staff.

(cont.)

FIGURE 8.2. Literacy coach survey. Adapted from Blamey, Meyer, and Walpole (2007).

- Listened and responded to the needs of parents.
- Understood and respected issues of confidentiality.
- Responded promptly to requests for assistance from teachers.
- Facilitated discussions on issues in adolescent literacy.
- Demonstrated positive expectations for students' learning.
- Applied concepts of adult learning and motivation to the design of professional development.
- Encouraged the reading specialist to serve as a resource for content-area teachers.
- Kept administrators informed and involved in literacy efforts.
- Remained current with professional literature on the latest research.
- Examined best practices.
- Examined curriculum materials.
- Met regularly (at least once a month) with other coaches in the school or district.
- Attended professional seminars, conventions, and other training in order to receive instruction on research-based literacy strategies.
- Attended professional seminars, conventions, and other training in order to receive instruction on how to work effectively with adult learners.

2. Out of the above activities, rank the top three activities with which you believe you need the most support in terms of your future professional learning.

3. As a *coach*, check all the activities you have participated in during the most recent school year
   - Worked with teachers individually, providing support on a full range of reading, writing, and communication strategies.
   - Worked with teachers in collaborative teams, providing support on a full range of reading, writing, and communication strategies.
   - Worked with teachers in departments, providing support on a full range of reading, writing, and communication strategies.
   - Assisted teachers in the analysis and selection of content-area texts and instructional materials that meet the diverse needs of students.
   - Assisted teachers in developing instruction designed to improve students' abilities to read and understand content-area text and to spur students' interest in more complex text.
   - Provided content-area teachers with professional development related to metacognitive reading strategies.
   - Facilitated professional development related to instructional strategies for literacy that content-area teachers could adopt and adapt for their classrooms.

(cont.)

FIGURE 8.2. *(cont.)*

- Explored with content-area teachers cross-cultural communication patterns in speaking and writing and their relationship with literacy skills in English.
- Developed a repertoire of reading strategies to share with and model for content-area teachers.
- Helped determine which reading strategies are best to use with the content being taught.
- Assisted teachers with improving writing instruction, student writing, and appropriateness of writing instruction and assignments.
- Facilitated professional development related to strategies to help students analyze and evaluate Internet sources.
- Linked teachers to current evidence-based research to help make research more tangible and applicable.
- Observed and provided feedback to teachers on instruction-related literacy development and content-area knowledge.
- Ensured teacher observations are nonthreatening (used as a tool to spark discussion).
- Regularly conducted observations of content-area classes to collect informal data on strategy implementation and student engagement.
- Before and after observations, engaged in reflective dialogue with teachers.
- Demonstrated instructional strategies.
- Provided ongoing support to teachers as they tried strategies out themselves.

4. Out of the above activities, rank the top three activities with which you believe you need the most support in terms of your future professional learning.

5. As an *evaluator,* check all the activities that you have participated in during the most recent school year.
   - Led faculty in the selection and use of a range of assessment tools in order to make sound decisions about students' literacy needs.
   - Developed a comprehensive assessment program that uses both informal and formal measures of achievement.
   - Set schedules for administering and analyzing both formative and summative assessments.
   - Aided in the design and/or implementation of formative assessments to determine the effectiveness of a strategy.
   - Helped teachers standardize the scoring of writing and other literacy measures.
   - Reviewed current research and trends in assessment methodologies.
   - Conducted regular meetings with content-area teachers to examine student work and to monitor progress.

(cont.)

FIGURE 8.2. *(cont.)*

- Introduced content-area teachers to ways to observe adolescent literacy skills.
- Introduced content-area teachers to ways to observe ELL's language development progress.
- Helped teachers analyze trends in content-area achievement tests.
- Helped teachers use the analysis of various assessment results to determine which strategies will support higher achievement.

6. Out of the above activities, rank the top three activities with which you believe you need the most support in terms of your future professional learning.

7. Check all that you feel competent in
   - Developing and implementing instructional strategies to improve academic literacy in English/ language arts.
   - Developing and implementing instructional strategies to improve academic literacy in mathematics.
   - Developing and implementing instructional strategies to improve academic literacy in science.
   - Developing and implementing instructional strategies to improve academic literacy in social studies.

8. In which area do you feel the need for greatest improvement?
   - Developing and implementing instructional strategies to improve academic literacy in English/ language arts.
   - Developing and implementing instructional strategies to improve academic literacy in mathematics.
   - Developing and implementing instructional strategies to improve academic literacy in science.
   - Developing and implementing instructional strategies to improve academic literacy in social studies.

FIGURE 8.2. *(cont.)*

Academic Coaching

Middle-grades coaches must be able to coach in the four core content subjects: English language arts, mathematics, science, and social studies; both our intuition and the results of the pilot survey referenced above (Blamey et al., 2007) indicate that most middle-grades coaches are more comfortable in their subject-specific knowledge of English language arts. Some of the standards affect all content learning, and others are specific to a given area. Relevant to every area is coaches' knowledge of content and how reading and writing "intersect" with content learning. They must be able to relate their knowledge of adolescent development, literacy development, language, and cultural background to knowledge acquisition in all content-specific subjects.

Within English language arts, coaches must be familiar with the IRA and NCTE standards (*www.ncte.org/about/over/standards*) and those of TESOL (*www.tesol. org/s_tesol/seccss.asp?CID=86&DID=1556*). They must be able to appraise text and textbook demands, beginning with readability and extending to the different demands of narrative and expository text—the task of distinguishing fact from opinion, the need to interpret technical vocabulary, the requirement of thinking critically and inferentially, and the ability to use visual aids and glossaries. Coaches must be able to help language arts teachers select multicultural texts, and they must demonstrate comprehension strategies related to specific text structures included in those texts (e.g., narrative, main idea–detail, comparison–contrast, chronological, cause–effect, argument–evidence, combined structures). Further, they must help teachers identify those structures and match their instruction to them. Finally, coaches must know and model ELL methods and process-writing strategies.

Within mathematics, coaches must be familiar with the NCTM standards (*www.nctm.org/standards/*) as well as state and local standards. They must understand the special demands that math textbooks place on students—a reality often overlooked in the fields of math education and literacy education. These demands involve concept density, how concepts build across a chapter or chapters, multiple-meaning words, equations and symbols, diagrams and graphs, using different representations such as words and diagrams, and the notation conventions used in mathematics.

Once these demands are identified, coaches must be prepared to demonstrate comprehension strategies to enable students to meet them. These entail an appreciation of the principal text structures used in math text, such as providing definitions, presenting main ideas and details, and the structure of word problems. Math comprehension strategies also involve how logic is used (e.g., conjecture, inductive reasoning, deductive arguments, proof by contradiction, understanding and producing proofs), and coaches must be able to model how to teach these strategies. They must also be able to model ways to actively engage students (e.g., jigsaw, think-pair-share, paired problem solving, fishbowl, and round-robin strategies) and varying ways to represent mathematical ideas (e.g., literal, symbolic, graphic).

Within science, coaches must be familiar with the National Science Education Standards (*www.nap.edu/catalog.php?record_id=4962#toc*), the Benchmarks for Science Literacy (*www.sciencenetlinks.com/benchmark_index.htm*), and state and local standards. They must know the specific demands of science textbooks (e.g., their dependence on prior knowledge, the density of ideas, the manner in which concepts build across a chapter or chapters, the need for continual review, the importance of distinguishing empirical facts from opinion, the need to use scientific knowledge to draw inferences and to discern cause–and–effect relationships, the importance of following lab instructions and of interpreting diagrams, abbreviations, and symbols). These demands are formidable, and, left unattended, they might discourage teachers and students from using the text at all. It is the job of the coach to highlight them for teachers and also to provide reasonable strategies for making these important texts more accessible and useful to students.

Coaches must also help science teachers use investigation, comprehension, writing, speaking, and listening strategies to become active learners of science. They must work collaboratively to implement effective strategies that help students understand materials. Strategies include identifying key concepts and the relationships among them, such as hierarchical concept relationships, cause and effect, and prediction, sequencing scientific information, and using scientific knowledge to analyze hypotheses. Coaches also work collaboratively to implement effective strategies that use logic and reasoning, such as testing hypotheses, reasoning inductively, making deductive arguments, establishing boundaries and conditions of knowledge, and using evidence to reject or support propositions. Coaches collaborate to implement effective strategies for writing in science contexts (e.g., questions, lab procedures, observations, reasoning) and for actively engaging students. Coaches also work collaboratively to implement model strategies for representing scientific concepts (e.g., textual, symbolic, graphic modes) and for teaching students to write or orally deliver for a wide range of audiences.

Within social studies, coaches must be familiar with the NCSS standards (*www.ncss.org/standards/*) as well as state and local standards. They must know the specific demands of social studies textbooks (e.g., the ability to distinguish fact from opinion, to distinguish primary from secondary sources, to think critically and inferentially, to acquire technical vocabulary, to navigate a wealth of factual information, including visual aids, glossaries, databases, indexes, and maps). Coaches must also assist social studies teachers by demonstrating how to teach students about a wide range of text structures (e.g., narrative, cause–effect, comparison–contrast, definition, main idea–detail, description, problem–solution, goal–action–outcome, proposition–and–support) typically included in social studies materials. They must follow up by helping teachers match instructional methods to these text structures. Coaches must know and model patterns of argument and rules of evidence used in social studies, and they must likewise know and model strategies for encouraging active student engagement, such as expressing and defending others' viewpoints, visual discovery, experiential exercises, group problem solving, and Internet quests. Finally, they must know and model strategies for interpreting maps, charts, graphs, and other nonlinguistic tools.

Whew! Is there really a single person with all of these abilities? The authors of the standards point out that these are the "ideal," and they acknowledge also that "few coaches will meet all of the standards—at least initially" (IRA, 2006, p. 5). We suspect that the road to achieving the entire list of standards will be an arduous one for nearly any coach; we hope, however, that the prospect of engaging in such a personal learning journey is exciting. Imagine how wonderful it would be to actually accomplish these things! Our suggestion is that a middle-grades literacy coach begin with a list of objectives and use this list to conduct a personal and private self-assessment. Then, rather than attempting to target all of the objectives a coach has self-rated as 1 or 2 ("not sufficiently knowledgeable" or "somewhat knowledgeable ... but need to know more"), a coach should select a manageable number of these to target for personal growth. One objective related to each of the nine criteria would make an excellent action plan for professional growth. The self-assessment can be revisited periodically and perhaps be supported by a personal journal. We have found it especially helpful for coaches to network together along the way with the goal of sharing concerns and successes. Given that our goal for middle-grades coaches is that they work with middle-grades teachers to support middle-grades achievement in all disciplines, we must be aggressive in setting our agenda. The challenges that these coaches face are real, and we describe them next.

Characteristics of Struggling Middle Schoolers

The number of middle-grade students who struggle with the reading and writing they are expected to do is staggering. In 2005, NAEP found that just over 32% of eighth graders enrolled in public schools read below a "basic" level. NAEP documents describe the basic level this way:

> "Eighth-grade students performing at the Basic level should demonstrate a literal understanding of what they read and be able to make some interpretations. When reading text appropriate to eighth grade, they should be able to identify specific aspects of the text that reflect overall meaning, extend the ideas in the text by making simple inferences, recognize and relate interpretations and connections among ideas in the text to personal experience, and draw conclusions based on the text." (NAEP Reading Achievement Levels by Grade: *nces.ed.gov/nationsreportcard/reading/achieveall.asp*)

This finding is not new. A similar statistic dates back to the origin of the NAEP in 1969. The reasons are complex. Some of these students did not achieve adequate fluency in the elementary grades. For many, vocabulary growth has been inadequate to keep pace with the demands of content reading. For a growing number, English must be acquired as a second language, placing them well behind the general language development of native English speakers.

In comparing weaker with stronger adolescent readers, Torgesen (2006) lists several key differences:

- They are almost always less fluent readers—with sight word vocabularies many thousands of words smaller than average readers.
- They usually know the meanings of fewer words.

- They usually have less conceptual knowledge.
- They are almost always less skilled in using strategies to enhance comprehension or repair it when it breaks down.
- And, there are students in every middle and high school who continue to struggle with basic word identification processes.

These differences did not occur overnight. The gap between good and poor readers gradually widens over time. One of the inevitable results of this is that those who struggle develop a limited sense of self-efficacy—that is, their own impression of how well they read is poor (Alvermann, 2001). This negative image leads to worsening attitudes, more behavior problems, and a tendency to drop out of school when they are legally able to do so and to disengage from school while they are there.

PLANNING A THREE-PRONGED ATTACK

Fostering reading proficiency in a middle school involves action on three major fronts: (1) content-literacy instruction, (2) intervention programs, and (3) language arts instruction. A coach should lead teachers to develop a plan that addresses all three. Content-literacy instruction concerns the role of reading and writing in subject matter classes, especially science and social studies. A coach must take stock of whether literacy plays a major role in content learning and whether teachers employ research-based practices; this stock-taking must lead to a reasonable plan to make improvements. Intervention programs provide additional assistance for students who struggle even with these improvements. The history of middle school literacy interventions is a checkered one, however, and many middle schools can benefit from inspecting which programs are in effect and how they operate (e.g., through Title I or special education); the trick is to match student needs and program offerings. Language arts instruction has a firm place in the instructional schedule, but such instruction might not be differentiated and might often involve selections that do not appeal to young adolescents.

In order to make progress in all three dimensions of the school program, the coach must work with teams of teachers. No coach can expect to bring about a significant level of change without working in tandem with other teachers. Working with teams of teachers is an effective way of distributing leadership and ensuring the level of buy-in needed for real change. Establishing a schoolwide literacy team is a good beginning (Sturtevant, 2003). But forming smaller teams is also possible, allowing teachers to focus on issues of immediate import.

Consider the case of Lake Blackshear Middle School, which has two teams at each grade level. Figure 8.3(a) shows the existing interdisciplinary team structure. The sixth-grade teachers of the Bear Team are already used to working together,

(a) Example of an existing interdisciplinary team

Grade	Team	ELA	Math	Science	Social studies
6	Bears	Jones	Smith	Ray	Lee
	Lions	Wilson	Brown	Wallace	Reed
7	Tigers	Wyatt	Ryals	Banks	Cruz
	Jaguars	Green	Combs	Thomas	Winn
8	Pumas	Hall	Jeffers	Good	Darden
	Eagles	Glenn	Hardy	Ordonez	Curry

(b) Example of a same-grade interdisciplinary team

Grade	Team	ELA	Math	Science	Social studies
6	Bears	Jones	Smith	Ray	Lee
	Lions	Wilson	Brown	Wallace	Reed
7	Tigers	Wyatt	Ryals	Banks	Cruz
	Jaguars	Green	Combs	Thomas	Winn
8	Pumas	Hall	Jeffers	Good	Darden
	Eagles	Glenn	Hardy	Ordonez	Curry

(c) Example of a cross-grade subject matter team

Grade	Team	ELA	Math	Science	Social studies
6	Bears	Jones	Smith	Ray	Lee
	Lions	Wilson	Brown	Wallace	Reed
7	Tigers	Wyatt	Ryals	Banks	Cruz
	Jaguars	Green	Combs	Thomas	Winn
8	Pumas	Hall	Jeffers	Good	Darden
	Eagles	Glenn	Hardy	Ordonez	Curry

(d) Example of a same-grade subject matter team

Grade	Team	ELA	Math	Science	Social studies
6	Bears	Jones	Smith	Ray	Lee
	Lions	Wilson	Brown	Wallace	Reed
7	Tigers	Wyatt	Ryals	Banks	Cruz
	Jaguars	Green	Combs	Thomas	Winn
8	Pumas	Hall	Jeffers	Good	Darden
	Eagles	Glenn	Hardy	Ordonez	Curry

FIGURE 8.3. Types of teacher teams.

and when a coach joins their meetings, they are positioned to share concerns and collaborate on solutions (Biancarosa & Snow, 2006). When members of the other sixth-grade team meet with the Bear teachers, as illustrated in Figure 8.3(b), they are in a position to discuss more broadly based concerns affecting their grade level. Such meetings will probably occur less often and may require logistical ingenuity. Figure 8.3(c) shows yet another possible team, all of the teachers in a given subject area across the three grades. Bringing these teachers together affords opportunities to explore curricular matters like vertical articulation, testing requirements, and intervention programs. Finally, Figure 8.3(d) shows a subgroup of a subject-matter team, limited to the same grade level. In this case, Jones and Wilson can meet with the coach to discuss issues specifically related to the sixth-grade language arts program. Their work might later be linked to that of the other two grade levels.

Content-Literacy Instruction

Part of the solution to these challenges lies in adapting content literacy as a middle school focus. In fact, the IRA standards we have described are all designed to ensure this focus. Content literacy is the ability to use reading and writing to acquire content knowledge (McKenna & Robinson, 1990, 2008). This ability requires a certain level of general reading proficiency but also knowledge and skills that are unique to a subject area. This means that content teachers are best positioned to incorporate reading and writing into their instruction. Typically, however, this idea has met with resistance. As Sturtevant (2003) puts it, "many content-area teachers do not believe that they should include literacy-related strategies in their repertoire of teaching practices" (p. 10).

Resistance to Content Literacy

What causes such resistance? Stewart and O'Brien (1989) surveyed content teachers and discovered three principal reasons. First, content teachers may feel inadequate. They frequently have little knowledge of reading and understandably doubt their ability to implement content-literacy approaches. Second, they often think that content-literacy activities infringe on subject-matter time. This objection is especially strong in an era when subject-matter competency tests must be passed. Consider a science teacher who makes the compelling point that more state standards can be achieved by more students if science instruction were largely based on lecture, demonstration, lab work, and discussion—and as little as possible on reading and writing. How might a coach respond to this argument? Finally, content teachers may deny the need for content-area reading and writing techniques. This objection stems from a misunderstanding concerning the nature of these techniques. Stewart and O'Brien's findings, though, represented a field largely without coaching; they need not be an unchangeable reality.

Overcoming resistance is a tall order and one that the middle-grades coach must take seriously. In the mid-twentieth century, educators who advocated for content literacy adopted an unfortunate slogan designed to foster awareness and responsibility among content specialists: "Every teacher a teacher of reading." This idea was misconstrued as a mandate for social studies and science teachers to devote time to basic reading skills instruction (e.g., developing general decoding or fluency skills). Although this was never the intent, the negative impression was hard to counter. We offer some practical suggestions for proactively addressing resistance to content-literacy techniques.

1. Be clear that content-literacy approaches do not entail skills instruction. They are instead a different means of providing content instruction. In most cases, these methods require no additional time compared with traditional lecture-and-demonstration approaches.

2. Stick with a small number of research-based approaches. A core of effective practices has been validated by multiple studies. Findings that confirm the usefulness of an approach in fostering content acquisition can be persuasive. We briefly describe key approaches in the next section.

3. Start with vocabulary techniques. Because every content subject has its own technical terminology, content teachers must ensure that students acquire word meanings and learn how concepts are connected. We might modify the old slogan to reflect this reality: "Every teacher a teacher of vocabulary." No content specialist is likely to refute this idea. A coach who is knowledgeable about effective vocabulary techniques might be able to establish a foundation from which to introduce other literacy activities.

4. Start with the willing. Approach teachers who are willing to investigate one or more content-literacy techniques. Encourage them to contrast these techniques with those that do not rely on reading or writing. Results of these action research studies, when shared during team meetings, can be useful in overcoming the resistance of other teachers.

5. Remember that collecting student data, such as unit test results, can be instrumental in grounding a productive and objective teacher conference. You'll recall that focusing on data is a key component of the subject-specific coaching model (Gabriel, 2005), described in Chapter 1.

6. Convey to content teachers that you are colearners in that you will depend on subject matter specialists' content expertise (Puig & Froelich, 2007). In other words, allow yourself to be coached.

7. And what about the objection that high-stakes tests require rapid content introduction without the use of time-consuming literacy activities? We think it can be powerful to remind teachers that the standards-based tests their students must take require adequate reading ability even if their focus is on content knowledge and skills. We might again revise the old motto: "Every test a test of reading."

Effective Content-Literacy Approaches

It is vital that a coach learn about broadly based, well-researched content-literacy strategies (see these texts for comprehensive samples: Buehl, 2000; McKenna, 2002; McKenna & Robinson, 2008; Tierney & Readence, 2004). They will then be in a position to model such strategies and to help teachers establish notebooks of materials that will help in implementing them (IRA, 2006). But which instructional approaches should a coach recommend? We suggest that content teachers be able to apply a small number of the most effective instructional approaches and that coaches focus on encouraging their use. We categorize them in three ways: (1) before–during–after lesson formats, (2) vocabulary approaches, and (3) comprehension approaches. The vocabulary and comprehension techniques are to be embedded within the before–during–after formats. Figure 8.4 presents our "all-star" list of instructional techniques that have been validated through multiple studies and in various content areas. This is not an exhaustive list but one that we suggest as a "starter set" for teacher study. The pages that follow present brief reproducible handouts that can be shared with teachers as they learn and try these new approaches.

Before–during–after lesson formats
DRA
DR–TA
Listen-read-discuss

Vocabulary approaches
Graphic organizers
Feature analysis
List-group-label
Semantic maps

Comprehension approaches
Reading guides
QARs
ReQuest

FIGURE 8.4. Suggested research-based content-area reading techniques.

DIRECTED READING ACTIVITY

Overview

The *Directed Reading Activity* (DRA) is the oldest before–during–after lesson format. In fact, it set the stage for more recent (though not necessarily better) techniques by providing a framework for how a teacher might prepare students to read a selection, focus their attention as they read, and then reinforce and monitor their comprehension afterward.

Applications

The DRA is an extraordinarily flexible lesson format. It can be used with fiction or nonfiction, and the time devoted to each step can be adjusted as appropriate.

Steps

The steps of a DRA are simple to follow and allow ample room for creative planning. Remember that these steps are only a shell; the lesson must be adapted in detail to a particular selection.

- Step 1. Develop readiness for the reading selection. Try to anticipate deficiencies in prior knowledge of the content and then shore them up by introducing vocabulary and providing factual information that the author assumes the reader knows. For nonfiction selections, especially those with subheadings and other visual organizers, conduct a walkthrough, pointing out how the selection is organized, discussing visual aids, etc.
- Step 2. Create a focus for reading. There are many ways to do this, such as asking students to answer specific questions, complete a chart, reach a conclusion, draw a picture, complete a reading guide, or test a hypothesis. Combinations of these approaches are often possible.
- Step 3. Allow students to read the selection. This should be an active process since students now have specific purposes on which to focus while they read.
- Step 4. Lead a discussion of the reading selection. The framework of this discussion will be the focus established in Step 2, but additional questions are a natural extension.
- Step 5. Provide extension or reinforcement activities. These can take many forms and could focus on word recognition, comprehension, or personal responses to content.

Comments

Some teachers believe that the DRA is too teacher centered; however, others view this characteristic as a plus. To be sure, the teacher has a clear idea of what students should gain from the selection, but the flexibility of the DRA allows for more student-centered lessons. For example, the teacher might focus students on a creative application of what they read.

DIRECTED READING–THINKING ACTIVITY

Overview

The *Directed Reading–Thinking Activity* (DR–TA) is a teaching strategy used to introduce a reading selection and to encourage students to form predictions as a means of making their reading more purposeful. It was proposed by Stauffer (1980) as an alternative to the DRA, one that encourages students to form and test hypotheses as they read. Doing so, he claimed, would make them more purposeful readers.

Applications

Because the DR–TA is based on prediction, it might be natural to assume that it is only appropriate for narrative selections, which are organized around a sequence of events. Stauffer had a much broader view, however. It is also possible, he argued, to make predictions about how the *facts* will turn out. This means that the DR–TA is useful with virtually any prose selection, though we do think it is easier to apply to narrative text. Remember that sequences of events are not limited to fiction. They also include science experiments ("What will happen if we mix these substances?"), natural processes ("What happens to water after it evaporates?"), and historical accounts ("Who do you think won this battle?").

Steps

The steps of a DR–TA are simple to plan. The first and last steps are similar to those of the DRA.

- Step 1. Develop readiness for the reading selection. As in the DRA, try to anticipate deficiencies in students' prior knowledge of the content and then shore them up by introducing vocabulary and providing factual information that the author assumes the students know. Be careful, however, not to reveal too much since the students must make predictions.
- Step 2. Ask the students to read to a key point and then stop. They are then to form predictions about how the narrative will end or how the facts will unfold. These predictions may be generated individually or by collaborative groups.
- Step 3. Permit the students to read the remainder of the selection for the purpose of testing their predictions.
- Step 4. Lead a discussion, focusing on the predictions students have made. Were they right or wrong? Why?
- Step 5. Provide extension or reinforcement activities. These can take many forms and could focus on word recognition, comprehension, or personal responses to content.

Comments

The DR–TA lacks some of the flexibility of the DRA. It is, we argue, easier to use with fiction or narrative nonfiction. On the other hand, the DR–TA is less teacher centered than the

(cont.)

DRA, and research evidence of its effectiveness is convincing. In fact, most of the head-to-head comparisons of the two techniques favor the DR–TA (McKenna & Robinson, 2008). In addition, a recent comparison of the DR–TA with "Know, want to know, learn" (K-W-L) (Stahl, 2004) revealed a significant advantage for the DR–TA. (Stahl and others have argued that K-W-L has very little empirical evidence of its effectiveness, which is why we chose not include it among these research-based techniques.)

LISTEN-READ-DISCUSS

Overview

Listen-read-discuss (Manzo & Casale, 1985) is a before–during–after instructional format especially designed for struggling readers. However, it is markedly different from the DRA or the DR–TA because of its first step. During the "listen" phase of the lesson, the teacher completely presents the content or story, almost as though there was to be no reading at all on the part of the students. Manzo and Casale have referred to this idea as "frontloading." Doing so boosts prior knowledge to a very high level, making the reading itself much easier.

Applications

Listen-read-discuss is suitable for any reading selection. It is most useful for students with limited background and prior knowledge. This means that it is particularly well suited to selections that present unfamiliar ideas or that relate experiences that students will not have sufficient background to interpret.

Steps

The following steps constitute the entire approach:

- Step 1. Present the content of the reading selection thoroughly. Use lecture, discussion, demonstration, and whatever other techniques promise to be effective.
- Step 2. Have students read the selection. Provide them with a specific focus, just as you would in a DRA. Asking them to make predictions, however, as you would in a DR–TA, is not an option since the students will know the content of the selection thoroughly when they begin to read it.
- Step 3. Lead a discussion based on the focusing activity you provided.

Comments

Listen-read-discuss may not sound like the most exciting instructional approach ever devised. It isn't. But its background-building capacity more than makes up for this deficit. Students report learning much more through listen-read-discuss than through alternative approaches, and test results support their claims. Reading is almost like a review since new concepts and ideas have already been thoroughly introduced. Decoding is also facilitated since new terms are pronounced and written on the board during the "listen" phase.

GRAPHIC ORGANIZERS

Overview

A *graphic organizer* is a diagram showing how key concepts are related. Ready-made examples abound in textbooks, though they can also be constructed by teachers and students. Some types of graphic organizers include time lines, tree diagrams, Venn diagrams, labeled pictures, graphs, and semantic maps (webs). Each of these types is used to introduce technical terms in clusters, showing students how the terms are related to one another. This approach does not mean that the definitions do not need to be taught. Rather, graphic organizers provide a means of going beyond the definitions, allowing students to grasp interrelationships among concepts.

Applications

Graphic organizers are useful whenever a group of terms is closely related. For this reason, they are not useful in teaching a list of unrelated words, as might be required in some general vocabulary lessons. They have a potential advantage for coaches trying to reach out to reluctant content-area teachers: They need not always be tied to reading selections. That is, they are always an excellent means of teaching content vocabulary.

Steps

Several simple steps should help you construct a good graphic organizer.

- Step 1. Make a list of key terms.
- Step 2. Identify clusters of closely related terms within the list.
- Step 3. Determine how the words in each cluster are related.
- Step 4. Arrange the words in each cluster into a diagram.

(Note that several graphic organizers may come from your original list.) Many reading selections include graphic organizers so that it is not necessary to construct one. Either way, the key is to build them into the before–during–after lesson you have selected. The following suggestions can make instruction with graphic organizers more effective:

- Decide when to introduce the organizer. In most cases it will work best toward the end of a chapter or unit, as a way of pulling content together. When students have adequate background knowledge, however, an organizer might be used effectively prior to assigned reading.
- Make sure you introduce an organizer with plenty of discussion and explanation. Do not assume that it will "teach itself."
- If you are constructing an organizer, look for ways of including some terms that are already familiar to students. Doing so will help them associate new learning with previous content.
- Encourage students to construct their own organizers. This will become feasible after you have exposed students to a variety of organizers over time. Begin by asking

(cont.)

students to complete partially constructed organizers, and move to situations in which students develop their own, given only a list of terms.

- Couple organizers with reading guides. Once students have caught on to how graphic organizers work, they can be expected to complete or construct them during guided reading of nonfiction. These two proven strategies—graphic organizers and reading guides—work well in combination!

Comments

There are many advantages to graphic organizers: (1) they help students see abstract content, (2) there is little to read, (3) they are easy to construct and discuss, (4) they allow technical terms to be taught in related clusters, and (5) they provide a way for students to organize content learning for better recall and understanding (McKenna & Robinson, 2008). For practical ideas about using graphic organizers, see Bromley, Irwin-De Vitis, and Modlo (1995).

FEATURE ANALYSIS

Overview

Feature analysis, introduced by Johnson and Pearson (1984), is a vocabulary strategy that is useful whenever a cluster of new terms represents members of the same category. Also called *semantic feature analysis*, this technique makes use of a simple chart. In the upper left-hand corner of the chart, the name of the category is written. The category members are written in the first column. Across the top of the chart, the column headings are various features that each concept might or might not possess. The chart is completed by placing a plus sign (+) in a particular position if the concept in that row has the feature for that column. If not, a minus sign (–) is used. Some teachers find the letter *s* helpful if a concept *sometimes* has that feature. The feature analysis chart permits comparisons of any pair of concepts by noting features shared, features possessed by only one of the concepts, and features possessed by neither concept. The chart also facilitates the analysis of each feature by considering which concepts possess it and which do not.

Applications

Feature analysis is useful whenever terms are members of the same category. This technique is more limited than graphic organizers, which merely require that the terms be related in some way. Feature analysis is typically used in content subjects, but it can be applied to literature, as well. For example, a chart could include the characters in a novel, books by the same author, genres, poetic devices, etc.

Steps

There is no single method of using feature analysis. It can be embedded within a before–during–after lesson format, or, like graphic organizers, it can be used as a vocabulary approach that is not connected with a specific reading selection. The following steps represent our view of best practice:

- Step 1. Place an empty chart on the board or project it with a transparency. In the upper left-hand corner, place the name of the category. Tell students they will be helping you fill in the chart with some of the words they have been studying.
- Step 2. Ask the students to suggest words that are examples of the word you have written in the upper left-hand box. Add additional examples the students do not mention but that you know need to be included in the chart.
- Step 3. Write down key features at the head of each of the remaining columns. You are the best judge of these.
- Step 4. Together with the students, complete the chart row by row, deciding together whether each category member possesses each of the key features. Discuss the terms as you go.
- Step 5. Make comparisons of category members based on the completed chart. Focus on which features they have in common and where they differ.

(cont.)

Figure 8.5 presents a feature analysis chart that reflects these steps. Once the chart has been completed, the teacher might use it to point out interesting facts. For example, there is no large-scale, renewable energy source that is free of air pollution.

Comments

Not only are feature analysis charts easy to build, but students find them long on thinking and short on tedium. An excellent way to use feature analysis charts is to establish a focus for reading. Whenever the content is appropriate, the students read a selection with the goal of completing the chart. Of course, the chart would need to be adequately introduced and at least one row filled in by the teacher as an example. This makes an excellent inferential reading activity, one that requires no tedious copying—just pluses and minuses. A limitation of feature analysis charts is evident in this example. Whenever two or more concepts have identical patterns of pluses and minuses, there is not enough information to tell them apart. In this case, solar, geothermal, and hydroelectric power appear to share a common set of features. One way to differentiate them, if a teacher felt it useful to do so, would be to add columns (new features) that capture differences. For a more detailed discussion of feature analysis, see Pittelman et al. (1991).

Energy sources	Air pollution	Large scale	Renewable
Nuclear	–	+	–
Coal	+	+	–
Hydroelectric	–	–	+
Solar	–	–	+
Geothermal	–	–	+

FIGURE 8.5. Example of a feature analysis chart.

LIST-GROUP-LABEL

Overview

Taba's (1967) simple three-part vocabulary strategy is based on what Stahl and Nagy (2005) identify as the most important cognitive skill in learning vocabulary: categorizing. List-group-label encourages students to actively organize what they have learned, making it easier to understand and remember.

Applications

List-group-label is effective at the end of a content unit in nearly any subject area. It works best when a fairly sizable number of new content vocabulary words have been introduced.

Steps

Although many variations are possible, the following steps are typical:

- Step 1. Begin by reminding the class of the major topic they have been studying. Ask students to brainstorm all of the words they have learned in connection with the topic. Write these words on the board or on a transparency until 25 to 30 have been recorded.
- Step 2. Have the students work together to rearrange the words into categories. Tell them not to worry about the exact nature of their groupings at this point—they are simply to group words that are connected in some meaningful way. Again, you are the scribe. Write these groups on the board or transparency. Erase or cross through the words in your original list as you rewrite them in groups.
- Step 3. Ask the students to suggest a label for each group. Some words may be left without a clear category membership, but vocabulary is messy and this is a natural result! Encourage students to generate labels for these leftover terms if they can.

Comments

List-group-label has several key strengths. It focuses on the interrelationships that exist among key terms; it stimulates active engagement and is well suited to collaborative, small-group variations; and it provides an easy way of linking new with past content. Figure 8.6 illustrates how the three steps of list-group-label might play out in the case of a simple example: mammals.

(cont.)

List	Group	Label
Students brainstorm terms related to the topic. Teacher records.	Students collaboratively group terms into meaningful categories. Teacher rewrites.	Students agree on category labels. Teachers writes label at the top of each group.
have hair rabbit bear people produce milk born, not hatched tiger monkey can live on land or in water whale	have hair milk born, not hatched can live on land or in water rabbit bear people tiger monkey whale	*Characteristics* have hair milk born, not hatched *Habitat* can live on land or in water *Types of mammals* rabbit bear people tiger monkey whale

FIGURE 8.6. Example of list-group-label.

SEMANTIC MAPS

Overview

Heimlich and Pittelman (1986) transformed list-group-label from a chart to a diagram format. The result is called a *semantic map* (or *web*), which places a key concept at the center and related concepts at the ends of radiating spokes. It is an easy diagram to make, and students can be engaged in suggesting words to be included in the map. Like list-group-label, semantic maps derive their instructional power by stressing the connections among word meanings. They help students organize what they know, making it more meaningful and more memorable.

Applications

Semantic mapping can be used with any nonfiction selection that introduces information about a specific topic. Like list-group-label, semantic maps work best when students are challenged by an abundance of new terms.

Steps

It can be applied either before or after reading—or both! If used beforehand, the technique activates (and helps the teacher assess) students' prior knowledge of the topic. If used afterward, it helps students reorganize the new words they have learned. Heimlich and Pittelman's description of the approach (1986) can be summarized in these steps:

- Step 1. Present a central concept and have students brainstorm words that are related to that concept. List these on the board.
- Step 2. Add words that you know to be important but that students do not mention.
- Step 3. Quickly supply working definitions of these terms.
- Step 4. Together with the children, develop the semantic map, starting with the central concept. Make public decisions about which words belong on which spokes.
- Step 5. Make sure that a key concept anchors the end of each spoke. Draw a box or oval around it.
- Step 6. If semantic mapping is used prior to reading, leave a spoke or two blank so that additional words can be added later.

Figure 8.7 provides an example of a semantic map based on the topic, mammals. You may find it useful to contrast it with Figure 8.6, which illustrates the same topic in a list-group-label lesson.

Comments

Stahl's (1999) summary of research into the effectiveness of semantic mapping led to the following conclusions: (1) semantic mapping can improve students' word knowledge, and (2) semantic mapping can improve students' comprehension of passages containing the words included in the map. These findings are not surprising given the engagement that this approach assures, its use of graphic organizers, and the reliance on categorizing as a key cognitive skill.

(cont.)

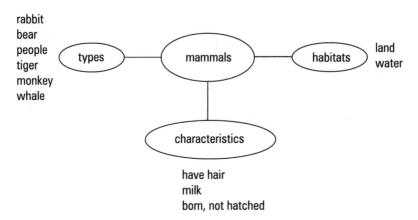

FIGURE 8.7. Example of a semantic map.

READING GUIDES

Overview

A *reading guide* (also called a *study guide*) is a list of questions and other tasks to which a student must respond *while reading*. The purpose is to focus a student's attention on key ideas during reading and to provide a tool for later review and discussion. Guides differ from postreading questions in that comprehension is fostered as the student reads, not afterward.

Applications

Reading guides are truly universal. Because they are tailored to fit, they can be used with any reading selection in any genre.

Steps

Constructing Guides

There is no formula for constructing a reading guide, no right or wrong way. Each guide is unique in that a teacher must first decide what it is important for the students to grasp and then construct tasks for helping them do so. These tasks might include: (1) questions to be answered, (2) charts to be completed, (3) diagrams to be constructed, (4) pictures to be drawn, or (5) responses to be written. There is really no limit to the ways such tasks can be created and interwoven, and there is certainly an element of creativity in constructing a good reading guide. The following steps might be helpful:

- Step 1. Read the selection carefully.
- Step 2. Decide which ideas and facts are important to know.
- Step 3. Create tasks that help students attain this knowledge.
- Step 4. Include a variety of tasks, not just questions.
- Step 5. Aim for simple wordings.
- Step 6. Leave plenty of space for children to write.
- Step 7. Arrange the tasks sequentially.
- Step 8. Include page numbers and/or subheads.
- Step 9. Where appropriate, include comprehension aids.

Using Guides

- Step 1. Model their use. Students must be instructed in what is expected of them as they complete a guide.
- Step 2. Monitor closely. Troubleshoot as students read and complete the guides in class.
- Step 3. Tie the guides to discussion. Ask students to place their completed guides on their desks prior to a discussion. Then, use the guides to anchor that discussion.

(cont.)

- Step 4. Encourage students to use the guides to review. Since guides provide notes about what the students have read, they can be used as a valuable aid in reviewing for tests or in writing about the selection.
- Step 5. Revise if necessary. Be alert to weaknesses in the guides you create. Make changes electronically so that an improved guide is ready the next time you teach the same selection.
- Step 6. Give guides time to work. The full impact of reading guides may not become evident until they have been used routinely for a few months. Once their use has become a part of in-class reading, students will complete them knowledgeably and may even complain when they are not provided!

Comments

Reading guides have numerous advantages, as teachers who use them regularly attest:

- They improve comprehension by focusing students' attention on important aspects of content.
- They make reading an active rather than passive process.
- They cause students to translate material into their own words, phrases, and sentences.
- They are a means of integrating reading and writing.
- They produce a useful tool for review.
- They provide a blueprint for postreading discussion and give students a valuable discussion aid.
- They model strategic, purposeful reading.
- They model effective notetaking.

Of course, reading guides have disadvantages, as well. They take time to create, they require paper, and they have to be copied. These drawbacks can be daunting, but we believe that using guides on a trial basis will soon persuade teachers that the advantages are worth it.

QUESTION–ANSWER RELATIONSHIPS

Overview

In *question–answer relationships* (QARs), Raphael (1984, 1986; Raphael, Highfield, & Au, 2006) suggests that students should be "let in" on the fact that different types of questions exist and that each type requires a different reading strategy. The four types of QARs are named with student-friendly designations in Figure 8.8. These types roughly correspond to the literal, inferential, and critical levels of comprehension. QARs can help students recognize that comprehension is not limited to the literal level, at which answers are routinely regurgitated.

Applications

QARs can be used with any reading selection, and they can be used before students read to focus their thinking or afterward to stimulate higher-order thinking during a discussion.

Steps

Students must be introduced to QARs systematically. A three-stage process is often used.

- Step 1. Define and model the four types of questions. Select short passages from reading selections and created clear-cut examples of each question type. Define the four types of QARs in simple terms and introduce examples to help clarify differences. In later selections interject examples at certain points, again pointing out how they conform to the definition of one of the four types.
- Step 2. Ask students to classify questions. In subsequent reading selections, pose questions of each type and ask students to classify them. They will need to locate the answer, or the basis of the answer, before they can do so, of course. Provide numerous opportunities for students to classify questions of each type. Give feedback and encourage discussion, even if classifying some questions seems a bit murky.
- Step 3. Give students opportunities to generate questions. Once students fully grasp the distinctions among the four types of questions, ask them to create their own examples, either individually or collaboratively.

Comments

Remember that the four types of QARs are meant as a guide to generating questions that rely on key comprehension processes. They are not meant to be a foolproof way of classifying questions. You will encounter murky examples that don't seem to fit into any of the four categories. Our advice is not to worry about this. Disputing question types can be healthy, but don't press the point too far.

(cont.)

In-the-book QARs	In-my-head QARs
Right there	*Author and you*
These are literal-level questions, and the answers can be found in the material. Indeed, they are "right there."	The reader must combine information from the material with prior knowledge.
Think and search	*On my own*
These are inferential questions that require students to make logical connections among the facts presented in the material.	These are questions that rely almost entirely on students' prior knowledge and experience. This category includes critical-level questions.

FIGURE 8.8. Four types of Question–Answer Relationships.

RECIPROCAL QUESTIONING

Overview

Manzo's (1969) technique of *reciprocal questioning* (ReQuest) has now been effectively used for more that three decades. It involves students actively asking questions of the teacher and/or one another during a discussion. The basic idea is that in order to ask good questions a reader must understand the content reasonably well. If a reader reads with the aim of asking questions, then comprehension is apt to be good. Not surprisingly, many variations of the technique have sprung up.

Applications

ReQuest is useful with any reading selection. It can used before reading as a means of focusing thinking, or it can be used after reading as part of a discussion.

Steps

There are no set steps in applying ReQuest. Instead, we describe its implementation in terms of a few of the variations that are possible.

- Variation 1. The teacher introduces the reading selection and asks the students to begin reading silently. At a predesignated point, the students stop reading, and one student is called on to ask questions of the teacher. The teacher must answer as many questions as the student can think to ask. When the student can think of no more questions, the teacher asks the student additional questions. For the next segment of the reading selection, another student is called on.
- Variation 2. After the selection has been completed, the teacher calls on a student at random. The student asks the teacher one question, and then the teacher asks the student a question. The teacher then calls on another student, and so forth.
- Variation 3. The teacher begins the postreading discussion by calling on a student. The student asks a question but, instead of answering it, the teacher deflects it to another student, who must try to answer. This second student may then ask a question, which the teacher deflects to a third student, and so forth. The teacher may use his or her knowledge of students' abilities to decide which questions to deflect to which students.

Comments

In the years following its introduction, research has continually validated ReQuest, and the National Reading Panel (NRP) (NICHHD, 2000) mentioned it specifically as an effective approach. It led to the creation of *reciprocal teaching* (RT), which combines question generation with other comprehension strategies as students work collaboratively.

Intervention Programs

Struggling readers often receive instruction from reading specialists and special educators on a pull-out basis. The intervention these teachers provide varies considerably in effectiveness, and certainly the odds of a successful outcome are reduced by the negative attitudes and self-efficacy of struggling students and by the wide gap between where they are functioning and the level required to succeed in middle-grades classrooms. However, these long odds do not excuse a lack of urgency among intervention providers. Federal mandates for RTI models to reduce the number of students needing special education services will likely begin to shed light on the efficacy of existing programs.

What is the role of a literacy coach with respect to this dimension of the middle-grades literacy program? We believe that a coach can be instrumental in helping these specialists bring about positive effects. First, they should ensure that the commercial programs in use are sound and likely to be engaging and effective. For many years, few materials were available for this purpose, but the problem nowadays is to choose among many possibilities. A good first step is to consult reviews, which not only size up products objectively but also make coaches aware of what's available. An excellent source is a book by Deshler, Palinscar, Biancarosa, and Nair (2007), in which over 40 programs are described and critiqued. Many of these programs are indeed commercial products (e.g., Read 180, Accelerated Reader, Corrective Reading), but many are noncommercial and require little or no financial investment (e.g., Project CRISS, QARs, concept-oriented reading instruction).

A related question is whether specialists should base their instruction on the selections students are expected to read in content classes. For example, a reading specialist might use a textbook chapter as the basis for developing comprehension strategies. This link between intervention instruction and classroom demands has the advantage of motivating reluctant students through their desire to pass content subjects (Allington, Boxer, & Broikou, 1987). Another advantage is that successful approaches, such as QARs and concept-oriented reading instruction, can be implemented by the specialist using class materials. A potential (and perhaps surprising) disadvantage is the negative reaction of content-area teachers, some of whom believe that the use of class materials affords weaker students an unfair advantage over their abler classmates, who do not receive extra assistance. It is a hard to fathom this objection, but we have found it to be widespread. The wise coach should anticipate it and attempt to win over teachers who harbor such a concern.

Language Arts Instruction

How can coaches help language arts teachers meet the challenges of their struggling students? A good way to begin is by observing. It is important to know whether teachers are providing students with choices in what they read, at least part of the time, and whether they take the steps necessary to facilitate comprehension. Like their peers in science and social studies, language arts teacher should likewise be employing before–during–after formats and implementing effective strategies for vocabulary and comprehension. Because language arts teachers are presumably more in tune with reading strategies than are teachers of other subjects, it is tempting to conclude that they already implement them, but the reality is that many do not, especially when it comes to facilitating the reading of weaker students.

It is also important to find out how much reading students actually do. Our observations suggest that the amount is alarmingly limited; we have witnessed many hours filled with work on grammar, discussion, literary criticism, and writing, but little actual reading. One of the goals of coaching is therefore likely to be a better balance between reading and other activities in language arts classrooms; we anticipate that the language arts classroom is the best place to ensure that middle-grade readers read both widely and deeply, in shared grade-level curriculum selections, in texts chosen for their reading level, and in self-selected texts chosen to foster motivation.

APPROACHES TO LITERACY COACHING IN THE MIDDLE GRADES

Many approaches to middle-grades coaching have begun to emerge. They vary in terms of the coach's role and expectations, and they are undoubtedly better suited to some contexts than others. We describe five approaches in this section but caution that this not an exhaustive list. Moreover, the best approach for a particular setting may well be a hybrid formed by combining elements of these. You might refer back to Chapter 1, where we discussed choices in choosing or developing a coaching model, as you think specifically about the middle grades. You will see that attempts to design and implement middle-grades coaching are in their infancy in the professional literature; rather than wait for research, most schools and districts simply have to forge their own way.

Subject-Matter Specialist Approach

In this approach, developed in Long Beach, California, by Scott Joftus (2002), each coach specializes in a specific subject. One coach might work only with social studies teachers, attempting to foster content-literacy methods. Given the reality of teacher resistance, the focus is on mentoring new teachers. An additional coach targets classroom management. For more information, visit *www.all4ed.org/files/ archive/publications/EveryChildAGraduate/every.pdf.*

Coaching Continuum Approach

Puig and Froelich (2007) have developed a model in which coaches move along a growth continuum toward full responsibility for all aspects of coaching. This approach is a bit slow going, but it acknowledges the fact that coaches, too, are adult learners who cannot be thrust into a complex and demanding context without being given time to develop their skills. The learning curve is simply too steep. During the first year, therefore, coaches implement effective practice in their own classrooms, which serve as laboratories. They also lead study groups, during which selections from professional literature are read and shared along with the coach's experiences with implementation. During the second year, coaches work with language arts teachers. Only during the third year does the coach interact with content teachers. The prevailing idea is to put off approaching the teachers most likely to resist until the coach is well accustomed to the school and its challenges.

Striving Readers Approach

Beginning in 2004, a federal program has employed coaching in Title I-eligible middle and high schools. Because of federal funding, a major component of this approach is evaluation of effectiveness in an attempt to identify workable models. The *Striving Readers program* does not embrace a single model of coaching, but, in most projects, coaches work with intervention teachers. The structure is similar to Reading First in that the coach supervises and analyzes assessments and provides a variety of professional development, including both in- and out-of-class activities. For more information, visit *www.ed.gov/programs/strivingreaders/index.html*.

Stafford Approach

All eight middle schools in Stafford County, Virginia, have taken part in an innovative coaching initiative led by Nancy Guth. The *Stafford Approach* has a strong affective component, acknowledging the fact that struggling readers are frequently disaffected. Accordingly, students are given choices of what to read whenever possible, and the amount of reading they do is greatly increased. Coaches team teach, model strategies, provide mentoring, and meet with interdisciplinary teams. Interacting with the coach is voluntary, but a ripple effect tends to convince resistant teachers that the coach is nonthreatening and helpful. Research has revealed significant improvements in student achievement for teachers who choose to team with the coach. For more information, visit *www.pen.k12.va.us/Div/Stafford/middle.html*.

Boston Approach

This approach to middle-grades coaching is part of the Boston Plan for Excellence. Although coaching is implemented somewhat differently across sites, key characteristics are shared. Coaches stress "workshop approaches" and take part in inquiry groups of teacher teams. They meet regularly with principals and attempt to forge a supportive bond. Coaches model instruction at laboratory sites and follow up within classrooms only on request. The prevailing philosophy is that positive change cannot reasonably be expected if teacher participation is compulsory. For more information, visit *www.bpe.org/*.

Building an Approach That's Right for Your School

These approaches to middle-grades literacy coaching were developed to meet the needs of specific contexts. They may not represent the right fit for your school. They do provide guidance concerning what has worked elsewhere, but the lessons they teach must be tailored to a new setting. The following suggestions may assist you in planning or refining a middle school coaching approach that's right for your situation:

1. Begin by completing a self-assessment of your coaching ability. Be honest about your shortcomings as a coach and be realistic in choosing a limited number of targets for your own professional growth. Look for peer support from other coaches in other schools. They will have much to offer (and gain).

2. Construct an achievement profile. Gather available data from standardized assessments and disaggregate the results by grade and subject. Track cohorts from grade to grade, and try to determine trouble spots. Include other relevant data if you have access to them. Try to analyze data based on participation in interventions to gauge the impact they are having. If these data are unavailable, plan for assessments aimed at establishing the effectiveness of interventions (e.g., pre–post individually administered batteries). We do not recommend creating achievement histories for individual teachers, at least initially, because of measurement challenges.

3. Find some extended quality time to meet with the principal. Discuss the achievement profile, and outline your coaching responsibilities. Stress the importance of operating as a team, of distancing yourself from teacher evaluations, and of respecting teacher confidences. If you have room to bargain, try to exclude yourself from teaching assignments.

4. Take stock of the intervention materials in use. Consult program reviews, and speak with the teachers who use them.

5. Start building new teams and working with existing ones. Make your role clear, and establish constructive dialogue, using the profiles you created as a focus. At these meetings, ask to observe.

6. Look for ways of creating an interest in reading among students, as in the Stafford Approach. You might be able to enlist the library media specialist's assistance in this campaign.

7. Conduct observations without feedback simply to learn what's going on. In content classrooms, observe to determine the uses of reading and writing and the implementation of effective content-literacy strategies. The results of these observations will help you plan study groups and give you perspective on individual teachers.

8. Select a few teachers who are open to working with you. These may be proficient veterans who do not feel threatened, or they may be new teachers, as in the Subject-Matter Specialist Approach. Include department chairs, if possible, because they are in a position to influence other teachers. You may want to limit yourself to a single content subject if you feel overwhelmed, as in the Coaching Continuum Approach. Prior to group meetings, look for ways of sharing classroom-based activities like modeling, observing, and conferencing. You might persuade a teacher to share something positive, for example.

9. Toward year's end, gather the data you need to gauge the school's progress. Summarize your findings at team meetings and for the principal.

10. Acquire data documenting your own effectiveness. These might include an end-of-year retrospective survey like the one in Figure 8.9, and they might include pre–post achievement means for teachers you've coached (the Stafford Approach employs this method). Because the link between coaching and student growth is not yet well researched, gathering your evidence will strengthen your case and make you aware of areas in which you can improve.

CONCLUSION

A middle-grades literacy coach faces an array of challenges. Foremost among these are resistant teachers, a wide range of student achievement, negative attitudes, and limited time. Moreover, while several promising approaches to coaching have been piloted, no definitive evidence has emerged concerning which is likely to be most effective. Regardless of the approach chosen, the best coaches must work with teacher teams. In team settings, the coach's responsibilities can be clearly communicated to teachers. Ideally, the coach's role will be limited to that of professional developer, and will not involve providing instruction directly to struggling students (Snow et al., 2006). Given the demanding standards of middle-grades coaching, even the best coach will need to add proficiencies over time. Conducting a candid self-assessment is a good first step toward taking stock and setting personal goals. The next step is to read widely, and the sources listed in Figure 8.10 are an excellent place to begin.

Subject:	Agree	Tend to agree	Tend to disagree	Disagree	NA
The coach respected confidences. *Comment:*					
The coach demonstrated adequate knowledge of my subject. *Comment:*					
The coach communicated with me objectively and professionally. *Comment:*					
The coach helped me improve my students' learning. *Comment:*					
Things I would not change about this coach:					
Things I would change about this coach:					
Additional comments:					

FIGURE 8.9. Middle school teacher survey of coaching effectiveness.

Alvermann, D. E. (2001). *Effective literacy instruction for adolescents*. Executive Summary and Paper Commissioned by the National Reading Conference. Chicago: National Reading Conference.

Biancarosa, C., & Snow, C. E. (2006). *Reading Next: A vision for action and research in middle and high school literacy* (2nd ed.). Washington, DC: Alliance for Excellent Education.

Deshler, D. D., Palinscar, A. S., Biancarosa, G., & Nair, M. (2007). *Informed choices for struggling adolescent readers: A research-based guide to instructional programs and practices*. New York: Carnegie Corporation of New York.

Heller, R., & Greenleaf, C. L. (2007). *Literacy instruction in the content areas: Getting to the core of middle and high school improvement*. Washington, DC: Alliance for Excellent Education. Available at *www.all4ed.org/publications/LiteracyContent/index.html*.

International Reading Association. (2006). *Standards for middle and high school literacy coaches*. Newark, DE: Author, in collaboration with NCTE, NCTM, NSTA, NCSS, and the Carnegie Corporation of New York.

Jetton, T. L., & Dole, J. A. (Eds.). (2004). *Adolescent literacy research and practice*. New York: Guilford Press.

Joftus, S. (2002). *Every child a graduate: A framework for an excellent education for all middle and high school students*. Washington, DC: Alliance for Excellent Education.

Raphael, T. E., Highfield, K., & Au, K. H. (2006). *QAR Now: Question answer relationships: A powerful and practical framework that develops comprehension and higher-level thinking in all students*. New York: Scholastic.

Worthy, J., Broaddus, K., & Ivey, G. (2001). *Pathways to independence: Reading, writing, and learning in grades 3–8*. New York: Guilford Press.

FIGURE 8.10. Suggested readings for literacy in the middle grades.

CHAPTER 9

The Challenge of Reluctant Teachers

Teacher reluctance can be one of a coach's most formidable challenges. A reluctance to participate in coaching can take many forms. It may consist of antagonistic comments during group presentations. It may be experienced in passive resistance as teachers avoid the coach and ignore suggestions. It may resonate in the excuses and objections—the "yes, but's"—voiced by teachers who feel threatened by change. In short, reluctance may be experienced in any and all of the interactions between teacher and coach. Teachers who resist interacting with the literacy coach can be a source of frustration and stress. In fact, it is the number one concern expressed by many coaches (Toll, 2005). In this chapter, we first explore how varying degrees of reluctance are related to the model of coaching that has been put in place in a school. We then examine the major reasons for reluctance and offer suggestions for meeting that challenge. These suggestions are compiled from several sources, including our own experiences with coaches and teachers.

TEACHER RELUCTANCE AND MODELS OF COACHING

We have observed that the number of reluctant teachers in a school and the degree of their resistance may be related to the model of coaching in use. In Chapter 1, we presented six basic models (not an all-inclusive list), and we return to them here to examine how each relates to the reluctance exhibited by some teachers to the prospect of being coached. Figure 9.1 presents a scale of teacher reluctance to coaching. It places the six models on a spectrum from a greater to a lesser likelihood of reluctance. We acknowledge that our placement of the models along this continuum is not scientific. We base it on the characteristics of each model and on the experiences of the teachers and coaches with whom we have worked.

On this basis, we believe that mentoring new teachers is likely to be met with the least resistance. There are several reasons for this prediction. First, new teachers are usually quick to realize that their preparation has not been detailed enough

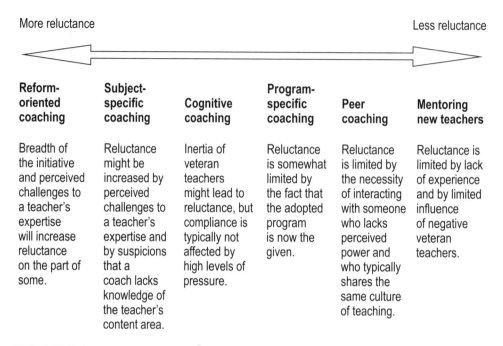

More reluctance   Less reluctance

Reform-oriented coaching	Subject-specific coaching	Cognitive coaching	Program-specific coaching	Peer coaching	Mentoring new teachers
Breadth of the initiative and perceived challenges to a teacher's expertise will increase reluctance on the part of some.	Reluctance might be increased by perceived challenges to a teacher's expertise and by suspicions that a coach lacks knowledge of the teacher's content area.	Inertia of veteran teachers might lead to reluctance, but compliance is typically not affected by high levels of pressure.	Reluctance is somewhat limited by the fact that the adopted program is now the given.	Reluctance is limited by the necessity of interacting with someone who lacks perceived power and who typically shares the same culture of teaching.	Reluctance is limited by lack of experience and by limited influence of negative veteran teachers.

FIGURE 9.1. Teacher reluctance and models of coaching.

to ready them for day-to-day life in the classroom. They are therefore open to any advice that might make their jobs easier and their teaching more effective. In addition, they have not yet been acculturated into the belief system prevalent among their colleagues. If these beliefs are marked by cynicism and indifference, the consequences after a time can be dire. It is no wonder that some coaching programs, like the Subject-Matter Specialist Approach (Joftus, 2002) described in Chapter 8, have focused exclusively on new teachers.

We view peer coaching as somewhat more likely to breed reluctance. However, because the coaching is done by a colleague rather than by a literacy coach, there is no power differential to contend with. That is, the colleague is charged with observing and offering feedback, to be sure, but this relationship is reciprocal. It is possible, however, that some teachers may fear being exposed as a poor teacher, even in this limited setting, because they sense that the peer with whom they will reciprocate is a more proficient teacher. In addition, they may feel that the lack of a power differential will prevent their coaching partner from reporting on them if, in fact, they refuse to engage in the process.

In program-specific coaching, where a new set of materials is in use, teachers may occasionally feel resistant to the materials themselves, and this resistance may lead to a negative response to coaching. However, since the program or materials have already been adopted and are therefore the new "given," resistance to the materials may not translate into antagonism toward the literacy coach.

Such teachers may come to view the new program as a "necessary evil" and therefore comply, if halfheartedly, with the targeted efforts of the coach to assist in implementation.

Cognitive coaching requires, above all, a teacher who is willing to reflect on classroom practice. Together with the coach, the teacher is led to reason carefully about why certain practices are more effective than others. Doing so means being honest and self-critical, two traits that are not terribly commonplace. There are therefore bound to be teachers whose reluctance (or inability) to examine their own practice is a barrier to cognitive coaching. We do not place this form of coaching at the most reluctant end of our scale, however, because cognitive coaching is not typically a high-stakes enterprise. There are few real pressures to participate and few, if any, consequences for failing to improve.

Subject-specific coaching, prevalent at the middle and high school levels, is more likely to encounter teacher reluctance, a possibility we addressed in Chapter 8. When the coaching is done by a content specialist (e.g., one science teacher coaching another), reluctance is likely to be no greater than in any peer-coaching situation. But when a literacy coach attempts to work with a science teacher, targeting content-area reading instruction, the reaction is often much more negative. Unless the coach has a comparable background in a given content subject—for example, when the coach happens to be a former science teacher—some teachers will be reluctant to respond to suggestions, even though such suggestions are well grounded in content-literacy research.

We view reform-oriented coaching—the model we have the most direct experience with—as the one most likely to foster reluctance. This is because school-wide literacy reform initiatives are comprehensive in nature. There is nowhere to hide from them. Teachers are often given many choices, but they may not be fully comfortable with any of them. And when some teachers are compelled to leave their comfort zone, they travel down the road to reluctance. We believe that the most effective reform-oriented coaches can be placed toward the "hard" end of the coaching scale we presented in Figure 1.9. The demands of the reform, if it is to be taken seriously, mean altered practice, and the price of altering the status quo is relentless coaching. Unfortunately, relentlessness can lead to reluctance, which is why we feel compelled to address this subject in detail. As Woodrow Wilson once observed, "If you want to make enemies, try to change something." We do not believe that coaching necessarily makes enemies, but in a climate of change, it is good to keep Wilson's adage in mind and take steps to ensure that even the most reluctant teachers are engaged with respect and ingenuity.

REASONS FOR TEACHER RELUCTANCE

A coach's life would be so much simpler if every teacher would take suggestions to heart with creativity and enthusiasm. Since the reality is otherwise, however, coaches must embrace the problem of reluctance with those very qualities—creativity and enthusiasm! We realize that the natural reaction is likely to be quite different. Coaches often see such teachers as the bane of their very existence. However, it is important to see such teachers in the same light that good teachers view their most challenging students—as puzzles to be solved.

We believe that the best place to start is by trying to determine the reason for resistance. It is vital to listen to reluctant teachers and learn about their beliefs and histories (Bean & DeFord, 2006). Other information can also be useful, such as the achievement record of their classes. Information assembled in this way can provide an idea—a theory—of why the teacher resists coaching efforts. Usher and Bryant (1989) use the term *practical theorizing* to refer to the process that adult educators, such as coaches, go through to become critically aware of the informal theories they have developed to guide their practice. The process begins as the coach wrestles with problems and contradictions associated with the job. The actions the coach takes may seem largely a matter of instinct, but critical reflection often reveals that they are attempts to address the theories held by the reluctant teacher. Becoming aware of the theories that guide actions can be useful in making better decisions. Usher and Bryant identify two ways of achieving this awareness: (1) comparing their informal theories with those held by others, and (2) using informal theories to better understand their own ideas.

In the case of reluctant teachers, the first option is problematic because it would mean sharing concerns with a third party. Above all, we do not suggest approaching the principal for information concerning evaluations, because doing so would threaten the coach's reputation for confidentiality—even if the coach merely listens. If a coach is networking with coaches in other schools, it may be possible to present the case in the abstract, so that the teacher's identity is protected, and to obtain advice from coaches outside the school context. We suspect, however, that it is impossible to mask the identity of any one teacher while speaking with educators inside the school context, and so it is better to avoid the risk.

Usher and Bryant's second suggestion, however, constitutes good advice for any coach. It entails developing a "practical theory" concerning the reasons for a particular teacher's reluctance. In developing such a theory, a coach should consider the most likely reasons for resistance. Based on our experience, we suggest six:

1. Fear of change
2. Low self-efficacy
3. Honest philosophical differences
4. Low expectations for students
5. A belief that as a certificated professional, a teacher's expertise is not to be questioned
6. Resentment by senior teachers at the idea of being coached by someone younger

In using these categories to help infer the reason for a teacher's reluctance, it is important to keep several thoughts in mind. First, remember that these reasons are not mutually exclusive. A combination of them might be true for a particular teacher. Second, remember that the actions you plan in order to overcome resistance should be based on the reason(s) you suspect apply—on your practical theory. Finally, remember that teachers who resist may not necessarily be ineffective (Toll, 2005). It would be a mistake to automatically equate resistance with poor teaching.

Fear of Change

"Change is good," runs an old Dilbert comic strip. "You go first." People are naturally cautious about making changes, especially when the status quo seems tolerable. What some teachers are willing to tolerate, however, for the sake of not having to change, is simply not in the best interests of the children they serve. A strong fear of change may manifest itself in behaviors that appear calculated to bring other teachers around to the same point of view. Brighouse and Woods (1999) speak of "energy consumers," teachers who drain energy from those around them, including coaches. They tend to make excessive use of other people's time. These individuals often have a negative view of the world and themselves. They resent change and make attempts to block it. They are unwilling and frequently unable to examine their own teaching and appear unwilling to improve their performance.

What can be done to overcome reluctance based on an unreasonable fear of change? We suggest working with cooperative teachers to begin with. Let the word spread that your involvement is not a threat (Bean & DeFord, 2006; NRFTAC, 2005). Also, check with reluctant teachers regularly. Unless you are using a "soft" model of coaching, convey the message that not participating is not an option. Make contact of some kind at least once a week. In short, you must be relentless. And, just as participation is required of teachers, it is also required of the coach. You must resist the temptation to dismiss such teachers as a waste of your time (Toll, 2005). Ultimately, connecting with them may prove to be one of your greatest accomplishments.

Toward this end, remember the importance of being tactful in your interactions with teachers for whom you may have limited patience. We acknowledge the reality that a coach is not likely to respect all teachers equally, but they must all be *treated* with equal respect. The philosopher Nietzsche put it well: "Good teachers do not always say what they think. They say what it is useful for their students to hear." This advice applies to coaching situations in which measured language is essential.

Low Self-Efficacy

Some teachers harbor a secret fear that they are incapable of improving. If you suspect that this is the case, the message you must convey is not that they aren't proficient but that they have the potential to improve. One way to tackle the problem of low self-efficacy is to offer to help. Who can resist a good-faith offer to lend a hand? Ask, "What can I do to help you?"—and mean it. For example, if you suspect that a teacher believes that he or she is incapable of implementing a technique, offer to coplan. Once a detailed lesson plan has been developed, the teacher is likely to feel far more capable of delivering a quality lesson. A variation on this strategy is to arrange for the teacher to coplan with or to observe a colleague he or she trusts. Even if both are resistant, their interaction may be productive.

Another way to combat low self-efficacy is to be the "good cop." Some teachers may associate your visits with visits by the principal, as part of evaluation. Make sure you communicate how your role differs from the principal's. It is especially important to make clear that your role is not to evaluate. Take steps to drive this point home. For example, if you take notes during an observation or conference, leave them with the teacher. These notes should accentuate positive aspects of the lesson whenever possible ("I really liked how you … "). These comments must be sincere, however. If they aren't, a teacher may well infer that you are being patronizing.

Contending with limited self-efficacy also requires building trust, especially among those teachers who are least confident. When all teachers learn that you respect confidences, an atmosphere of trust will be created. It will be fragile, however, and you must protect it by not talking about teachers. Once teachers come to trust you, those who resist will have less to fear (Bean & DeFord, 2006).

Finally, the time will eventually arrive when your work with a particular teacher bears fruit in the form of achievement results. It is vital to signal progress on these occasions. When assessment trends become positive, for a classroom or a child, there is cause for celebration. Be sure to share positive trends with the teacher and, where appropriate, to attribute the gains to altered practice. We believe there is no better way to bolster self-efficacy than by presenting evidence of effectiveness.

Philosophical Differences

The history of reading instruction is rife with antagonism, and the "reading wars" are still claiming casualties. Teachers may take issue with certain aspects of a reform initiative, depending on where they studied and which authorities they value. Undoubtedly, the worst approach to philosophical resistance is direct confrontation. Pointing out that research does not support their viewpoint is not likely to be persuasive. Rather, it may provoke a combative response in which contradictory studies are produced. This type of debate is pointless, inconclusive, and divisive. It also risks permanently alienating the very teacher you are attempting to engage. It is far more productive, we believe, to take a more invitational approach. Involve resistant teachers in group activities, for example. Try giving them a role in grade-level meetings and study groups. Seek their input about issues and problems. Acknowledge alternative views, but note that the reform effort in your school has taken a particular course.

In approaching teachers whose views concerning instruction differ, it is important to focus on data. Assessment results afford the opportunity to speak objectively with teachers about a documented problem. Such assessments also allow you and the teacher to work as fellow professionals to set goals and to examine children's profiles (Bean & DeFord, 2006). Of course, resistant teachers can attempt to dismiss assessment results, but when the achievement pattern of their students differs visibly from similar students served by other teachers, the door is open for frank discussion.

Low Expectations for Students

Teachers sometimes believe that nothing will work. This was typically not the case when they began their careers, but years of unsuccessful attempts to serve the needs of their most challenging students have resulted in a resignation to defeat. Unfortunately, they tend to place the blame on the students and not on the instructional techniques they have used. We believe that the best approach to connecting with such teachers is to anticipate their objections and to appear to agree. Of course, you can then spin the situation to your own goals. Some examples appear in Figure 9.2.

It is a good idea to restate what a resistant teacher says in order to signal that you are listening—and also to make sure you understand the concern. Here are a few examples of how you might do so:

- Say more about that.
- Let me see if I understand.
- I'd be interested in hearing more about ...
- So, are you saying/suggesting ...
- When I say _____, I mean _____. When you say _____, what do you mean?
- I'm intrigued by/interested in/wonder about ... (Wilkinson, 2007)

Another strategy is to model a particular method while the teacher watches. It is difficult to argue that the method will not work with a particular group of students when there is visible evidence to the contrary. The next step is to follow up with an observation during which the teacher has committed to implementing the same method. This is required for the teacher to take ownership of the approach and to employ it independently.

Teacher	Coach
"I just don't have time to try this."	"I know you don't. You're already doing so much. What if I come in and manage a group for you while you try it?"
"I just don't have time to talk to you."	"I know you're busy. When's a good time to come back?"
"This won't work with my kids."	"I know. You've got a tough group this year. But I wonder if it might work with a few of them if you gave it a try."
"I like my approach better."	"I'd like to learn more about it. Can I come in while you're using it?"

FIGURE 9.2. Coaching responses to teacher objections.

Finally, data can be convincing. Demonstrating positive achievement trends can be an effective means of dispelling low expectations, just as they can be effective in addressing issues of low teacher self-efficacy.

Professional Autonomy

As certificated professionals, teachers sometimes cling to the view that their judgment is sacrosanct and not to be questioned. As with philosophical differences, our experience suggests that direct confrontation is unlikely to be productive. Pointing out that even the world's finest athletes have coaches is simply not an analogy that will resonate with such teachers. It is better to offer them leadership roles, through which their expertise is respected—and channeled in a productive direction. For example, asking them to lead a book study places them in a position to teach teachers, and, at the same time, it brings them into the boundaries of the reform initiative by acquainting them with important ideas. Asking them to pilot a new technique in an action research study can also have the effect of massaging egos, and if the new technique proves superior, a vocal convert will be born.

Resentment Based on Seniority

Some teachers find it difficult to accept coaching from an individual many years their junior. The fact that the coach may be more knowledgeable is not recognized, for book knowledge cannot trump experience. And in a way, this is true. Years of classroom experience have taught valuable lessons, and savvy coaches honor these lessons as they interact with veteran teachers. Asking a teacher to recount a successful experience during a grade-level meeting sends a message to peers that the teacher's expertise matters. Occasionally deferring to a senior colleague ("What do you think, Abby?") can have a similar effect, as can inviting the teacher to exchange roles ("You're so good at read-alouds, Abby. Would you mind observing while I do one and then give me feedback?").

Above all, be modest. No one expects you to be a guru. Make it clear that you are a fellow learner and that you bring to classrooms the simple advantage of another set of eyes. Avoid giving the impression that you are the expert, who is there to give teachers the word and tell them what they are doing wrong (Bean & DeFord, 2006). Be quick to admit that you don't know the answer to a question—and then offer to research it!

CONTENDING WITH RELUCTANCE IN GROUP SETTINGS

When groups convene, reluctant teachers may seize the floor in order to express their resistance to ideas, vent their concerns, or try your patience. It is a good idea to anticipate these incidents and to acquire, in advance, some on-your-feet strategies for defusing them. How a coach responds in such situations will have a ripple effect among other teachers, who may harbor similar concerns but are unwilling to voice them. Anticipating problems also avoids having to arrive at an insightful response extemporaneously, something few of us are good at.

A good strategy is to use redirecting language that acknowledges the concern but deflects it for the present:

"I understand that you are concerned with _____. That will be addressed _____. Here we have a chance to work on _____."

Another is to write down the issue and tell teachers that you will communicate about it later. We have used a "parking lot" for issues that concern policy, require research, or that are not germane to the topic. Post-it Notes containing concerns or questions are placed on a wall, easel, or marker board and collected later. Making the parking lot a routine part of group meetings soon creates a behavior set among teachers that heads off many problems.

Wilkinson (2007) points out that it is vital to remain calm and objective. This is not always easy, especially if you suspect that you are being baited. But it is important, she contends, not to rise to the bait but to stay focused on the problem at hand. A certain amount of venting during group sessions can actually be healthy and the opportunity will be appreciated, but it may require refocusing after a minute or two. Propelling concerns in a positive direction can be an effective means of redirecting a meeting. For example, you might list possible solutions on chart paper, suggest resources and training opportunities, or brainstorm some of the positives that might offset the concerns.

ADDITIONAL SUGGESTIONS

We asked a group of experienced literacy coaches to list the strategies they found successful in engaging reluctant teachers. These ideas are compiled in Figure 9.3. It continually amazes us how resourceful coaches can be in their efforts to connect with teachers who initially resist. As you are coaching, you should make note of additional strategies that provide results for you. In fact, you could add to our list and then use it as a safety net when you are at the end of your rope. Take a suggestion, and try to make it work for you and for your reluctant teacher.

But even this type of ingenuity doesn't always work. As a coach, you cannot afford to wait indefinitely for a teacher to become cooperative. So remember to document your efforts. If all else fails, your record of attempts can be shared with the principal, who bears the ultimate responsibility for action (Walpole & McKenna, 2004). Communicating in writing with both the teacher and the principal shifts control to the latter. This will be a hard step to take, but remember that the children served by your teachers deserve the most effective instruction we can provide them. Even though they don't know it, these children are depending on you to take the necessary steps to provide such instruction. On days when your coaching seems ineffective (and there will be such days) remember to count the positive changes that you have made in the lives of teachers and children to balance your attention to the puzzles that remain.

A FINAL WORD

We began this chapter by revisiting the basic models of coaching introduced in Chapter 1. These models vary in many respects, including the level of teacher reluctance they are likely to evoke. These differences offer the choices necessary to select a model that is right for your school, and still more choices are possible by combining elements to create a hybrid that may work better in your context than any of the individual models. We leave you in the hope that this book has extended your thinking about coaching, about the range of possibilities it presents, and about its connection with school leadership.

1. I try to be a good listener. Allowing someone to vent a little and then moving the conversation in a productive direction can work wonders.

2. One of my teachers didn't want to talk about data and would try to not focus on them. In the course of the conversation, she told me that all she really needed was a pencil sharpener that worked. Unbeknownst to her, I went to the office, filled out a Title I purchase order for a pencil sharpener and then delivered it to her when it arrived. It gave me a lot of credibility as a support person and has since given me a big "foot in the door."

3. I have successfully tried a coteaching approach with a particularly apathetic teacher. Her students were literally falling asleep. We divided the lesson so that we alternated instruction. Her goal was to watch the students when I was teaching, which I proceeded to do with excessive enthusiasm! The atmosphere of her classroom has since changed after she saw how the students sat taller, answered more quickly, and stayed awake.

4. I pick my battles. It's important not to get into power struggles, nit-picking every disagreement.

5. I get to know my teachers and allow them to know me. I share personal information about myself and learn as much as I can about them. I have learned the names of their children, for example, and make a point to ask about them.

6. It helps to be very specific (in writing) about the steps I want the teacher to take and to then keep coming back—relentlessly.

7. I keep chocolate in my room so that even reluctant teachers come to visit me. I use these drop-ins to sneak in questions and offer suggestions.

8. Chocolate is a favorite, but some teachers are trying to lose weight and others are diabetic. I make a point to keep sugar-free candy and small crackers on hand, as well.

9. If I want teachers to try a new approach, I provide them with concrete materials they will need when they teach. For example, if they need word cards for a sorting lesson, I create them. I make sure they have exactly what they need to teach.

10. When my teachers express reluctance to implement a new program, I challenge them to try the program experimentally and tell them that, together, we will see what the data show about student achievement.

11. When I model an approach, I sometimes invite a second teacher to observe as well as the classroom teacher. I choose someone whom the reluctant teacher respects. After the lesson, we have a three-way conversation.

12. I build group activities into every professional development session. I strategically arrange the room so that two to three people can work together to complete a task.

13. When teachers come to my room, I give them my full attention. I stop what I'm doing, make eye contact, and show them I care. This demonstrates that I respect them and that I truly want to provide support.

14. Some teachers truly think they do nothing right. They need to hear about their strengths.

15. I find out what my teachers want to know more about. Then I do the legwork and deliver the goods!

16. After an observation, I leave a note on the teacher's desk with a positive comment and a question to ponder.

FIGURE 9.3. Advice from coaches about meeting the challenge of reluctant teachers.

References

Achinstein, B., & Athanases, S. B. (Eds.). (2006) *Mentors in the making: developing new leaders for new teachers.* New York: Teachers College Press.

Allington, R., Boxer, N., & Broikou, K. (1987). Jeremy, remedial reading and subject area classes. *Journal of Reading, 30,* 643–645.

Alvermann, D. E. (2001). *Effective literacy instruction for adolescents.* Executive Summary and Paper Commissioned by the National Reading Conference. Chicago: National Reading Conference.

Bean, R. M., & DeFord, D. (2006). *Do's and don'ts for literacy coaches: Advice from the field.* Policy Brief, International Reading Association and National Council of Teachers of English, Literacy Coaching Clearinghouse. Available at *www.literacycoachingonline. org/briefs/DosandDontsFinal.pdf.*

Bear, D. R., Invernizzi, M., Templeton, S., & Johnston, F. (2007). *Words their way: Word study for phonics, vocabulary, and spelling instruction* (4th ed.). Upper Saddle River, NJ: Pearson.

Beck, I. L., McKeown, M. G., & Kucan, L. (2002). *Bringing words to life: Robust vocabulary instruction.* New York: Guilford Press.

Berman, P., & McLaughlin, M. W. (1980). Factors affecting the process of change. In M. M. Milstein (Ed.), *Schools, conflict, and change* (pp. 57–71). New York: Teachers College Press.

Biancarosa, C., & Snow, C. E. (2006). *Reading Next: A vision for action and research in middle and high school literacy* (2nd ed.). Washington, DC: Alliance for Excellent Education.

Blamey, K. L., Meyer, C. K., & Walpole, S. (2007). *Middle- and high-school literacy coaches: An initial survey.* Manuscript in preparation.

Block, C. C., Oakar, M., & Hurt, N. (2002). The expertise of literacy teachers: A continuum from preschool to grade 5. *Reading Research Quarterly, 37,* 178–206.

Borman, G. D., Slavin, R. E., Cheung, A., Chamberlain, A. M., Madden, N. A., & Chambers, B. (2005a). Success for All: First-year results from the national randomized field trial. *Educational Evaluation and Policy Analysis, 27,* 1–22.

Borman, G. D., Slavin, R. E., Cheung, A., Chamberlain, A. M., Madden, N. A., & Chambers, B. (2005b). The national randomized field trial of Success for All: Second-year outcomes. *American Educational Research Journal, 42,* 673–696.

Brighouse, T., & Woods, D. (1999). *How to improve your school*. London: Routledge.

Bromley, K., Irwin-De Vitis, L., & Modlo, M. (1995). *Graphic organizers: Visual strategies for active learning*. New York: Scholastic.

Buehl, D. (2000). *Classroom strategies for interactive learning* (2nd ed.). Newark, DE: International Reading Association.

Cassidy, J., & Cassidy, D. (2007). What's hot, what's not for 2007. *Reading Today, 24*(4), 1, 10–12.

Chall, J. E. (1983/1996). *Stages of reading development*. New York: McGraw-Hill.

Cobb, C. (2005). Professional Development for Literacy—Who's in charge? *Reading Teacher, 59*, 388–390.

Copland, M. A. (2003). The Bay Area School Reform Collaborative: Building the capacity to lead. In J. Murphy & A. Datnow (Eds.), *Leadership lessons from comprehensive school reform* (pp. 159–183). Thousand Oaks, CA: Corwin Press.

Copland, M. A. (2004). Distributed leadership for instructional improvement: The principal's role. In D. S. Strickland & M. L. Kamil (Eds.), *Improving reading achievement through professional development* (pp. 213–231). Norwood, MA: Christopher-Gordon.

Costa, A., & Garmston, R. (1997). *Cognitive coaching: A foundation for Renaissance schools* (3rd ed.). Norwood, MA: Christopher-Gordon.

Costa, A. L., & Garmston, R. J. (2002). *Cognitive coaching: A foundation for Renaissance schools*. Norwood, MA: Christopher-Gordon.

Council for Chief State School Officers. (1996). *Interstate school leaders licensure consortium: Standards for school leaders*. Washington, DC: Author. Available at *www. ccsso.org/content/pdfs/isllcstd.pdf*

Deshler, D. D., Palinscar, A. S., Biancarosa, G., & Nair, M. (2007). *Informed choices for struggling adolescent readers: A research-based guide to instructional programs and practices*. New York: Carnegie Corporation of New York.

Desimone, L. (2002). How can comprehensive school reform models be successfully implemented? *Review of Educational Research, 72*, 433–479.

Deussen. T., Coskie, T., Robinson, L., & Autio, E. (2007). *"Coach" can mean many things: Five categories of literacy coaches in Reading First*. (Issues & Answers Report, REL 2007–No. 005) Washington, DC: U.S. Department of Education, Institute of Education Sciences, National Center for Education Evaluation and Regional Assistance, Regional Educational Laboratory Northwest. Retrieved July 6, 2007, from *ies.ed.gov/ncee/edlabs*

Dole, J. A., & Donaldson, R. (2006). "What am I supposed to do all day?": Three big ideas for the reading coach. *The Reading Teacher, 59*, 486–488.

Donaldson, G. A. (2001). *Cultivating leadership in schools: Connecting people, purpose, and practice*. New York: Teachers College Press.

Doubek, M. B., & Cooper, E. J. (2007). Closing the gap through professional development: Implications for reading research. *Reading Research Quarterly, 42*, 411–415.

Doyle, M., & Strauss, D. (1993). *How to make meetings work: The new interaction method*. New York: Berkeley.

Duffy, G. G. (2004). Teachers who improve reading achievement: What research says about what they do and how to develop them. In D. S. Strickland & M. L. Kamil (Eds.), *Improving reading achievement through professional development* (pp. 3–22). Norwood, MA: Christopher-Gordon.

Eitington, J. (1984). *The winner trainer*. Houston: Gulf Publishing.

Eller, J. (2004). *Effective group facilitation in education: How to energize and manage difficult groups.* Thousand Oaks, CA: Corwin Press.

Fountas, I. C., & Pinnell, G. S. (1996). *Guided reading: Good first teaching for all children.* Portsmouth, NH: Heinemann.

Fuchs, D., & Fuchs, L. (2005). Peer-assisted learning strategies: promoting word recognition, fluency, and reading comprehension in young children. *Journal of Special Education, 39*(1), 34–44.

Fuchs, D., & Fuchs, L. S. (2006). Introduction to response to intervention: What, why, and how valid is it? *Reading Research Quarterly, 41,* 93–99.

Fullan, M. (2005). *Leadership and sustainability: System thinkers in action.* Thousand Oaks, CA: Corwin Press and Ontario Principals' Council.

Gabriel, J. G. (2005). *How to thrive as a teacher leader.* Alexandria, VA: Association for Supervision and Curriculum Development.

Garmston, R. J. (2005). *The presenter's fieldbook: A practical guide* (2nd ed.). Norwood, MA: Christopher-Gordon.

Gersten, R., Baker, S. K., Shanahan, T., Linan-Thompson, S., Collins, P., & Scarcella, R. (2007). *Effective literacy and English language instruction for English learners in the elementary grades: A practice guide* (NCEE 2007-4011). Washington, DC: National Center for Education Evaluation and Regional Assistance, Institute of Education Sciences, U.S. Department of Education. Retrieved from *ies.ed.gov/ncee*

Gersten, R., & Dimino, J. A. (2006). RTI (Response to Intervention): Rethinking special education for students with reading difficulties (yet again). *Reading Research Quarterly, 41,* 99–108.

Goleman, D., Boyatzis, R., & McKee, A. (2002). *Primal leadership.* Boston: Harvard Business School Press.

Guskey, T. R. (2000). *Evaluating professional development.* Thousand Oaks, CA: Corwin Press.

Guskey, T. R., & Sparks, D. (1996). Exploring the relationship between staff development and improvements in student learning. *Journal of Staff Development, 17*(4), 34–38.

Hasbrouck, J., & Denton, C. A. (2007). Student-focused coaching: A model for reading coaches. *The Reading Teacher, 60,* 690–693.

Hasbrouck, J., & Tindal, G. A. (2006). Oral reading fluency norms: A valuable assessment tool for reading teachers. *The Reading Teacher, 59,* 636–644.

Hay Group Management. (2004). *A culture for learning.* London: Author.

Heifetz, R., & Linsky, M. (2002). *Leadership on the line: Staying alive through the dangers of leading.* Boston: Harvard Business School Press.

Heimlich, J. E., & Pittelman, S. D. (1986). *Semantic mapping: Classroom applications.* Newark, DE: International Reading Association.

Hoffman, J., & Pearson, P. D. (2000). Reading teachers education in the next millennium: What your grandmother's teacher didn't know that your granddaughter's teacher should. *Reading Research Quarterly, 35,* 28–44.

Hosp, M. K., Hosp, J. L., & Howell, K. V. (2007). *The ABCs of CBM: A practical guide to curriculum-based measurement.* New York: Guilford Press.

International Reading Association. (2000a). *Excellent reading teachers: A position statement of the International Reading Association.* Newark, DE: Author.

International Reading Association. (2000b). *Teaching all children to read: The roles of the reading specialist.* Newark, DE: Author. Available at *www.reading.org/resources/issues/positions_specialist.html*

International Reading Association. (2004). *The role and qualifications of the reading coach in the United States.* Newark, DE: Author. Available at *www.reading.org/resources/ issues/positions_coach.html*

International Reading Association. (2006). *Standards for middle and high school literacy coaches.* Newark, DE: Author, in collaboration with NCTE, NCTM, NSTA, NCSS, and the Carnegie Corporation of New York.

Invernizzi, M., & Meier, J. (2000). *Phonological awareness literacy screening: Grades 1 to 3.* Charlottesville: University of Virginia.

Joftus, S. (2002). *Every child a graduate: A framework for an excellent education for all middle and high school students.* Washington, DC: Alliance for Excellent Education.

Johnson, D. D., & Pearson, P. D. (1984). *Teaching reading vocabulary* (2nd ed.). New York: Holt, Rinehart & Winston.

Joyce, B., & Showers, B. (1996). Staff development as a comprehensive service organization. *Journal of Staff Development, 17*(1), 2–6.

Joyce, B., & Showers, B. (2002). *Student achievement through staff development* (3rd ed.). Alexandria, VA: Association for Supervision and Curriculum Development.

Kame'enui, E. J., Francis, D. J., Fuchs, L., Good, R. H., O'Connor, R. E., & Simmons, D. C., Tinday. G., & Torgesen, J. K. (2006). The adequacy of tools for assessing reading competence: A framework and review. *Educational Researcher, 35,* 3–11.

Kean, M. H., Summers, A. A., Raivetz, M. J., & Farber, I. J. (1979). *What works in reading?* Philadelphia: School District of Philadelphia and the Federal Reserve Bank.

Killgallon, D. (1997). Sentence composing for middle school. Portsmouth, NH: Heinemann.

Kinnucan-Welsch, K., Rosemary, C. A., & Grogan, P. R. (2006). Accountability by design in literacy professional development. *The Reading Teacher, 59,* 426–435.

Klingner, J. K., & Edwards, P. A. (2006). Cultural considerations with response to intervention models. *Reading Research Quarterly, 41,* 108–117.

Knowles, M. S. (1989). *The making of an adult educator.* San Francisco: Jossey-Bass.

Learning First Alliance. (1998). *Every child reading: An action plan.* Washington, DC: Learning First Alliance. Available at *www.learningfirst.org/publications/reading/*

Lewis, C. C. (2002). *Lesson study: A handbook of teacher-led instructional change.* Philadelphia: Research for Better Schools.

MacKeracher, D. (2004). *Making sense of adult learning* (2nd ed.).Toronto: University of Toronto Press.

Manzo, A. V. (1969). The ReQuest procedure. *Journal of Reading, 13,* 123–126.

Manzo, A. V., & Casale, U. P. (1985). Listen-Read-Discuss: A content reading heuristic. *Journal of Reading, 28,* 732–734.

Marzano, R. J. (2004). *Building background knowledge for academic achievement: Research on what works in schools.* Alexandria, VA: Association for Supervision and Curriculum Development.

McEneaney, J. E., Lose, M. K., & Schwartz, R. M. (2006). A transactional perspective on reading difficulties and response to intervention. *Reading Research Quarterly, 41,* 117–128.

McKenna, M. C. (2002). *Help for struggling readers: Strategies for grades 3–8.* New York: Guilford Press.

McKenna, M. C., & Robinson, R. D. (1990). Content literacy: A definition and implications. *Journal of Reading, 34,* 184–186.

McKenna, M. C., & Robinson, R. D. (2008). *Content area reading: Helping students learn through text*. Upper Saddle River, NJ: Pearson/Vango.

McKenna, M. C., & Stahl, S. A. (2003). *Assessment for reading instruction*. New York: Guilford Press.

McKenna, M. C., Stahl, S. A., & Stahl, K. A. D. (in press). *Assessment for reading instruction* (2nd ed.). New York: Guilford Press.

McKenna, M. C., & Walpole, S. (2005). How well does assessment inform our reading instruction? *The Reading Teacher, 59*, 84–86.

McLaughlin, M. W., & Talbert, J. E. (2001). *Professional communities and the work of high school teaching*. Chicago: University of Chicago Press.

McMahon, S. I., & Raphael, T. E. (Eds.). (1997). *The book club connection: Literacy learning and classroom talk*. New York: Teachers College Press.

Merriam, S. B. (2001). Something old, something new: Adult learning theory for the twenty-first century. In S. B. Merriam (Ed.), *The new update on adult learning theory* (pp. 93–96). New Directions for Adult and Continuing Education, No. 89. San Francisco: Jossey-Bass.

Mesmer, H. A., & Karchmer, R. A. (2003). REAlity: How the Reading Excellence Act took form in two schools. *The Reading Teacher, 56*, 636–645.

Moore, M. T. (2007). Issues and trends in writing instruction. In R. D. Robinson & M. C. McKenna (Eds.), *Issues and trends in literacy education* (4th ed., pp. 281–293). Boston: Allyn & Bacon.

Murphy, J. (2004). *Leadership for literacy: Research-based practice, PreK–3*. Thousand Oaks, CA: Corwin Press.

Murphy, J., & Datnow, A. (2003a). The development of comprehensive school reform. In J. Murphy & A. Datnow (Eds.), *Leadership lessons from comprehensive school reform* (pp. 3–18). Thousand Oaks, CA: Corwin Press.

Murphy, J., & Datnow, A. (2003b). Leadership lessons from comprehensive school reform designs. In J. Murphy & A. Datnow (Eds.), *Leadership lessons from comprehensive school reform* (pp. 263–278). Thousand Oaks, CA: Corwin Press.

National Institute of Child Health and Human Development. (2000). *Report of the National Reading Panel. Teaching children to read: An evidence-based assessment of the scientific research literature on reading and its implications for reading instruction* (NIH Publication No. 00-4769). Washington, DC: U.S. Government Printing Office.

National Reading First Technical Assistance Center (2005). *An introductory guide for Reading First coaches*. Washington, DC: U.S. Department of Education.

National Staff Development Council (NSDC). (2001). *Standards for staff development* (rev. ed.). Oxford, OH: Author. Available at *www.nsdc.org/standards/index.cfm*

National Staff Development Council (NSDC). (2003). *Moving NSDC's staff development standards into practice: Innovation configurations*. Oxford, OH: Author.

Neufeld, B., & Roper, D. (2003). *Coaching: A strategy for developing instructional capacity: Promises and practicalities*. Washington, DC: Aspen Institute Program on Education and Annenberg Institute for School Reform. Available at *www.annenberginstitute.org/images/Coaching.pdf*

Opitz, M. F., & Lee, V. G. (2005). Engaging readers. *The Reading Teacher, 59*, 294–295.

Ouchi, W. (2003). *Making schools work*. New York: Wiley.

Pinnell, G. S. (1985). Helping teachers help children at risk: Insights from the Reading Recovery program. *Peabody Journal of Education, 62*, 70–85.

Pinnell, G. S., Fried, M. D., & Estice, R. M. (1990). Reading Recovery: Learning how to make a difference. *The Reading Teacher, 43,* 282–295.

Pittelman, S. D., Heimlich, J. E., Berglund, R. L., & French, M. P. (1991). *Semantic feature analysis: Classroom applications.* Newark, DE: International Reading Association.

Poglinco, S. M., Bach, A. J., Hovde, K., Rosenblum, S., Saunders, M., & Supovitz, J. A. (2003, May). *The heart of the matter: The coaching model in America's choice schools.* Philadelphia: Consortium for Policy Research in Education.

Popham, W. J. (2007). *Classroom assessment: What teachers need to know.* Boston: Allyn & Bacon.

Puig, E. A., & Froelich, K. S. (2007). *The literacy coach: Guiding in the right direction.* Boston: Pearson/Allyn & Bacon.

Raphael, T. E. (1984). Teaching learners about sources of information for answering comprehension questions. *Journal of Reading, 27,* 303–311.

Raphael, T. E. (1986). Teaching question-answer relationships, revisited. *The Reading Teacher, 39,* 516–523.

Raphael, T. E., Highfield, K., & Au, K. H. (2006). *QAR Now: Question answer relationships: A powerful and practical framework that develops comprehension and higher-level thinking in all students.* New York: Scholastic.

Rathvon, N. (2004). *Early reading assessment: A practitioner's handbook.* New York: Guilford Press.

Reading Recovery Council of North America. (2004). *Standards and guidelines of Reading Recovery© in the United States.* Columbus, OH: Author.

Roberts, S. M., & Pruitt, E. Z. (2003). *Schools as professional learning communities: Collaborative activities and strategies for professional development.* Thousand Oaks, CA: Corwin Press.

Roy, P., & Hord, S. M. (2003). *Moving NSDC's staff development standards into practice: Innovation configurations, Volume I.* Oxford, OH: National Staff Development Council.

Roy, P., & Hord, S. M. (2004). Innovation configurations: Chart a measured course toward change. *Journal of Staff Development, 25,* 54–58.

Schwartz, S., McCarthy, M., Gould, T., Politziner, S., & Enyeart, C. (2003). *Where the rubber hits the road: An in-depth look at collaborative coaching and learning and workshop instruction in a sample of effective practice schools.* Boston, MA: Boston Plan for Excellence.

Simmons, D. C., Kuykendall, K., King, K., Cornachione, C., & Kame'enui, E. J. (2000). Implementation of a schoolwide reading improvement model: "No one ever told us it would be this hard!" *Learning Disabilities Research and Practice, 15,* 92–100.

Simon, H. A. (1947). *Administrative behavior: A study of decision-making processes in administrative organizations.* New York: Free Press.

Slavin, R. E. (1995). *Cooperative learning: Theory, research, and practice* (2nd ed.). Boston: Allyn & Bacon.

Snow, C. E., Ippolito, J., & Schwartz, R. (2006). *What we know and what we need to know about literacy coaches in middle and high schools: A research synthesis and proposed research agenda.* Newark, DE: International Reading Association.

Spandel, V. (2004). *Creating writers through 6-trait writing assessment and instruction.* Upper Saddle River, NJ: Prentice Hall.

Speck, M. (1996, Spring). Best practice in professional development for sustained educational change. *ERS Spectrum,* 33–41.

Stahl, K. A. D. (2004). Proof, practice, and promise: Comprehension strategy instruction in the primary grades. *The Reading Teacher, 57,* 598–609.

Stahl, S. A. (1999). *Vocabulary development.* Cambridge, MA: Brookline Books.

Stahl, S. A., & Nagy, W. E. (2005). *Teaching word meanings.* Mahwah, NJ: Erlbaum.

Stauffer, R. G. (1980). *The language experience approach to the teaching of reading* (2nd ed.). New York: Harper & Row.

Stewart, R. A., & O'Brien, D. G. (1989). Resistance to content area reading: A focus on preservice teachers. *Journal of Reading, 32,* 396–401.

Sturtevant, E. G. (2003). *The literacy coach: Key to improving teaching and learning in secondary schools.* Washington, DC: Alliance for Excellent Education. Available at *www.all4ed.org/publications/LiteracyCoach.pdf*

Taba, H. (1967). *Teacher's handbook for elementary social studies.* Reading, MA: Addison-Wesley.

Taylor, B. M., Frye, B. J., Peterson, B. S., & Pearson, P. D. (2004). *Steps for schoolwide reading improvement.* Washington, DC: National Education Association.

Tennant, M. (2006). *Psychology and adult learning* (3rd ed.). London: Taylor & Francis.

Terehoff, I. I. (2002). Elements of adult learning in teacher professional development. *NASSP Bulletin, 86*(232), 65–77.

Tierney, R. J., & Readence, J. E. (2004). *Reading strategies and practices: A compendium* (6th ed.). Boston: Allyn & Bacon.

Togneri, W. (2003). *Beyond islands of excellence: What districts can do to improve instruction and achievement in all schools—A leadership brief.* Washington, DC: Learning First Alliance. Available at *www.learningfirst.org/publications/districts/*

Toll, C. A. (2005). *The literacy coach's survival guide: Essential questions and practical answers.* Newark, DE: International Reading Association.

Torgesen, J. K. (2006). *Improving adolescent literacy: Suggestions from research.* Florida Center for Reading Research. Available at *www.fcrr.org/science/sciencePresentationsTorgesen. htm*

Trotter, Y. D. (2006). Adult learning theories: Impacting professional development programs. *Delta Kappa Gamma Bulletin, 72*(2), 8–13.

Usher, R. S., & Bryant, I. (1989). *Adult education as theory, practice and research: The captive triangle.* New York: Routledge.

Walpole, S., & Blamey, K. L. (2007a). Assessing implementation of literacy curricula. In K. Pence (Ed.), *Assessment in emergent and early literacy* (pp. 189–226). San Diego, CA: Plural Publishing.

Walpole, S., & Blamey, K. L. (2007b). *Building-level literacy coaches: Fostering site-specific choices.* Manuscript under review.

Walpole, S., & McKenna, M. C. (2004). *The literacy coach's handbook: A guide to research-based practice.* New York: Guilford Press.

Walpole, S., & McKenna, M. C. (2007). *Differentiated reading instruction: Strategies for the primary grades.* New York: Guilford Press.

Walpole, S., & McKenna, M. C. (2008). Literacy coaches: Their emerging leadership roles. In S. B. Wepner & D. Strickland (Eds.), *Administration and supervision of reading programs* (4th ed., pp. 45–54). New York: Teachers College Press.

Walpole, S., & Meyer, C. K. (2008). Models for coaching: Making them work for preschools. In L. Justice & C. Vukelich (Eds.), *Achieving excellence in preschool literacy instruction* (pp. 69–83). New York: Guilford Press.

Wiggins, G., & McTighe, J. (2005). *Understanding by design* (Expanded 2nd ed.). Alexandria, VA: Association for Supervision and Curriculum Development.

Wilkinson, C. (2007). *Coaching tools for energizing reluctant colleagues.* Paper presented at the National Reading First Conference, St. Louis.

Wood, K. D., Lapp, D., & Flood, J. (1992). *Guiding readers through text: A review of study guides.* Newark, DE: International Reading Association.

Yopp, H. K. (1995). Yopp–Singer test of phoneme segmentation. *The Reading Teacher, 49,* 20–29.

Index